D0713016

A GUIDE TO THE
BIRDS AND MAMMALS OF
COASTAL PATAGONIA

A GUIDE TO THE

Birds and Mammals of Coastal Patagonia

GRAHAM HARRIS

ILLUSTRATIONS BY
THE AUTHOR

WITH A FOREWORD BY
WILLIAM CONWAY

PRINCETON UNIVERSITY PRESS

Copyright © 1998 by Princeton University Press
Published by Princeton University Press, 41 William Street,
Princeton, New Jersey 08540
In the United Kingdom: Princeton University Press,
Chichester, West Sussex

All Rights Reserved

Library of Congress Cataloging-in-Publication Data

Harris, Graham, 1953–
A guide to the birds and mammals of coastal Patagonia /
Graham Harris ; with a foreword by William Conway ;
illustrations by the author.
p.   cm.
Includes bibliographical references (p.   ) and index.
ISBN 0-691-05831-8 (cl : alk. paper)
1. Birds—Patagonia (Argentina and Chile)   2. Mammals—Patagonia
(Argentina and Chile)   I. Title.   I. Title: Guide to the
birds and mammals of coastal Patagonia.
QL689.P37H37   1998
599′.0982′7—DC21   97-43118

This book has been composed in Baskerville
Designed by Jan Lilly

Princeton University Press books are printed on
acid-free paper and meet the guidelines for permanence
and durability of the Committee on Production
Guidelines for Book Longevity of the
Council on Library Resources

http://pup.princeton.edu

Printed in the United States of America

10   9   8   7   6   5   4   3   2   1

To Pat

Contents

From the Fortabat Foundation

IN LATE 1979 I spent an afternoon in a small boat in the company of Southern Right Whales that come to breed each year at Península Valdés. I saw many whales that afternoon but one in particular I shall never forget. We had stopped our boat a little distance from shore, forty yards or so from this young whale. Almost immediately it turned toward us. I called out, "Come, darling, come; we love you." Then it swam forwards beneath the boat and circled us several times, its movements surprisingly careful. Finally it raised its head out of the water near my side of the boat, as though offering its friendship. I was moved to tears as I caressed its head and was stunned by the curiosity and gentleness of this animal whose size dwarfed our vessel. I could not help but think that in spite of the cruelty whales have known from man, they remain friendly toward us. Those magical moments spent among whales off the shores of Patagonia have lived with me since, and I resolved from that day on I would do what I could to ensure that these animals are protected.

The Fortabat Foundation has supported Graham Harris's work as a wildlife researcher and spokesman for nature in Patagonia since 1981. We have followed his progress and in particular the preparation of this book with great interest. He is a great artist and his descriptions bring you to Península Valdés as in a dream. It is our belief that this guide will contribute significantly to the understanding of the birds and mammals of Patagonia and will stimulate many people to care for the protection of this wildlife and visit this magnificent place.

Amalia Lacroze de Fortabat
January 1998

Foreword

PARCHED lonely shores, famously high winds, and cold rough seas are home to Patagonia's spectacular coastal wildlife. Guanacos, maras, armadillos, and mouse-opossums share a harsh desert scrub with Darwin's rheas, tinamous, and earthcreepers on land, while whales, elephant seals, penguins, giant petrels, and steamerducks occupy the edge of the sea and its coastal waters.

There are one hundred and fifty colonies of marine birds and seventy-five colonies of seals and sea lions from Península Valdés to the Straits of Magellan. They include 1.6 million Magellanic penguins, 80,000 southern sea lions, and over 40,000 huge elephant seals, and they protect 2000 rare right whales and fewer than 2000 dolphin gulls. This singular seacoast with its little-known tinamous, canasteros, and cachalotes includes the world's largest continental penguin colony and its only continental colonies of elephant seals. Today, most Patagonian coastal wildlife concentrations are remarkably accessible to sensitive tourism—or destruction and slaughter.

Graham Harris, an Argentine Patagonian born and bred, is both author and artist of this first guide to Patagonia's coastal mammals and birds. As a long-term conservation scientist on the staff of New York's Wildlife Conservation Society and as president of a Patagonian conservation organization, Fundación Patagonia Natural, he brings to this book a unique combination of credentials: a scientist's perception, an artist's eye, and a Patagonian's insight. His book reflects a knowledge not only of what Patagonia's wild birds and mammals are and do, but also how they are doing in this depressing time of global wildlife extinctions.

No tool is more fundamental to the tasks of environmental care and wildlife conservation than an understanding of what is at stake. The stimulus for Harris's book was the belief that it would accelerate an understanding of Patagonia's avian and mammalian wildlife and help to assure its survival in this rapidly developing frontier area, where a major coastal ecosystem of pristine shores and inspiring wild creatures can still be seen and may yet be preserved.

William Conway
Wildlife Conservation Society
New York

Preface

PATAGONIA is the name of a vast region of South America that begins along an ill-defined boundary roughly at 40°S and extends down through southern Argentina and Chile as far as Cape Horn. With an area covering over half a million square miles, Patagonia is larger than Spain and Portugal together. Although the name is usually given to the dry, windswept, scrub desert that covers most of the region, Patagonia also includes moist, forest-clad mountains, a myriad of islands, and even a frozen continental ice sheet.

This book is about the 185 species of birds and 61 species of mammals known to inhabit the part of eastern or coastal Patagonia that extends from Península Valdés to the Strait of Magellan, and from 70°W as far as one may see from shore looking eastward over the Atlantic Ocean. This area corresponds to the eastern parts of the provinces of Chubut and Santa Cruz in Argentina.

Coastal Patagonia is sparsely inhabited. There are thirteen towns scattered along 3000 miles of coast. The largest of these, Comodoro Rivadavia, has over 100,000 inhabitants; over half of the remaining towns have fewer than 5000 people each. Many of these places seem to have been forgotten in time, thus Patagonia is still a true frontier. The harsh, desert environment makes it a land of contrasts, compelling Darwin to refer to it as one of the most uninviting places on earth. Yet, in his old age, he came to admit that of all the places he had known, it was the memories of far-away Patagonia that captivated him most.

As this guide was being produced, a number of important changes occurred in the region affecting the wildlife. Industrial development, particularly along the coast, has attracted workers from other parts of Argentina; towns have grown enormously, sometimes at the rate of four families a day. New housing facilities have sprouted, ports have been built to accommodate increased shipping, and new roads have been opened. Furthermore, oil extraction on land and offshore in southern Patagonia, and the transport of oil by ship to Buenos Aires and Bahía Blanca, have increased. These changes have in turn brought pressure on the region's wildlife.

During this period, tourism, generated by sightseers in search of wildlife, has multiplied. With new and better accommodations for visitors, and with tour agencies competing aggressively to provide better services, the tourist industry has trebled. Wildlife has become an economic resource.

This in itself is good news for the animals and may help ensure their protection, but a note of caution is necessary. Tourism is centered around marine birds and mammals that gather in colonies to breed. If the industry is badly managed, the resulting disturbances to the animals and habitat will affect reproductive success.

The region is vast and difficult to control. Traditionally, budgets for provincial wildlife reserves have been low. Low budgets result in poor management, which produces less income, which in turn lowers the budgets further. Instead of exploiting a few properly managed reserves to a maximum degree and restricting access to the rest, managers have allowed the entire coastal region to come under severe pressure because of lack of control. As a result, in recent years entire breeding colonies along the coast have been abandoned because of disturbances produced by people who have had uncontrolled access.

Wildlife as a tourist resource has been undervalued in Patagonia, and this situation must change. Entrance fees to reserves must be strictly applied, and they must be sufficiently high so that visitors can be provided with adequate services while reserves are efficiently managed and wildlife is protected. When properly directed, revenue from tourism can ensure control, provide support for research, and monitor the wildlife of the entire coastal region. If informed and sensitive wildlife management is not implemented soon—if the wildlife and its needs are not protected—the animals will leave or die out.

Acknowledgments

DURING the 1970s, while I was reading Veterinary Science at Buenos Aires University, I guided ornithological tours through Argentina during the holidays to earn some money for my studies. It was on one of these tours in late 1979 that I met William Conway, the General Director of the Wildlife Conservation Society, at the time called the New York Zoological Society. When I produced some bird sketches, Bill Conway asked me if I would like to live at the Society's station at Península Valdés and paint illustrations for a guidebook of the wildlife of the area. This is where the idea for this volume began. In the years that followed, I went on to work for the Society, and Bill became my friend and mentor, all the time coaxing and encouraging me to complete the task. Bill, Kix Conway, and I have traveled thousands of miles of Patagonian roads together; we have watched cormorants on lonely windswept beaches, we have crawled on our bellies to photograph sea lions, and we have climbed hills for a glimpse of a Buff-necked Ibis colony. Although the responsibility for the contents of this book is mine, I like to think the results are also a little of Patagonia seen through Bill's eyes.

In 1981 I met Amalia Lacroze de Fortabat. Amalita had recently gone whale watching in Península Valdés when a friendly right whale had swum up to and around the boat in which she was a passenger. Touched by the gentleness and curiosity of these whales, which had been hunted for centuries almost to extinction, Amalita decided she wanted to help protect them. Consequently, since 1982 the Fortabat Foundation has supported my work in protecting the right whales and other wildlife of Patagonia, and in particular it has supported the preparation of this book. Amalita's support has continued through the years, and I hope that with the publication of this guide I have met her expectations.

Amalita's philanthropy extends to many corners of Argentina. Just as her efforts to protect wildlife in Patagonia are almost unknown to the general public, she has helped many people as well, seeking no recognition in return. She is keenly sensitive toward the wildlife of Patagonia, and her kindness is a rare jewel in a country where giving for nature is an unusual occurrence.

Maurice Rumboll has been my professor and friend ever since I was in school back in 1964. One of Argentina's truly great naturalists and teachers, Maurice kindled my interest in wildlife in those early years and continues to be one of the true naturalists I most respect.

I cherish the memory of my friend "mi amigo" Don Alberto Pereyra Iraola and his wife, Agustina. They helped me and stood by me in 1981, when we were just starting out on this venture. Their friendship meant a lot to me and my family.

I first met Roger Payne one evening in the late 1970s, at a whale conference he was hosting in Buenos Aires. Roger is an unusually articulate and charismatic person and has probably done more to protect whales than anyone else alive in the world today. His talk on whales that night was memorable. Roger and his wife, Katy Payne, and their four children generously shared with me and my young family their affection for whale camp, the whales, and their friends all those years ago.

Since the late 1960s, each of the successive governments of the province of Chubut has been consistently in the forefront of wildlife conservation in Argentina. More recently, the province of Santa Cruz has become equally committed to the protection of its coastal wildlife. I thank the leaders of both provinces for the opportunity they have given me to see and enjoy the wildlife that inhabits their lands. I hope this book does it justice.

The Museo Argentino de Ciencias Naturales "Bernardino Rivadavia" has been extremely supportive throughout the years. In particular, I thank Jorge Navas for his help with the collections. The Museum of Natural History in New York also gave me access to its valuable collections.

The Ella Lyman Cabot Trust provided support in 1981 to help get me started.

The following contributed generously to this book by either providing data or by reading and correcting the manuscript: Dee Boersma, Claudio Campagna, Esteban Frere, Patricia Gandini, Miguel Haller, Miguel Iñiguez, Oliver Pearson, Osvaldo Reig, Andrew Taber, Sarah Taber, Peter Thomas, Bernd and Melany Würsig, and Pablo Yorio.

Marcelo Canevari, Pablo Canevari, Jorge Rodriguez Mata, Gustavo Rodolfo Carrizo, and Roberto Straneck generously shared their knowledge of birds with me.

I am also indebted to the following people of Patagonia: Carlos and Delia Garcia, José Ferrero, "Pichón" Peralta, Pancho Quiñenao, G. Martinelli, A. Torrejón, Marcos Oliva Day, and Carol Passera. I have benefited from their rich understanding of the land.

Keith Franklin, without complaint, translated the manuscript into Spanish, twice over; he proofread, typed corrections, and was always there to help out. Most importantly, he urged me to continue. I could not have done so without him.

Annette Harris proofread the manuscript twice and provided helpful ideas on style. Among other things, I am indebted to her for breathing life, and English, into me.

My father, who died before this book went to press, instilled in me my first love for animals when, long ago, he would take Mother and my brother and sisters and me camping in the Patagonian wilderness.

Finally, I would like to thank my family for providing me with encouragement and support during the lengthy preparation of this book. My wife Pat and I had the enormous good fortune of living in the small, isolated research station built by the Wildlife Conservation Society on Península Valdés, the "whale camp." From 1981 to 1987 we raised our two children, Edward and Sabrina, in this cinder-block and tin-roof facility by the sea, surrounded by animals. We took some of these animals into our home as orphans, and others just adopted us. Later on we moved into town, 100 miles away, to give our children schooling, but we continued to get out, whenever we could, among the animals. This book is about the birds and mammals we came to know.

A GUIDE TO THE
BIRDS AND MAMMALS OF
COASTAL PATAGONIA

Plan of the Book

THIS BOOK is an illustrated guide for the identification of birds and mammals of eastern Patagonia. Because the wildlife of any area is governed to a great extent by the characteristics of its environment, an introduction to the climate, vegetation, and geomorphology helps in comprehending the particular mix of species and their natural history. This book begins with a short section on the geology and geography of the area followed by an illustrated selection of the dominant plant species, and finally by a description of the principal habitats.

The main part of the book is dedicated to the birds and mammals themselves. All of the most common species have been illustrated. The text contains a brief description of each bird or mammal species, its behavior, details of its reproduction, habitat, and range. It also provides information on status; the more common or conspicuous species have been treated in a more detailed fashion. None of the animals has been described exhaustively, the intent being to provide an overview of the natural history of the more frequently seen or common species rather than an in-depth study. Consequently, information on the less evident species has been purposely restricted, even for those animals that may be common or well known elsewhere but are not a significant part of the fauna of this particular region. The result is a deliberate disproportion in the text in favor of the birds and mammals that I have felt the reader would most like to know about. In some cases, pen-and-ink illustrations have been added to emphasize points made in the text.

Much is yet to be learned about the birds and mammals of Patagonia. With a few notable exceptions, for example R. C. Murphy's classic, two-volume *Oceanic Birds of South America,* the available information is limited and restricted to a few museum collections, a handful of scientific reports and papers, and a scattering of records and sightings. In recent years, the field of wildlife research in Patagonia has opened up, and some species have been the subject of new and fascinating studies. When appropriate, the results of this research have been included.

NAMES

Each animal is listed by its English, Spanish, and scientific name.

Classification of mammals follows Corbet and Hill (1980); that of the birds follows the "standard" sequence published, for example, by R. Meyer de Schauensee (1970) and used in the American Ornithologists' Union Checklist (1983); for the passerines I have followed Ridgely and Tudor (1989, 1994). Outdated nomenclature appears in parentheses. Common names of the birds and mammals have been carefully selected. In some cases, particularly in Spanish, more than one common name figures in the literature. I have given preference to those that seem most appropriate; however, when faced with two equally well-known names, I provide both, although the first is my own choice.

In general, the common English names of birds follow *A Guide to the Birds of South America* by R. Meyer de Schauensee and *Seabirds, an Identification Guide* by P. Harrison.

Common Spanish names of birds have been selected from *Lista Patrón de Nombres Comunes de las Aves Argentinas* by J. Navas et al. and *Guía para la Identificación de las Aves de Argentina y Uruguay* by T. Narosky and D. Yzurieta.

In general, common English names of the mammals follow usage in *The Encyclopedia of Mammals* by D. MacDonald. When I have been unable to find a common name in the literature, as, for example, with some of the mice, I have provided my own.

Common Spanish names of mammals follow *Mamíferos Sudamericanos* by A. Cabrera and J. Yepes and *Guía de los Mamíferos Argentinos* by C. C. Olrog and M. M. Lucero.

FAMILY ACCOUNTS

Family accounts contain broad comments on description, behavior, and habitat characteristic of each group. The total number of species in the family and the number found in the region covered by the book are provided in this section.

SPECIES ACCOUNTS

Each species is treated individually. The text is divided into sections as described below to facilitate reading. Information from the literature has been consulted for these accounts. Some species accounts contain my own comments and personal observations, with details of behavior or habitat. Each of these observations is printed in italics in the text. When the reference is an unpublished source, the initials and last name or names of the people who provided the observation appear in parentheses, with a year when available, for example (*D. Boersma*, 1984). If the information is from a published source, the last name is followed by the date of publication not separated by a comma, for example (*Payne 1985*). When no name follows the reference, the observation was made by me personally. A bibliography appears in the back of the book.

Description

The measurements provided are averages and should be considered only as indicative. They figure first in English measures, followed by the metric equivalent in parentheses, rounded off for simplicity. For the birds, the first measurement provided is the approximate length from bill tip to tail tip in the live bird. For birds that glide, "wingspan" measurement is included and refers to the distance from tip to tip of both outstretched wings. For the mammals, "body" measurement refers to the average length, taken from the tip of the head to the base of the tail. Additional measurements include "tail," measured from base to tip; "height," measured at the shoulder; and "wingspan" for bats. For some species the average weight is given.

Measurements are followed by a short, selective text describing the distinctive markings of the species in its most common phase, restricted to key features for identification. When male and female are similar, there is only a single description and the sex is not mentioned. When they are different, the male is described first. Then, following the subheading "female," there is a brief outline of her distinctive measurements and markings. In the same way, when a species of bird presents distinct breeding and nonbreeding plumage, it is described in its most common phase; this is then followed by a short summary of the differences corresponding to the opposing phase. A description of the juvenile is included only if it is different from the adult and is limited to its distinctive markings.

Behavior

This section varies substantially in length and detail according to the species. In most cases the text is limited to behaviors that help find and identify the bird or mammal; however, the better known or more conspicuous species are discussed in greater depth. Breeding information is included only for those species that reproduce in Patagonia.

Status and Habitat

Little is known about the exact status of most birds and mammals of this region. First, certain habitats make estimating difficult; this is true, for example, for many whales and dolphins. Second, research effort is uneven, so that some areas are better known than others. Third, some species are more conspicuous than others. In some species, the behavior, voice, and coloration may vary with the season so that sometimes they seem to be more abundant when they are, in fact, merely more conspicuous.

The following terms refer to the probability of sighting. They are guidelines to be used in the habitats and ranges where one might expect to see the species.

Common. Those species sighted almost unfailingly in the right habitat and season.

Fairly common. Species with a 50/50 chance of sighting in the right habitat and season.

Uncommon. Species with less than a 20% likelihood of sighting in the right habitat and season. Count yourself fairly lucky if you see one of these.

Rare or scarce. Species with few sight records.

Local. Species that, within their range, are restricted to particular places either because thay have very specific habitat needs or have behavioral or external constraints.

Irregular or *erratic.* Migratory or wandering species that appear and disappear in an area without a regular pattern.

Accidental. Refers to isolated records of species that normally inhabit a very different habitat.

Hypothetical. Species whose presence is not yet supported by photographic records or collected specimens.

Resident. Species that remain in the area year-round.

Migrant. Species that regularly spend only a part of the year in the region;

the term is usually accompanied by the season when it is present (e.g., "summer migrant"). There can be "breeding" or "nonbreeding" migrants. A question mark is used when the information is insufficient.

Rare, accidental, and hypothetical sight records, when available, are set in italics followed by the name of the observer in parentheses.

An animal may be "common" even if not more than one or two individuals are seen at any given time (e.g., many hawks); likewise, "uncommon" species may sometimes be seen in large numbers (e.g., some shorebirds). On the other hand, species may be "rare" in Patagonia but "common" elsewhere, or they may be "common" but very restricted in distribution.

The principal habitats where the species are found or have been recorded are discussed in this section.

Range

Provides the geographical limits of the area where the species is known to exist. Range for eastern Patagonia is provided first, followed by the overall range. Migration ranges and dates are provided in this section.

Similar Species

Includes specific details to help distinguish species that are hard to tell apart in the field, in particular when distribution overlaps.

Note

Contains comments of interest, recent revisions in classification, etc.

MAPS

A range map is included for each species. Dark shading indicates breeding range. Light shading represents non breeding range. Hatching indicates probable range. Each map contains the name of the species to which it applies and the number that precedes the name in the text.

PLATES

All of the birds and mammals that occur regularly and are commonly seen in the area covered by the book can be found in the color plates. When different, the male, female, and/or juvenile are illustrated. Some of the birds are shown in flight. Brief descriptions facing each plate provide key information for the identification of each species, including the species/range map number.

APPENDIXES

This section contains a list of rare or accidental species, as well as a list of recommended readings.

Description of Eastern Patagonia

TOPOGRAPHY

Eastern Patagonia forms a flat plain that slopes gently toward the Atlantic Ocean. Interspersed here and there are outcrops and weathered peaks of ancient mountain chains that rise 1500–4500 ft (500–1500 m) above sea level, and in many places the remnants of cliffs can be seen where ancient seas once washed prehistoric shores.

Very few rivers traverse this vast territory. With their source in the Andes to the west, they make their way eastward across the desert until they reach the Atlantic. Following millennia of seasonal floods, these rivers have gouged valleys into the steppes that are sometimes several miles wide. These valleys have been put under irrigation and are developed for farming. The largest rivers are the Río Negro near the northern border of Patagonia, and the Río Santa Cruz near the Strait of Magellan in the south. The few rivers in between are small, some of them mere seasonal trickles.

Along the eastern seaboard, a harsh, unspoiled shore separates Patagonia from the South Atlantic. Much of this coastline is even and unbroken, but in parts it swings around to form bays, peninsulas, and capes, and in a few places the nearby ocean is peppered with small islands. Crumbling cliffs of loose, sedimentary rock, interspersed with beaches of rounded stones or sand, make up most of the coast. In some places areas of ancient volcanic rock lie exposed, forming capes, points, and islands. The sea encroaches on some of the river mouths to form large inlets. These shores are washed by tides, which in some places range as much as 21 ft and form large mudflats.

Beyond the eastern shore lies a vast continental shelf that stretches over 200 miles into the Atlantic Ocean. Relatively flat, this huge shelf lies under shallow water averaging barely 55–82 fathoms (100–150 m) in depth. One of the deeper parts of this shelf is found only a few miles from shore in the middle of the almost land-locked Golfo Nuevo, to the south of Península Valdés. Here, the depth of water reaches 95 fathoms (170 m).

Depressions of the earth's surface such as these also pepper the mainland. Some are small, others large—even many miles across—and often contain a lake or salt pan in the center. Two such depressions occur in the center of Península Valdés, the Salina Grande and the Salina Chica. The bottom of the Salina Grande lies 150 ft (48 m) below sea level.

The morphology of the region is constantly changing. In geological terms it is being rapidly transformed, and even in recent times the shape of much of the

ARGENTINA

PATAGONIA

CHUBUT

SANTA CRUZ

San Antonio Oeste

Río Negro

Viedma

Golfo San Matías
Punta Norte
Golfo San José
Península Valdés
Caleta Valdés
Punta Delgada
Puerto Pirámide
Golfo Nuevo
Punta Ninfas

Puerto Madryn

Trelew

Rawson
Punta Tombo

Camarones
Bahía Melo
Bahía Bustamante

Cabo Dos Bahías
Isla Tova

Comodoro Rivadavia

Golfo San Jorge

Caleta Olivia

Monte Loaysa

Cabo Blanco

Ría Deseado

Puerto Deseado
Isla Pingüino
Punta Medanosa

Puerto San Julián

ATLANTIC OCEAN

Río Santa Cruz
Puerto Santa Cruz

Monte León

Río Gallegos

Cabo Vírgenes
Strait of Magellan
Tierra Del Fuego

1. Coast of Patagonia from Península Valdés to the Strait of Magellan.
2. South America.

coast has changed remarkably. The most dramatic effects can be seen on the cliffs, where almost daily new pieces crumble, collapse, and tumble into the sea. Waves, huge tides, and strong currents tug at the coastline with such power that in some places visible changes occur from one year to the next.

GEOLOGY

Although geology is beyond the scope of this book, a brief background of the geological history of the region provides useful insights into the present situation affecting the wildlife.

For millennia, parts of Patagonia have risen and receded numerous times. Each time the land subsided, the sea advanced and covered part of the region; when it rose, the sea retreated, leaving marine deposits many miles from the present shores. There are fossil shells to be found even as far inland as the center of the province of Neuquen, many hundreds of miles northwest across the desert—a mute reminder of the extent of the upheaval.

The Geological History of Patagonia during the Tertiary

During the past 60 million years, Patagonia has been subjected to major marine incursions that coincided with the rising of the Andean mountain chain.

The sequence of events is as follows. At the end of the Cretaceous period, the Andes had not yet begun to rise and western Patagonia was probably fairly flat. At that time there was a marked descent of a great part of the region, with seas covering much of the land on two separate occasions.

The first buckling of the earth's crust, which gave rise to the Andes, started 70 million years ago and lasted for 20 million years (from the late Cretaceous into the mid-Tertiary). The mountains that were formed were probably not very high. Fossil remains of trees that subsequently grew in many parts of the plains of Patagonia indicate warm or temperate, damp climates.

About 20 million years ago, during the Miocene, the land subsided once more. This time the ocean advanced from the east and formed a large sea known to geologists as the Patagonian Sea. This period was followed by a gradual uplifting of the land, and the Atlantic Ocean receded eastward across the Patagonian plain.

Toward the end of the Miocene, 10 million years ago, a period of renewed activity took place in the Andes, and things really began to change for Patagonia. The rising mountain range caused prevailing westerly winds to release their moisture on the mountains' western slopes. As a result, grassland and forest turned to desert as the climate grew progressively drier.

This second period of intense mountain building has continued intermittently up to the present day. Erosion across the Patagonian plain has been intense. Mountain debris—rocks, stones, and sand—was carried eastward by rivers and glaciers. In the process, the stones were tumbled and worn so that now, rounded and polished, they form an almost continuous layer, known as *tehuelche* gravel or shingle, that covers the plains of Patagonia.

Tehuelche gravel is markedly heterogeneous. Only the hardest stones have survived this prolonged transport from the Andes, as the softer stones were worn away. Consequently, the shingle is made up mostly of rounded fragments of granite, basalt, and porphyritic rock, depending on the source. Petrified wood and fossil shells also form part of tehuelche gravel.

The times of occurrence of these geological events have been established by comparing the sequence of layers of sediment within which fossils are found. Each layer of sediment represents a period of time. Unless the land has been radically disturbed, the lower the sedimentary layer, the older it is. Cliffs or river beds provide excellent opportunities for viewing these different layers.

Many layers are the result of volcanic action or sediment transported by rivers, glaciers, wind, etc., and not all of them contain fossils. Fossils are formed only under the right conditions: when hard tissues such as bone and wood and, far more rarely, soft tissues lie undisturbed and covered by sediment for thousands of years. Minerals gradually replace the tissues of the organism, forming an "imprint" or image of the original, that is, a fossil. According to the surrounding sediment, fossils can be made up of different minerals and some reflect the original tissue more perfectly than others.

Most of the discoveries that led to our present-day knowledge of the origins of ancient South American mammals were made west of Comodoro Rivadavia near the lakes of Musters and Colhue Huapi. Here, at the turn of the century, Carlos Ameghino and his brother Florentino and, later on, many notable paleontologists from all over the world, discovered fossil remains that drew a remarkable picture of what Patagonia must have looked like through the ages.

It is fascinating to imagine that during that time, when parts of present-day Patagonia were under the ocean, the shores of a strange and wonderful land stood close at hand. Trees and grasslands flourished in the warm, damp climate. Large herds of peculiar, now long extinct, horse- and camel-like herbivores grazed the fertile plains, much the same as herds of herbivores graze around Africa today. Furthermore, crocodiles basked along the shores of streams and rivers; birds were abundant in the trees; and cuís and mara-like animals, uncannily similar to those of today, chased about on the ground.

CLIMATE

The most notorious feature of Patagonian weather is the wind. Wind has probably affected the lives of living creatures in the region more than any other factor. It is almost constant, with very few calm spells, and usually blows from the west with a moderate to strong force all year round. The region is generally arid because these prevailing westerlies shed their moisture on the Andes before they blow across the plains of Patagonia.

Rains are mostly restricted to the autumn and winter months of May to August. Summer is the driest season of the year, although occasional thunderstorms will occur. Annual rainfall ranges between 6 and 12 inches (150 and 300 mm).

Temperatures are affected by the prevailing winds and the proximity of the sea. In the northern parts of the region, summer temperatures average 65°F (17.4°C) and can rise above 85°F (30°C). The winters are comparatively mild, with an average of 12.4 days in the year registering temperatures below freezing; it very rarely snows.

In the southern parts of eastern Patagonia, summers are cool, with temperatures rarely rising above 75°F (25°C). In winter, temperatures often drop below freezing, and snow may lie for weeks.

THE HABITATS OF COASTAL PATAGONIA

The following are the main habitat types found in eastern Patagonia.

Oceanic

The region is under the influence of two currents and significant tides:

BRAZIL CURRENT

The Brazil current flows southward along the eastern edge of South America, and its force and direction vary seasonally. It is strongest off Brazil from Isla Abrholos to the latitude of Río de Janeiro. From the Tropic of Capricorn southward it becomes progressively weaker. It meets the cold Malvinas current off the coast of Argentina and is forced eastward into the Atlantic, forming gigantic slow-moving swirls and eddies. Although the two currents normally meet near the latitude of the province of Buenos Aires, the influence of the Brazil current is still felt along the coast of northern Patagonia.

The Brazil current is warm and clear and relatively poor in plankton and fish life. Consequently, seabirds and marine mammals are not abundant within this current except where it comes under the influence of rivers.

FALKLAND (MALVINAS) CURRENT

The Falkland or Malvinas current is cold and flows slowly northward up the coast of Patagonia. It is strongest along the outer edge of the continental shelf, where it travels at a speed of about one knot. Prevailing westerly winds produce upwelling of cold, Antarctic water along the edge of the shelf, which carries nutrients to the surface. This constant supply of nourishment along the shelf break forms the basis of the rich Southwest Atlantic ecosystem; it supplies the life support to its large fish populations and in turn supports spectacular populations of albatrosses, petrels, whales, elephant seals, and other wildlife. Many of these species seek the coastal waters and shores of Patagonia to breed.

The merging of the Brazil and Falkland (Malvinas) currents is over a wide and variable area and consequently has a substantial effect on the fauna of the region. Some scientists believe that occasional mass reproductive failures in seabird colonies on the coast of Patagonia may be the result of shifts in ocean currents. This shift in currents, likened to the periodic El Niño effect produced by the Humboldt Current off Peru, appears to be the cause of a general impoverishment of the food chain.

TIDES

In many places along the coast of Patagonia, tides are pronounced. Ranges between high and low can be greater than 21 feet (7 meters). Tides have a considerable effect upon the fauna that inhabit the coastline. For example, many birds find nourishment in areas exposed at low tide.

Reefs

At different places along the coast, often near points and projecting from the base of cliffs, there are broad, wave-cut platforms of compacted marine sediment, fine clays, sand, and fossils.

Many of these reefs are exposed at low tide. Inhabited by invertebrates and fish, they provide food for gulls and oystercatchers that gather there to feed.

Cliffs

Much of the coast is lined with sheer cliffs that rise 180–300 ft (60–100 m) from sea level. These cliffs are made up of different layers of sediment of Tertiary origin, some of which contain a variety of marine fossils including extinct Giant Oysters, crabs, and even whale skeletons.

Cliffs provide nesting and roosting places for many species of birds.

Outcrops of Volcanic Rock

Volcanic outcrops occur at many places along the coast of Patagonia. These outcrops, which are remnants of ancient volcanic activity, form the hard substrata of many of the points and islands such as Punta Tombo, Cabo Dos Bahías, Cabo Blanco, and the islands near Cabo Dos Bahías and Puerto Deseado. Points and islands such as these form the natural refuge for many species of marine birds and mammals.

Beaches

GRAVEL BEACHES

Along the base of many of the cliffs and interspersed along the coastline, tehuelche gravel has accumulated to form beaches. Where these beaches are most exposed and wave action is greatest, the gravel is large. Gravel beaches are used by many species of marine birds and mammals as roosts and rookeries.

SANDY BEACHES

Sandy beaches make up a small portion of the coast of Patagonia. These exist in sheltered bays where wave action is shielded by outcrops of firm substrate. Such beaches are usually backed by shifting sand dunes.

INTERTIDAL MUDFLATS

Intertidal mudflats occur within shallow bays or inlets that are sheltered from wave action. Sediment eroded from cliffs and beaches by wind and water accumulates in such places to form gently sloping muddy shores. Because there are few sheltered bays and inlets along the coast of Patagonia between Península Valdés and the Strait of Magellan, intertidal mudflats are uncommon; they are mostly restricted to the bays and inlets around the Península Valdés and a few isolated inlets. At low tide, large expanses of mud, rich in invertebrates, lie exposed.

A number of shorebirds and gulls specialize in feeding on the invertebrates that inhabit this environment.

Steppe

PREDOMINANT VEGETATION

The plants of the region are adapted to a dry climate with low seasonal rainfall. The grasses are coarse; they grow quickly in spring, and seed in early summer. Most bushes sprout in early spring, flower in summer, and go to seed in autumn. Some species are low and domeshaped, others are spindly, in both cases offering minimum resistance to constant winds. Many plants trap wind-blown soil around their base, providing nourishment for their roots.

Most of the northern parts of eastern Patagonia are bush covered. Predominant in the Península Valdés area are the "Creosote" bushes (*Larrea divaricata and L. nitida*), "Zampa" (*Atriplex lampa*), and "Quillimbai" (*Chuquiraga avellanedae*). Less abundant bushes include "Uña de Gato" (*Chuquiraga erinacea*), "Hume" (*Suaeda divaricata*), "Piquillin" (*Conllalia microphylla*), "Llaollín" (*Lycium chilense*), and "Molle" (*Schinus polygamus*). Grasses such as "Flechilla" (*Stipa tenuis*), "Coiron Pluma" (*Stipa neaei*), and "Coiron Amargo" (*Stipa humilis, S. speciosa, and S. chrysophylla*) dominate the lower stratum, whereas wild thyme (*Acantholippia seriphioides*) is common in some areas. Sandy terrain near the coast, such as in parts of Península Valdés, are covered with the dune grasses "Junquillo" (*Sporobolus rigens*) and "Olivillo" (*Hyalis argentea*).

In the district around Punta Tombo and Cabo Dos Bahías the dominant bush in many places is "Duraznillo" (*Colliguaya integerrima*), although "Zampa" and "Quillimbai" are still common. Farther south, bushes begin giving way to open countryside of short coarse grasses, interspersed with patches of "Duraznillo," "Llaollín," "Molle," and "Algarrobillo" (*Prosopis denudans*) bushes.

Much of the southern part of eastern Patagonia as far as the Strait of Magellan is covered by short coarse grasses and plants that hug the ground. "Coirón Blanco" (*Festuca palescens*) and pin-cushion plants (*Bolax sp.*) are common. "Mata Negra" (*Junellia tridens*) is the predominant shrub and in some areas forms a low, dense covering. This dark bush is covered with small pink and white blossoms in summer that flush the countryside with color.

Freshwater Lakes and Irrigated Areas

Permanent fresh water is scarce in much of eastern Patagonia. There are a few weeks each year, following the rains that usually come during autumn and winter, when the shallow lake beds that pepper the plains fill with water. For brief periods, fresh water is plentiful, but with the coming of wind and sun, almost all of these lakes dry up, leaving their exposed bed cracked and hardened.

Freshwater springs are very rare and seldom produce enough water to settle in permanent ponds; however, vegetation in these areas is more abundant and provides food for grassland animals. There are freshwater springs around the Salina Grande in Península Valdés.

Jarilla
Larrea divaricata

False Jarilla
Larrea nitida

Piquillín
Condalia microphylla

Quillimbai
*Chuquiraga
avellanedae*

Llaollín
Lycium chilense

Hume
Suaeda divaricata

Zampa
Atriplex lampa

3. Bushes common to northeastern Patagonia.

The only constant source of fresh water in much of the region is provided by rivers that descend from the Andes. Some of these rivers seep into the desert or evaporate and disappear; others make their way across the plains and flow into the Atlantic.

One of these rivers, the Chubut, flows into the sea just south of Península Valdés. The lower reaches of this small river wind through farmland that extends across the bottom of a wide valley. This green oasis supports a variety of birds that are not found in the surrounding desert, birds that are common to the grasslands and trees of the pampas farther north. Some parts of this irrigated valley are permanently or semipermanently inundated and are inhabited by migratory and resident birds. The largest river in the region by far, and the only other permanent one, is the Santa Cruz in southern Patagonia. This river does not traverse irrigated areas.

Migrations and Wildlife Viewing

As IN MANY temperate regions of the world, many of the birds and mammals of eastern Patagonia migrate seasonally. Some travel large distances each year between breeding and nonbreeding grounds. Some species of terns and shorebirds journey almost from one pole to the other and back again each year. Most travel in flocks or groups. Some animals such as penguins and right whales migrate at sea.

How animals navigate large distances under such varied conditions is not well understood. Some probably travel traditional routes using landmarks to guide their way; it has also been found that some birds navigate by the sun and stars.

Weather affects migration; birds will choose favorable winds for travel. Most migratory birds travel high in the sky: some species, such as ibis, flock in V-shaped patterns; others, such as many shorebirds, fly in compact groups. Some birds migrate during the day, others do so at night. During migration, birds may land and rest, though some travel great distances nonstop.

Some of these migrations, such as those of the upland and ashy-headed geese and red knots, are a striking part of the autumn and spring seasons.

HOW, WHEN, AND WHERE TO VIEW COASTAL WILDLIFE

The best viewing opportunities for coastal wildlife can be found at the wildlife reserves created for this purpose. Here the animals, though absolutely wild, have become accustomed to the presence of people and don't feel threatened. But visitors should not leave the trails; this will only frighten the animals. Not only will one's viewing opportunities be lessened—and the visitor will probably be reprimanded or fined—but, more importantly, disturbances may cause serious damage to wildlife. Information is provided throughout this book on the best reserves from which to view coastal species at any given time of year.

VIEWING COLONIAL SPECIES OF WILDLIFE

Wildlife colonies offer a spectacular oportunity for viewing animals in their natural surroundings. They are often placed in predictable locations at predictable times.

But a cautionary note is necessary. All colonies—particularly those of nesting birds—are extremely vulnerable. At the sight of a person, the animals may become nervous; mammals may stampede, injuring their pups, and birds are liable to abandon their nests, leaving eggs or chicks at the mercy of gulls and other predators. Careless approach can cause whole colonies to be destroyed. Seek advice from wildlife wardens. If none are available and you are approaching a colony that is not a designated reserve, move slowly and keep low. At the very first sign that the animals are becoming nervous, remain still or retreat slowly.

HOW, WHEN, AND WHERE TO LOOK FOR PETRELS AND ALBATROSSES

The basic requirement for seeing petrels and albatrosses from the coast is wind. Choose a day with a good stiff blow, stand on a windward shore, and gaze out to sea. Windward shores are not the norm in Patagonia with its prevailing westerlies, so judge the direction of the wind; study a map and you may be rewarded. Binoculars or a spotting scope can be a great help, and a place out of the wind makes for greater comfort.

At virtually any time of year you will see petrels and albatrosses dipping and rising above the waves; some are large and stately, others are small and fast. Sometimes they occur in great numbers, each bird swinging up above the skyline, then down to brush the waves, crisscrossing the paths of others, so that at any time some are up and others are down. Some glide stiffly, others beat their wings rapidly; some venture close to shore, while others stay well away.

HOW, WHEN, AND WHERE TO VIEW WHALES AND DOLPHINS

Many cetaceans can be seen from shore. Some sightings are predictable, but in most cases you need a fair dose of luck. In general, flat calm weather is best. Again, a spotting scope or a pair of binoculars is a great help, and so is patience.

HOW, WHEN, AND WHERE TO VIEW SHOREBIRDS AND WATERBIRDS

Spring and fall migrations are, of course, the best time to see shorebirds. Mudflats are a must. Access to many of these areas is through private land, and some areas are inside wildlife reserves; few, if any, have proper control facilities. Use tact and good judgment, and always seek permission when entering private property.

Many of the waterbirds can be viewed, without leaving public roads, through the irrigated areas along the Chubut River. The months of September through March provide the best viewing time for waterbirds.

HOW, WHEN, AND WHERE TO VIEW TERRESTRIAL WILDLIFE

Hunting is common in the region, making wildlife shy of man. Many animals seek cover in the sparse vegetation or try to keep as much distance as possible between themselves and the observer.

Most terrestrial birds and mammals can usually be seen best on the roadside from within a vehicle. Remember that many animals are more afraid of people than of cars and buses. Quiet roads off the beaten track provide better viewing opportunities for bird-watchers; permission should be obtained from landowners before entering private property.

> **Reminder.** General information on distribution is found in each species account under the heading "Range." Information on viewing specific birds and mammals is under "Status and Habitat," and records (personal observations within the species accounts) can help find rare or uncommon species.

WILDLIFE RESERVES AND PROTECTED AREAS

The following wildlife reserves exist on or near the coast of continental Patagonia.

Chubut

Península Valdés Provincial Reserve. Created in 1983. Land is privately owned but the wildlife is declared of "provincial interest"; access to the coast is restricted. The following areas are open for tourism: Punta Norte, where South American Sea Lions, Southern Elephant Seals, and occasionally Orcas can often be seen in February and March capturing sea lion pups on the shore. Caleta Valdés, where Southern Elephant Seals can be seen all year round; Punta Pirámide, where South American Sea Lions can be viewed during their breeding season; Isla de los Pájaros, where Kelp Gulls, Neotropic Cormorants, and Black-crowned Night-Herons, among others, can be seen.

Golfo San José Provincial Park. Created in 1974. One of the most important calving grounds of the Southern Right Whale. Selected areas such as Isla de los Pájaros are open to tourism and boating is restricted.

Punta Tombo Provincial Reserve. Created in 1979. Protects parts of the largest Magellanic Penguin colony in Patagonia. Parts of the reserve are open to tourism. Visitors must follow the instructions of their guides and keep to the trails.

Punta Loma Provincial Reserve. Created in 1967. Open to tourism. South American Sea Lions are the principal attraction and can be viewed all year round.

Punta León Provincial Reserve. Created in 1985. Mixed colony of sea birds and mammals. Wildlife very vulnerable to disturbance. Not open to visitors.

Bosque Petrificado Sarmiento. Created in 1983. An area with fallen fossil tree trunks. Parts are open to the public.

Cabo Dos Bahías Provincial Reserve. Created in 1983. Protects a Magellanic Penguin colony and a nonbreeding rookery of South American Fur Seals. Parts of the colony are open to tourism along well-marked trails.

Santa Cruz

Monumento Natural Bosque Petrificado de Madre e Hija. Created in 1954. An area with large fallen fossil tree trunks. Parts are open to the public.

Reserva Natural Intangible Cabo Blanco. Created in 1977. One of the only South American Fur Seal colonies along the coast of Argentina.

Ría Deseado Provincial Reserve. Created in 1977. One of the few colonies of Red-legged Cormorants in Argentina.

Bahía Laura. Created in 1977. Protects Imperial Cormorant colonies.

Bahía San Julián Provincial Reserve. Created in 1986. Magellanic Penguin colonies within the bay and one of the largest Red-legged Cormorant colonies at Cabo Curioso.

Cabo Virgenes Provincial Reserve. Created in 1986. One of the largest colonies of Magellanic Penguins in Santa Cruz and the second in size after Punta Tombo.

Areas under Consideration as Wildlife Reserves at the Time of This Writing

Punta Medanosa Provincial Reserve (Santa Cruz). Magellanic Penguin colony and cormorant colonies.

Monte León (Santa Cruz). Under consideration as a national park. Colonies of Magellanic Penguins, Imperial and Rock Cormorants, and Dolphin Gulls; also a sea lion rookery, all in a spectacular setting.

BIRDS / Aves

(Class Aves)

Animals with backbones. Warm-blooded, bodies
insulated with feathers. Forelimbs modified as wings;
most birds are capable of flight. Reproduction is
through egg-laying.

Wing plume of rhea

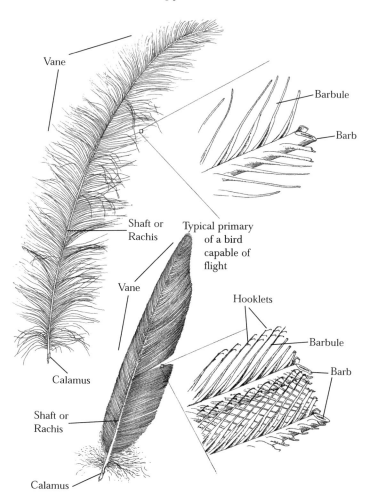

Vane

Barbule

Barb

Shaft or
Rachis

Typical primary
of a bird
capable of
flight

Vane

Hooklets

Barbule

Barb

Calamus

Shaft or
Rachis

Calamus

4. Rhea feathers lack the small hooklets on each barbule that maintain the vanelike feather structure in birds capable of flight.

RHEIFORMES

RHEAS / Ñandúes
(Family Rheidae)

Large, flightless birds with rounded bodies, very long necks, and comparatively small heads with straight, flattened beaks. They have long, powerful legs; toes are tipped with large, blunt claws. Rheas are swift runners. Their wing and tail feathers lack the compact structure found in most birds and are characteristically open-vaned. Rheas are gregarious and found in groups. Males incubate the eggs and rear the chicks. The family is exclusively South American, with 2 species (some authors consider 3), one of which is found in eastern Patagonia.

1. DARWIN'S RHEA / Choique o Ñandú Petizo
Pterocnemia pennata   *Plate 1*

Description. 47″ (120 cm). Very large and round-bodied. No tail. Dull gray-brown plumage, speckled with white. *Chick:* Back striped gray and white. *Juvenile:* Uniform gray at one month.

Behavior. Diurnal. Usually in flocks of 2–4 to sometimes over 50. Extremely shy. Runs from danger, briefly unfolding and spreading each wing. Capable of bursts of speed over 30 mph (50 kph).

Forages during the day on grass, leaves, berries, and seeds. Diet includes leaves and blossoms of "Quillimbai" (*Chuquiraga avellanedae*) and "Piquillin" berries (*Condalia microphylla*) as well as insects.

Conditions its plumage by preening and dust bathing to free it of old feathers and ectoparasites. Molt occurs between September and March.

Usually silent. Breeding male produces a loud drumming sound when courting and harsh hissing sounds when defending a nest. When dispersed, chicks produce high, thin wavering calls that serve to regroup the flock.

Breeding begins in July. Harem polygynous; each male mates with between 2 and 6 females.

Constructed by male, nest is a shallow scrape, 20″ (50 cm) in diameter, lined with downy feathers and dry grasses. Each female lays 10–12 eggs, one every 2 days, each egg weighing about 1.5 lb (600 g). They are bright green, bleaching to whitish yellow after a few days. A single nest can contain over 40 eggs.

Male incubates eggs and rears chicks. Females begin laying in their third year. When they have finished laying in one nest, females abandon the male and begin searching for another mate.

Incubation lasts 41–42 days. If disturbed during this period, male may abandon the nest.

Chicks start emitting sounds from within the egg, triggering synchronous hatching; all eggs in the clutch hatch within 24 hr. Chicks abandon the nest less than a day later and immediately begin feeding on their own under protection

5. Darwin's Rhea. (a) Chick. (b) One-month juvenile. (c) Yearling. (d) Adult.

of the male. When threatened, chicks run for cover while male attempts to distract the predator. Males often incorporate chicks of other flocks into their own. Flocks of over 105 chicks of varying ages have been reported.

Status and Habitat. Common resident. Grassy steppe and arid bush-covered areas. Often on dry, shallow lake beds carpeted with short grasses; also in areas with dunes.

Range. All of Patagonia, parts of western Argentina, and corresponding regions of Chile. Introduced on Tierra del Fuego. The altiplano subspecies, or Andean Lesser Rhea / Suri (*P. p. garleppi*), considered a separate species by some authors, is found in open, dry Andean regions of northwestern Argentina, northern Chile, western Bolivia, and southern Peru.

6. When resting, the Darwin's Rhea sits back on its tarsi and sleeps with its neck curled over its back.

7. As it runs, the Darwin's Rhea briefly opens its wings with each rapid change of direction.

TINAMIFORMES

TINAMOUS / Perdices y Martinetas
(Family Tinamidae)

Rounded birds with slender necks, relatively small heads, short legs, and very short tails. They are cryptically patterned in dull to rufous browns and grays. Sexes are similar. Tinamous are mainly terrestrial, but capable of flight. They are polygynous and the male incubates the eggs and rears the chicks. These birds are similar to the partridge of Eurasia, but are not related; they

8. When walking, the rhea jerks its head back and forth.

are exclusive to South America. Of the 41 species, 3 are found in eastern Patagonia.

2. DARWIN'S TINAMOU / Perdíz Chica Pálida
Nothura darwinii   *Plate 1*

Description. 10.2″ (26 cm). No crest. Short legs. Cryptic coloring. Head and neck pale buff, streaked brown. Chin white. Upperparts spotted and streaked with pale gray, brown, and white; underparts sandy brown, barred brown on flanks. Primaries and secondaries heavily barred.

Behavior. Usually alone. Stands very upright. Very shy; walks away, crouching low, hidden in the grass, or runs quickly for cover. If necessary, will fly up with rapid, buzzing wing beats interspaced with brief glides and land out of sight a short distance away. Alarm call, produced in flight, is a long string of uniform, rapid, high whistles, "Fee fee fee fee . . . "

Diet includes seeds, grasses, buds, and insects.

Breeding begins in September. Nest is a rough scrape in ground lined with grasses, partially hidden in vegetation. Average clutch 6–8 eggs. Eggs shiny, violaceous, gray brown.

Status and Habitat. Uncommon breeding resident. *One nest was found at Punta Delgada, Chubut, in October 1989 (F. Quiñenao). Lone individuals recorded by roadside in mixed grass and quillimbai bush area near Puerto Pirámides, Chubut, November 1982 and October 1985. Also recorded at Caleta Valdés, Chubut, November 1986.* Arid grasslands, mixed scrub, and open woodland. Grass-covered roadsides.

Range. Northeastern Chubut, central to northwestern Argentina. Also Chile, Bolivia, and Peru.

3. ELEGANT CRESTED-TINAMOU / Martineta o Copetona Común
Eudromia elegans   *Plate 1*

Description. 15.8″ (40 cm). Long neck. Cryptic coloring. Noticeable crest of black plumes, normally held erect. Long white eyebrow and malar stripe. Chin whitish. Upperparts and chest very barred and streaked brownish gray. Rest of underparts whitish, barred gray. Legs pale horn. *Chick:* Noticeable crest present at hatching. Upperparts very streaked pale buff, gray, and white. *Juvenile:* Similar to adult though smaller and paler.

Behavior. Fairly tame. Usually in threes or family groups from August to January; rest of year birds of either sex gather in flocks, sometimes of several dozen. Rarely alone.

Diurnal. Spends most of time feeding on leaves, flowers, and seeds of a variety of desert grasses and bushes. When alarmed, stands very erect and bows head and neck rapidly, at the same time producing alarm calls, "Wheet!" Prefers to run from danger, holding itself very upright and zigzagging rapidly between the bushes. Will fly if necessary, bursting suddenly into the air with rapid, noisy wingbeats interspaced with short glides. Traveling straight and low over the ground, it usually drops down again out of sight a short distance away. Both sexes produce contact calls, an intermittent, high whistle with one- or two-second intervals, lasting up to 2 min "Wheet . . . Wheet . . . Wheet . . . " *Molt occurs in December (P. Long & F. Long 1978).*

Breeding begins in August. Male establishes territory covering 4–16 acres. He emits a "whistle-warble", one long whistle followed by two quick short whistles, "Feee-Feefee!" Females travel in pairs that remain together through the breeding season. Male emits a low, lulling call to incite females to copulate. When he is accepted, he mates with each female. The trio remains together 1–3 weeks. During that time both females lay eggs in a single nest; when finished, they move on to find another male. Females take no part in the care of eggs or young and can mate successively with as many as 7 or 8 different males in one season.

Nest is a bowl-shaped hollow in the ground, lined with feathers and grasses, usually at base of a clump of grass or a bush. Clutch is complete when it contains about a dozen eggs; only then does the male begin sitting. Eggs are a remarkably bright glossy green.

Incubation lasts 21 days; all chicks in a brood hatch within 12 hr and nest is abandoned within the next 24 hr. Chicks immediately begin feeding on their own but keep close to the male, which constantly emits "contact" calls. When threatened, chicks disperse with twittering calls. Sitting close to the ground, they keep very still and become almost invisible. Male distracts attention from the chicks, sometimes using a "broken wing" display, then produces a quiet, surprisingly catlike mewing to regroup the scattered chicks. The flock roosts on the ground at night. If food is abundant, male can rear up to 3 broods per season.

Status and Habitat. Common, breeding resident in coastal regions of northern Patagonia; less common farther south. *In 1976 population density around Punta Norte on Península Valdés, Chubut, was estimated at 7 acres (3.6 hectares) per bird (P. Long & F. Long).* Arid, mixed-scrub grassland and open woodland; frequently among seeding grasses along roadsides November–February.

Range. All Patagonia north of Santa Cruz River; central and western Argentina to southeastern Salta. Also in Chile.

4. PATAGONIAN TINAMOU / Keú Patagónico
Tinamotis ingoufi *Plate 1*

Description. 15″ (38 cm). Rounded body; long neck and relatively small head. No crest. Three white stripes extending above, through, and below the eye down sides of head and neck. Upperparts buff, heavily barred, and spotted brown. Flanks whitish, barred gray. Lower abdomen rufous. Short legs, pale horn. *Chick:* Head and neck brown with noticeable white eye stripes. Upperparts streaked black, brown, and white.

Behavior. In groups of 3 and small family flocks from September to February; large flocks of 30 or more between March and August; rarely alone.

Runs fast, holding itself erect. When startled, the group scatters, producing alarm calls; each bird seeks cover in vegetation. Will drop down and keep very still, freezing into its surroundings. If necessary will fly up, alternating noisy wing beats with brief glides, and land a short distance away. Alarm call a sharp whistle. At night or in bad weather, several may group together seeking cover under clumps of grass or bushes. Diet includes seeds, berries, and shoots.

Nest is a scrape, dug in the ground, lined with grasses, concealed against a clump of grass or a bush. Up to 14 shiny, pale green eggs in clutch. Male incubates eggs and rears chicks. Brood keeps in contact with repeated whistles.

Status and Habitat. Uncommon breeding resident. *One adult with 5 young chicks in short, coarse grassy area with scattered Mata Negra bushes, near Cabo Blanco, Santa Cruz, December 1987 (W. Conway & G. Harris).* Arid, mixed bush and grassy steppe from sea level to 1500 ft (500 m).

Range. Province of Santa Cruz from Atlantic coast as far as foothills of Andes. Southern continental Chile.

SPHENISCIFORMES

PENGUINS / Pingüinos
(Family Spheniscidae)

Flightless seabirds with strong beaks, robust bodies, and flipper-shaped wings. Their feet are webbed and the strong legs are set far back on the body. They can stand and walk upright on land. The smallest living penguin, the Little Blue Penguin of Australia and New Zealand, stands around 12″ (30 cm) high and weighs about 2 lb (1 kg). The largest, the Emperor Penguin of Antarctica,

9. Pointing its head skyward and extending its flippers, the Magellanic Penguin produces its braying call.

(a)

(b)

10. Magellanic Penguins. (a) Female, has a slightly smaller beak. (b) Male, often has a pronounced forehead.

stands over 36″ (90 cm) high and weighs as much as 90 lb (40 kg). The sexes are similar although in general the males are larger and heavier built than the females. Their bodies are covered in a thick layer of small, almost scale-like feathers which they constantly preen and rub with water-proofing oils from a gland above the tail. A thick layer of fat under the skin helps keep the bird warm. Most species are pelagic and spend many months at sea; however, all must return to land—or ice—part of the year in order to breed and molt. They feed on fish, squid, and crustaceans. Penguins are monogamous and form colonies to breed. The same sites are used year after year. All make rudimentary nests that may contain some leaves, pebbles, or feathers; some in warmer latitudes dig burrows. These birds are virtually restricted to the Southern Hemisphere. The greatest variety of species occurs in the sub-Antarctic; however, several range farther north, and one species, the Galapagos Penguin, occurs on the equator. Of the 18 species, 2 breed on the coasts of Patagonia, one in small numbers. Three are occasional visitors.

5. MAGELLANIC PENGUIN / Pingüino de Magallanes
Spheniscus magellanicus   *Plate 2*

Description. 17″ (44 cm). Thick bill ending in hook. Upperparts and double pectoral band black. A white band arches around sides of head behind eyes. Underparts white. Average weight 9 lb (4.4 kg). *Female:* Very similar to male but slighter build, "forehead" less prominent, and bill not as heavy and more slender. *First-year juvenile:* Head and back pearl gray fading to white on belly and cheeks.

Behavior. Alone or in groups, sometimes large. Relatively unafraid. When threatened, moves head from side to side, looking first with one eye, then the other. As part of mutual recognition, hierarchy establishment, or threat display, 2 or 3 birds will face one another and "duel" rapidly with their bills.

Occasionally emits a single "haaa" sound at sea which serves as a contact call.

11. Magellanic Penguin. (a) Chick. (b) First-year plumage. (c) Adult.

Swims at 4–5 mph (6–8 kph) and dives up to 240 ft (80 m). "Porpoises" above surface when swimming fast. Feeds principally on Argentine anchovy (*Engraullis anchoita*) and young hake (*Merluccius hubbsi*), crustaceans, and squid (*Loligo brasiliensis, L. gahi, Loliguncula brevis* and *Paraledone charcott*).

Nests in colonies—some of which are very large—in same places every year. Season is as follows: At beginning of September the first males arrive from the sea and take possession of their nests. Females start arriving 2 weeks later. Female selects her mate, which is often the same one as in previous year, and both

12. Courting Magellanic Penguins often step ceremoniously around each other with bowed heads.

13. Magellanic Penguins often duel rapidly with their beaks.

take turns reconditioning the nest. Using bill and feet, they dig a shallow burrow or scrape out a nest beneath a bush which serves as protection for their young from predators and the hot summer sun. The same nests are used year after year. During courtship the pair face each other, incline their heads ceremoniously, circle each other slowly, and then mate. Within the colony, male vocalizes more than female. Both produce loud trumpeting calls reminiscent of a donkey's bray. Fights over mates or nesting sites common—often with bloody results.

Laying commences at beginning of October. Two white eggs are laid 4 days apart. Both parents take turns on nest. Incubation lasts 40–42 days. Hatching takes place through November. During the first weeks, the parents take turns brooding on the nest, then both parents forage at sea and only return for brief periods to feed their young. The adult can carry as much as 2 lb (1 kg) in its stomach to feed the chicks.

Fledging begins mid-January, 80–110 days after hatching. Once fledged, chick leaves for the ocean to feed on its own and does not return until following season. Juvenile—1-year-old-bird—molts mainly in February, and breeding adult molts in March and April—a process lasting 2–3 weeks—then it, too, migrates. Activity in colony decreases until it is deserted at end of April.

All birds are out at sea between April and August, only returning to land if sick or oiled. A few females begin reproducing after third year, males not until 4 or even 7 years old. Can live over 30 years.

Status and Habitat. Very common. Total population in Patagonia estimated at 1.8 million. *Largest colony is found at Punta Tombo, Chubut, with about 400,000 breeding adults (D. Boersma et al. 1990).* One of the most serious dangers it faces is pollution of the ocean by oil. *Between 1983 and 1990, 41,000 birds died each year due to chronic oil spills at sea (Gandini et al. 1994).*

Range. Breeding colonies occur between latitudes of Península Valdés south-

14. Magellanic Penguins spend part of their time ashore preening.

ward to Tierra del Fuego, and from there northward along Pacific to Valparaiso (33°05′S). Outside the breeding season, migrates northward over 2500 miles (4000 km) up to latitude of Río de Janeiro, Brazil.

6. KING PENGUIN / Pingüino Rey
Aptenodytes patagonicus   *Plate 2*

Description. 30″ (75 cm). Very large. Head black with crescent-shaped, yellow auricular patches. Chest yellow turning to white on belly, upperparts gray. Beak long, slightly down-curved; lower mandible rusty orange. Eye brown. Feet gray.
Behavior. Solitary on shore or at sea. Relatively unafraid of people. When swimming rapidly, "porpoises" at surface. Feeds mainly on squid. Molts between November and March. Usually silent. Pointing its beak skyward, emits a high, drawn-out trumpeting call.

15. Many penguins have metal bands on the left flipper placed there by scientists studying their biology.

Status and Habitat. Rare, nonbreeding visitor. *Lone adults on Playa Unión, Chubut in early 1986 and January 1990; and Isla Chaffers, Ría Deseado, Santa Cruz in late 1993.* Once a common breeding resident in waters surrounding the tip of continental South America (R. C. Murphy, 1936). Slaughtered by sailors 1700s–1800s, and boiled down for oil. No longer hunted, populations are now expanding on South Georgia and Falkland Islands (Islas Malvinas).

Range. Circumpolar. Península Valdés is northern limit of its range. Breeds on sub-Antarctic islands. The nearest are South Georgia, South Sandwich, and Falkland Islands (Islas Malvinas). Historical breeding records for Staten Island, coast of Tierra del Fuego, and Strait of Magellan.

7. MACARONI PENGUIN / Pingüino de Penacho Anaranjado
Eudyptes chrysolophus   Plate 3

Description. 18″ (45 cm). Hood black, ending in point at top of chest. Crown of orange plumes extending across forehead. Back blackish; belly white. Thick reddish brown beak, with bare, flesh-colored skin at the gape. Eye brown. Feet pink.

Behavior. Solitary. Usually moves on land with stiff hops; can climb steep rocky slopes. Only comes ashore in Patagonia if sick, oiled, or occasionally to molt. Produces a very loud, harsh, deep trumpeting.

Status and Habitat. Accidental visitor. Pelagic from May to September. Appears on gently slopping beaches or rocky shores of difficult access. *One breeding pair in late 1990s on Isla Pingüino, Santa Cruz. One bird molting at Punta Tombo in February 1990 (D. Boersma).*

Range. Range at sea is more southerly than the next species. Breeds on islands in Atlantic and Indian quadrant of the sub-Antarctic seas. Closest colonies are at South Georgia, South Shetland, South Orkney, Falkland (Islas Malvinas), and South Sandwich Islands.

Similar Species. Larger than the following species; orange rather than yellow crown plumes form a crescent across forehead, and black area ends in a point on center of chest.

8. ROCKHOPPER PENGUIN / Pingüino de Penacho Amarillo
Eudyptes chrysocome   Plate 2

Description. 16″ (40 cm). Relatively small and stocky. Black hood with golden eyebrows ending in long, back-swept, golden plumes. Back black, front white. Hooked orange-red beak.

Behavior. Alone or in groups. At sea between April and September; often hundreds of miles from land. At this time does not come ashore unless sick, oiled, or to molt. Feeds primarily on crustaceans and fish.

Can climb fairly steep terrain. Flexible and prehensile toes provide grip on steep rocky surfaces. Leaps from the crest of a wave directly onto dry land and climbs with small leaps. Points its beak skyward and produces a string of loud, harsh, nasal calls. Molt occurs in January and lasts about 2 weeks.

Arrives in October to breed. Nest is a rough bowl sometimes lined with pebbles and grass. Does not burrow. Normally 2 eggs are laid. Chicks fledge and leave colony by end of March.

Status and Habitat. Very local. Nests in colonies on steep, rocky shores of islands. *The only colony on the coast of Chubut and Santa Cruz, in a rocky canyon on Isla Pingüino near Puerto Deseado, Santa Cruz, had 300–400 breeding birds in 1985 (M. Oliva Day). Colonies on Falkland Islands (Islas Malvinas) and Staten Island; also Cape Horn, January 1989 (M. Oliva Day).* Occasional visitor on remaining coast of Patagonia. *One bird found molting in 1987 at Punta Tombo, Chubut, where 1–2 birds visit every year (D. Boersma).*

Range. Colonies on islands around Tierra del Fuego, also other islands in the South Atlantic, southern Indian Ocean, and off New Zealand. Ranges widely through the southern oceans and reaches the latitude of southern Brazil.

Similar Species. Smaller than the previous species; crest plumes yellow and restricted to eyebrows (not across forehead), and black ends area in a straight line on upper chest.

9. GENTOO PENGUIN / Pingüino de Pico Rojo
Pygoscelis papua   Plate 3

Description. 19″ (48 cm). Relatively large and heavily built. Head and back black with a conspicuous white line across top of crown from eye to eye. Belly white. Beak orange-red, tipped with black. Feet orange.

Behavior. Timid. Walks on land or, if in a hurry, falls forward onto its belly and toboggans on all fours. Prefers to come ashore on gently sloping beaches rather than steep rocky shores. Feeds on crustaceans and fish. Stretches up and points its beak skyward to produce a harsh, nasal braying call. Other voices include hisses and short calls, "Caw."

Status and Habitat. Rare, nonbreeding visitor. *One lone individual at Punta León, Chubut (E. Crespo); and another at Cabo Blanco, Santa Cruz, December 1989 (M. Oliva Day). One breeding pair at Isla Martillo, Tierra del Fuego (A. Schiavini & P. Yorio).*

Range. Breeds on Falkland Islands (Islas Malvinas), Staten Island, and in Antarctica. Also on other islands in South Atlantic and southern Indian Ocean.

PODICIPEDIFORMES

GREBES / Macaes
(Family Podicipedidae)

Small to medium-sized aquatic birds with short tails and pointed beaks. The feet are placed far aft and each segment of the toe is widened and paddle-like (lobed). Grebes dive frequently and swim well underwater with the wings clasped to the body, propelling themselves with their feet. They rarely come ashore and are extremely awkward on land. Although capable of flying, they rarely do so and prefer to escape by diving or scuttling across the water, rapidly beating their wings. Of the 18 species in the world, 5 are found in Patagonia.

10. WHITE-TUFTED GREBE / Macá Común
Podiceps rolland   *Plate 2*

Description. 9" (23 cm). Small. Upperparts black; underparts rufous. Short hind-crest, usually held erect. Conspicuous white auricular tufts. Eye red. *Nonbreeding:* Upperparts brown, white below. Sides of head streaked white.

Behavior. In pairs or family groups in breeding season. Rest of year either alone or more often in small to large, loose flocks. Dives with rapid flick of body, entering water head first. Feeds on aquatic plants, small fish, and invertebrates. Is fairly unafraid if undisturbed. Produces a quiet, nasal call.

Breeds between September and December on inland fresh water. Gathers up aquatic vegetation to form a small, damp, floating nest platform. Lays 4–6 eggs which are concealed with nesting material when the bird is not sitting.

Status and Habitat. Common breeding resident. Part of population migrates northward in March, returning in September. Found on standing freshwater ponds and lagoons, in densely vegetated areas, although also out in open water. Large flocks sometimes gather on the sea, close to shore, in March to May and September to November.

Range. From Tierra del Fuego, all Argentina and Chile to Bolivia and southern Peru.

11. SILVERY GREBE / Macá Plateado
Podiceps occipitalis   *Plate 2*

Description. 11" (28 cm). Small and rounded, with a slender beak. Foreneck, belly, and flanks white; back gray. Nape and hindneck black. Eye red. Yellow auricular plumes. *Nonbreeding:* Overall paler. Lacks yellow auricular plumes.

Behavior. In loose, often large flocks; occasionally alone. Dives frequently with rapid forward leap, entering water head first. Feeds on aquatic plants, small fish, eggs, and crustaceans. Produces a brief, high pitched call, "Chiop."

Builds a small platform of floating vegetation on inland fresh water. Lays 4–6 eggs, usually concealed among the nest material when parents are absent. Chicks can swim directly after hatching but also travel on a parent's back.

Status and Habitat. Common breeding resident. Found on standing freshwater lakes among aquatic vegetation and in the open. *Sewage ponds, Trelew, Chubut, November 1979.* Occasionally in numbers at sea close to shore from March to June and September to November. *A flock of 30 in Caleta Valdés, Chubut, June 1994, and 20 close to shore off Playa Doradillo, Golfo Nuevo, Chubut, September 1996.*

Range. From Tierra del Fuego to central Argentina; migrates to northeastern Argentina from March to September; *P. o. junensis* in northwestern Argentina to Ecuador.

Similar Species. Slightly smaller than following species and less distinctly marked; gray and white rather than black and white. Lacks well-defined hood and unmistakable forecrest.

12. HOODED GREBE / Macá Tobiano
Podiceps gallardoi   *Plate 2*

Description. 13″ (33 cm). Medium-sized grebe, with slender beak. Elegantly marked; distinct hood, hindneck stripe, and black back. Underparts white, flecked black on sides. Orange crest usually held erect. Eye red.

Behavior. Gregarious. Fairly curious and unafraid on lakes where undisturbed. Feeds on small gastropods and other aquatic invertebrates. In breeding season produces a bubbling call, "Too-rrééééé-roo."

Status and Habitat. Visitor between April and October. Known population is small. Breeds on open, freshwater lagoons on the high Patagonian plateau that contain "Vinagrilla" (*Myriophyllum elatinoides*), a red, aquatic plant that forms dense mats on the surface.

Range. Breeds in western Santa Cruz and southwestern Chubut. Ranges as far as the coast of Patagonia between April and September. *One bird sighted near Río Gallegos on an open freshwater pond a few miles from the Atlantic in July 1988 (P. Sutton, FVSA). Flock seen in Ría Coyle, Santa Cruz, May 1994 (A. Serret & A. Johnson, FVSA).*

Similar Species. Can be confused with Silvery Grebe but is larger, coloring more definitely black and white, and crest is distinctive.

Note. Recently discovered species (M. Rumboll, 1974).

13. GREAT GREBE / Macá Grande
Podiceps major   *Plate 2*

Description. 24″ (60 cm). Relatively large grebe. Long neck and long, slender beak. Head gray and short crest black. Hindneck and upperparts blackish. Sides of neck rufous, turning to cinnamon on sides of chest. Eye reddish brown. Belly white, mottled brown on flanks. In flight shows a large white wingpatch. *Nonbreeding:* Crown and hindneck gray. Back brown. Face, neck, and underparts white.

Behavior. Alone or in pairs, occasionally in loose flocks. Very awkward on land; only ventures ashore if sick. Reluctant flyer; scuttles short distances across water, rapidly beating its wings. Dives with flick of body, entering water head first. Feeds mainly on small fish.

Very territorial during breeding; pairs maintain some distance from each other, and brief chases and displays are common. Partners engage in ritualized courtship displays: facing each other, they alternately dip their beaks, then, with their necks held very upright, swim side by side, changing course together. When resting, curls neck back and tucks head under a wing; on rough sea, bobs up and down buoyantly. Produces a drawn-out, melancholy call which carries far over still water.

Builds a floating platform of aquatic vegetation on inland fresh water. Mating takes place on the nest. Usually 3 cream-colored eggs are laid. When unattended, parent covers eggs with nesting material. Chicks leave nest after hatching and often travel on the back of one of the parents.

Status and Habitat. Common year-round. Open, freshwater lakes and lagoons. At sea, close to shore, where it is more abundant from October to April.

Range. Ranges from Tierra del Fuego to Peru and southern Brazil.

14. PIED-BILLED GREBE / Macá de Pico Grueso
Podilymbus podiceps   *Plate 2*

Description. 13″ (32 cm). Relatively rounded. Crown and back dark grayish brown. Throat black. Underparts mottled gray. Short, thick beak, pale horn, with noticeable black subterminal band. Iris dark brown. Feet black. Wings gray brown with paler flight feathers and white patch on secondaries and tertiaries. *Nonbreeding:* Throat whitish. Bill lacks black band. Back brown fading to white below. *Juvenile:* Similar to nonbreeding with white stripes on side of head and neck.

Behavior. Solitary, in pairs, or in family groups. Does not form large flocks like other grebes. Prefers to remain within floating aquatic vegetation, but occasionally swims out into open water. Reluctant flyer; sinks inconspicuously below surface to escape danger, reappearing some distance away with just its head showing above water. Feeds on small fish and invertebrates. Loud clucking, "Kuk, kuk"; also a low, nasal contact call.

Gathers aquatic vegetation to form a floating nest platform among the rushes. As many as 8 dull white, slightly rough eggs are laid. When left unattended, eggs are covered with nesting material by parent. Both parents feed the chicks. Chicks often travel on a parent's back.

Status and Habitat. Uncommon resident. Freshwater lakes, rivers, and lagoons with abundant emergent and floating vegetation.

Range. From the Strait of Magellan, most of South and North America to Canada.

PROCELLARIIFORMES

Seabirds with characteristic, tubelike nostrils and complex beaks made up of a series of plates. Sizes range from the albatrosses, with over 9 ft (3 m) wingspans, to the almost finch-sized storm petrels. Legs are relatively weak; toes are webbed. Most are very awkward on their feet. They are mainly pelagic outside the breeding season. Albatrosses and petrels breed on land, usually on islands; smaller species dig burrows. Although cosmopolitan, two-thirds of all procellariiformes breed in the Southern Hemisphere.

ALBATROSSES / Albatros
(Family Diomedeidae)

Large seabirds with long, slender wings. The Wandering Albatross has the greatest wingspan of all living creatures. The beaks are large, made up of several plates, and end in a hook. The nostrils protrude as short tubes on each side of the beak. Albatrosses are mostly black and white, or gray. Excellent gliders, they alternately soar high above the skyline and then dip low close to the waves. They alight on the ocean to feed on fish, squid, and crustaceans. Albatrosses come ashore only to breed. On land their gait is awkward; they require a short run for take-off. Colonies are generally on isolated coasts and islands. Thirteen species occur worldwide. None breed in Patagonia; however, one of them is commonly seen and 3 are rare or occasional visitors.

15. WANDERING ALBATROSS / Albatros Errante
Diomedea exulans   *Plate 3*

Description. 53″ (135 cm); wingspan 137″ (350 cm). Very large. Weight 12–14 lb (6–7 kg). Entirely white except for the primaries and trailing edge of wing, which are black; outer tail feathers usually black except in old birds. Bill pale uniform pink. Feet bluish gray. *Juvenile:* Plumage goes through various stages lasting several years. Entirely chocolate brown with the exception of face, forehead, throat, and lining of wings, which are white. Subsequently mottled white and brown; darker on chest. Tail band black. Later, upper wing surface black, with a white patch near the base, becoming larger with age until eventually all the coverts turn white.

Behavior. Alone or in loose flocks. Stately flight on stiff, slender wings; alternately soars high above the skyline and then dips low over the waves. Covers enormous distances. *One bird was recorded to have flown 3150 nautical miles (5837 km) in 12 days (J. Croxal & P. Prince).* Speed through air is estimated to exceed 100 mph (160 kph). Settles on water to feed mostly on squid; diet also includes fish, crustaceans, and mollusks.

Status and Habitat. Scarce nonbreeding visitor. Rarely seen from shore. Common along edge of continental shelf. Pelagic, remains on high sea. Population in startling decline due to incidental capture by "long-line" fishing vessels off Argentina and Uruguay.

Range. Circumpolar from Tropic of Capricorn to 60°S. Breeds on northern Antarctic islands. Nearest colonies are at South Georgia.

Similar Species. Difficult to distinguish, at a distance, from Royal Albatross but underwing coverts at all ages are always white. Cutting edge of bill is distinctive at close quarters.

16. ROYAL ALBATROSS / Albatros Real
Diomedea epomophora   *Plate 3*

Description. 45″ (115 cm); wingspan 118″ (300 cm). Very large. White, except for black tips and trailing edges of wings. Tail white. Bill yellow with black line along cutting edge of upper mandible. *Juvenile:* Upperparts of wing black, turning gradually more white with age. Tail black.

Behavior. Alone or in loose flocks. Continuous, slow, stately glide, on stiff, outstretched wings, similar to Wandering Albatross; swings high in the sky, then dips close to the waves. In light winds, lazily flaps wings 2–3 times and glides. Alights on the water to feed.

Status and Habitat. Rare visitor. Seldom seen from shore. *A solitary adult seen 2–3 miles (3–4 km) from coast, in winds of 40 mph (60 kph), in Golfo San José, Chubut, November 1985. One adult found dead at Punta Tombo, Chubut, September 1989; was banded in New Zealand (D. Boersma).* Pelagic.

Range. Southeastern Atlantic and Pacific Ocean south of Tropic of Capricorn. Breeds on sub-Antarctic islands.

Similar Species. Differs from more common Black-browed Albatross and rare Gray-headed Albatross by its greater size and absence of black tail band. Hard to distinguish in field from Wandering Albatross; white on upper wing on leading edge rather than at center of base.

17. BLACK-BROWED ALBATROSS / Albatros Chico o de Ceja Negra
Diomedea melanophrys   *Plate 4*

Description. 33″ (85 cm); wingspan 98″ (250 cm). Pure white, with uniform black across wings and back. Conspicuous black eyebrow. Black terminal band on tail. Bill yellow, tipped salmon pink. Legs and feet bluish gray. *Juvenile:* Back of head and neck suffused with gray. Bill ivory to grayish.

Behavior. Usually in disperse flocks, spread over many miles of ocean. Graceful, soaring flight on outstretched wings held very straight. Flies in near shore when wind rises above 15–20 knots (30–40 kph). With light winds intersperses slow wing beats with gliding. Rests on the sea when wind drops altogether. Pelagic. Flies within surf zone but normally not over beaches, but on occasion on hot summer days sails on updrafts along cliff edges and rides thermals, circling vulturelike, high into the sky over the coast and some distance inland. *Fifty or 60 albatrosses circling several hundred feet high, 5 miles from sea, on a warm still day, Península Valdés, Chubut, February 1983.* Occasionally found sick or exhausted on the ground, sometimes many miles inland.

Lands on ocean to feed. Sitting buoyantly on water, it jabs at crustaceans, Argentine anchovy (*Engraulis anchoita*), and other fish with its beak, sometimes burying neck and part of body under surface in pursuit of prey. *Together with shearwaters and Kelp Gulls, often joins Dusky Dolphins or cormorants that feed on schooling fish around Península Valdés between October and March (B. Würsig & G. Harris). Together with Kelp Gull, the most common seabird feeding on bycatch discarded by coastal fishing vessels in 1995 and 1996 (P. Yorio & G. Caille).* Will follow ships for many days. Usually silent at sea.

Status and Habitat. Very common year-round nonbreeding visitor. More abundant in warmer months, when sometimes hundreds can be seen at once. Enters bays; can be seen from shore, particularly on windward coasts.

Range. Found through southern oceans from Tropic of Capricorn to 60°S. Breeds on sub-Antarctic islands. Nearest breeding colonies are on Isla de los

Estados (Tierra del Fuego) and Falkland Islands (Islas Malvinas).
Similar Species. Pure white head and black eyebrow distinguish it from the following species. Black band across tail and smaller size differentiate it from Royal and Wandering Albatrosses.

18. GRAY-HEADED ALBATROSS / Albatros de Cabeza Gris
Diomedea chrysostoma   *Plate 3*

Description. 29″ (75 cm); wingspan 79″ (200 cm). Head and neck bluish gray. Upper wing surface and back black. Rump and underparts white. Underwing white, edged black. Black band across the tip of the tail. Bill black with bright yellow culmen and rami. Feet bluish gray. *Juvenile:* Head darker than adult. Underwing surface brown. Bill blackish.

Behavior. Alone or in disperse flocks. Pelagic. Gliding flight, swinging up and down above the waves, flapping its wings every now and then if wind is light. Follows ships. Alighting, holds wings raised above back and folds them when it has settled. Feeds at surface of ocean on fish, crustaceans, squid, and offal. To rise from water, it makes a short run, flaps wings awkwardly, and launches itself into the air on stiff wings.

Status and Habitat. Rare nonbreeding visitor. Seldom seen from shore. *One lone individual glided back and forth several times, coming well within the surf zone, in winds exceeding 40 mph (60 kph); Golfo San José, Chubut, February 1988.*

Range. Southern oceans from edge of pack ice to 35°S. Breeding colonies on Diego Ramirez (off Cape Horn) and South Georgia; also islands in the South Pacific and southern Indian oceans.

Similar Species. Distinguished by pearl gray head—and yellow and black beak at close range—from otherwise very similar black-browed Albatross.

PETRELS, SHEARWATERS, AND PRIONS / Petreles
(Family Procellariidae)

Seabirds of very varied size and coloring, mostly dull blue-grays, browns, and whites. Their beaks are made up of several plates and surmounted with characteristic, tubelike nostrils, differing in shape and size with each species. The wings are long and slender and feet are webbed. All feed at sea; the Giant Petrel also feeds on carrion ashore. These birds are found in all oceans. Of the 57 species, 10 are found regularly off Patagonia, 5 of them commonly.

19. SOUTHERN GIANT PETREL / Petrel Gigante del Sur
Macronectes giganteus   *Plate 4*

Description. 37″ (95 cm); wingspan 83″ (210 cm). Large. In flight holds head slightly outstretched showing a distinct neck. Outstretched wings are long, stiff, and held bent. Grayish brown, turning to gray or whitish on the head and neck. Bill large and strong, yellowish horn to pale green; pronounced nasal tubes. Feet

gray. Iris gray, whitish, or brown. Female a little smaller and has a lighter bill. *Juvenile:* Dark brown or black, including head and neck. Legs dark gray. Iris brown.
Behavior. Alone or in—sometimes large—flocks. Usually the first petrel to glide in close to shore when wind rises. Although not as graceful as the albatrosses, it is a superb glider and soars effortlessly up and down above waves. Able to glide in very little wind, beating its wings occasionally. Rides updrafts along cliff edges and tops of beaches, its wing tips passing within inches of ground. Occasionally rides thermals, towering vulture-like, high into sky. Frequently comes ashore. Walks in awkward, ungainly fashion with outstretched wings. Sometimes in flocks, rests on solitary beaches.

Feeds principally on carrion; congregates in numbers to squabble over carcasses. Will kill weak or sick seabirds at sea. *A juvenile attacked an adult penguin on a beach, dragged it into the water, and drowned it. Golfo San José, Chubut, November 1986.* Also feeds on squid and crustaceans caught at surface of ocean. Produces rattling and grating sounds when quarreling over food. Courting adult produces sounds like the whinnying of a colt.

Nests in colonies on high, flat ground within sight of sea. Nests placed 6–9 ft (2–3 m) from one another and vary from hollow mound of mud and vegetation to shallow scrape lined with pebbles and vegetation. Arrival and mating occur in September and October. A single egg is laid; chicks hatch in December. If disturbed on nest, ejects a dark oily strong-smelling fluid from its beak to a distance of 6 ft (2 m). Both parents brood young. Chicks begin to molt in February and are abandoned by adults in April. Chicks remain unfed for a month or two until, driven by hunger, they begin flying and leave the colony.
Status and Habitat. Common breeding resident; seen from shore all year round. Flies within the surf zone and over beaches. Overall dark, juveniles are particularly common near shore. Abundant near seabird and mammal colonies, also around carcasses on shore or in water. *Seventy or 80 birds including many white-headed individuals observed for several weeks around carcass of a dead whale; Caleta Valdés, Chubut, September 1985.* Open ocean, coastal waters, and beaches. Breeds on islands. *Common in February at Punta Tombo, Chubut, where they come close to shore and rest on beaches while feeding on fledging chicks and molting penguins (D. Boersma).*
Range. From 30°S to Antarctica. *Colonies on Isla Gran Robledo, 600 nests in 1989, and Isla Arce, 150 nests, off Cabo Dos Bahías, Chubut. February 1987 and November 1989.* Also breeds on Antarctic continent and islands in Antarctic and sub-Antarctic.
Similar Species. All dark juveniles can be confused with White-chinned Petrel, but the latter is smaller, has a shorter neck, holds its wings straighter, and does not fly over the beaches.

20. SOUTHERN FULMAR / Petrel Plateado
Fulmarus glacialoides   Plate 4

Description. 20″ (50 cm); wingspan 57″ (145 cm). Gull-like. Pale gray with white head and distinctive light "windows" at base of primaries. Bill plates yellow horn, outlined black.

Behavior. Alone or in small flocks (gregarious in other parts of range). Settles on water to feed. Diet principally pelagic crustaceans, but will attack and eat weak birds; probably also feeds on small fish. Takes off easily even in light breezes. Stands and walks with difficulty on land; rests on its tarsi and helps itself along with its wings.

Status and Habitat. Uncommon nonbreeding visitor. Lone individuals or small flocks occasionally appear during strong winds, flying into the surf zone but not as far as the beach. *Lone individuals and pairs sighted in Golfo San José, and at Cabo Dos Bahías, Chubut, from September to March.*

Range. Circumpolar south of 30°S. Ranges northward where cool currents bathe continental shores. Breeds in Antarctica and islands in sub-Antarctic. Nearest breeding colonies are on Antarctic peninsula and South Georgia.

21. CAPE PETREL / Petrel Damero, del Cabo o Pintado

Daption capense *Plate 5*

Description. 16″ (40 cm); wingspan 35″ (90 cm). Head black. Upper wing surface black with striking white markings. Back speckled and terminal band across tip of tail black. Underparts white. Bill and legs black.

Behavior. Alone or in small groups (flocks in other parts of range). Agile glide, undulating quickly up and down, keeping fairly close to surface of sea, with occasional bursts of rapid wing beats. In strong winds glides higher into sky. Often lands on water and sits buoyantly. Voracious appetite. Feeds at surface of sea and makes shallow dives. Filters small food from water with its pouchlike mouth; diet includes crustaceans, cephalopods, and scraps. Only accidentally comes ashore in Patagonia. On land, hobbles clumsily on its tarsi, using its wings to help its progress.

Status and Habitat. Uncommon visitor. Appears only with high winds and rough seas. *Lone individuals sighted from the shore, flying into the surf zone but never over the shore, Golfo San José, Chubut, September to March.* Open ocean.

Range. Ranges widely in all southern oceans from Antarctica to northern limits of cool southern currents and occasionally beyond. Breeds on Antarctic shores and sub-Antarctic islands.

22. WHITE-CHINNED PETREL (SHOEMAKER) / Petrel Negro

Procellaria aequinoctialis *Plate 4*

Description. 19″ (50 cm); wingspan 53″ (135 cm). Entirely dark brown with chin variably white, sometimes extending up sides of head (hard to see in the field). Bill plates yellow horn, outlined black.

Behavior. In loose flocks, often mixed with other petrels and albatrosses. Flies like a small albatross, holding its wings straight and stiff as it wheels up and down over the waves in graceful arcs. When wind drops, may be seen sitting alone on calm water. Rides buoyantly on ocean. Feeds mainly on cephalopods, crustaceans, and fish. Silent at sea.

Status and Habitat. Common year-round nonbreeding visitor. Open ocean to coastal waters. Flies into surf zone but does not fly over beach.

Range. Ranges from Antarctic circle to 30°S. Breeds in Antarctic and on sub-Antarctic islands. Nearest breeding colonies on Falkland Islands (Islas Malvinas).

Similar Species. Easily confused with juvenile Southern Giant Petrel but is smaller, has noticeably shorter neck, wings are held straighter in flight, and does not fly over beaches.

23. GRAY PETREL (PEDIUNKER) / Petrel Gris
Procellaria (Adamastor) cinerea   Plate 3

Description. 18″ (45 cm); wingspan 47″ (120 cm). Ash gray upperparts. Underparts white with gray underwing and undertail coverts. Bill yellowish horn. Legs and toes fleshy gray or whitish.

Behavior. Solitary or in small groups. Flight similar to larger shearwaters. Dives from the wing straight into water in pursuit of prey. Feeds on cephalopods and fish.

Status and Habitat. Rare nonbreeding visitor; more abundant offshore. Occasional washups. *One exhausted adult on beaches of Golfo San José, Chubut, June 1981.* Strictly pelagic, rarely entering bays and channels.

Range. Southern oceans between 25° and 55°S. Nearest breeding colonies on Tristan da Cunha.

24. GREATER SHEARWATER / Pardela de Cabeza Negra
Puffinus gravis   Plate 5

Description. 17″ (44 cm); wingspan 43″ (110 cm). Upperparts gray. Well-defined black cap. Rump white. Terminal tail band black. Chin and rest of underparts white. Feet bluish.

Behavior. In flocks, mixed with other shearwaters and petrels. Glides for long periods in strong winds, swinging up and down rapidly, rising high in the sky as do Sooty Shearwaters. Diet includes fish and squid. Joins mixed flocks of seabirds that collect to feed on Argentine anchovy (*Engraulis anchoita*) being preyed upon by Dusky Dolphins or Imperial Cormorants. Sights prey from air, lands on water, and dives. "Flies" under water using wings as paddles. Silent in flight. Produces cackling and croaking sounds when feeding in flocks at sea.

Status and Habitat. Common year-round nonbreeding visitor. *Usually seen with the more numerous Sooty Shearwater (P. griseus) around Península Valdés, Chubut.* Open ocean to inshore waters. Flies close to but not within surf zone.

Range. Atlantic Ocean from Tierra del Fuego to Arctic Circle. Nearest breeding colonies on Tristan da Cunha and Falkland Islands (Islas Malvinas).

Similar Species. Very similar to Little Shearwater but noticeably larger, with white rump and distinct cap.

25. SOOTY SHEARWATER / Pardela Oscura
Puffinus griseus   Plate 5

Description. 18″ (45 cm); wingspan 37″ (95 cm). Long slender wings. All brown with pale silvery underwings. Long slender black bill. Short nose tubes as with other shearwaters. Legs black.

Behavior. In flocks, often very large and dispersed over many miles of sea. Agile glide, faster in high winds, swinging rapidly up above skyline and down close to waves in a ceaseless undulating pattern. Alternates glides with 5–8 rapid wing beats. When air is still, sits in large groups on water some distance from shore. Diet includes fish, crustaceans, and cephalopods. Gathers with other shearwaters, gulls, terns, and Black-browed Albatrosses to prey on schools of Argentine anchovy (*Engraulis anchoita*) herded to surface by feeding Dusky Dolphins or Imperial Cormorants. As the flock feeds, birds in rear take off and fly quickly to front of the group where they land and dive, disappearing from view. A few moments later they reappear a little way ahead, where they may rest before taking off again. Will follow a school of fish for several hours. Produces cackling sounds. Flock makes noisy cackling chorus, heard over a mile away when sea is still.

Status and Habitat. Common year-round nonbreeding visitor. *One or more thousand seen passing in same direction in a never-ending stream in Golfo San José, Chubut, March 1981.* Open ocean to coastal waters. In rough weather comes close to, but not within, the surf zone.

Range. All oceans except the Arctic and northern Indian. Nearest breeding colonies on islands that fringe Tierra del Fuego.

26. LITTLE SHEARWATER / Pardela Chica
Puffinus assimilis elegans   *Plate 5*

Description. 10″ (27 cm); wingspan 23″ (58 cm). Small. Upperparts black extending below the eye. Underparts white with black underwing tip and margins. Bill black. Legs pink with outer edge black.

Behavior. In flocks, often mixed with other shearwaters. Agile, fast flight. Swings up and down close to waves, alternating short glides on rigid wings with bursts of rapid wing beats. When following a school of fish, flies rapidly, close to surface, and dives straight into water, disappearing from view. Reappears a few moments later, a few lengths ahead, and immediately takes off, wings beating as fast as before. *Gathers with other shearwaters, gulls, terns, and albatrosses to prey on Argentine anchovy (Engraulis anchoita) herded to surface by feeding Dusky Dolphins or cormorants when sea is calm, between October and March. Península Valdés, Chubut.*

Status and Habitat. Uncommon nonbreeding visitor. Open ocean up to, but not within, the surf zone.

Range. Southern oceans between Tropic of Capricorn and 50°S. Also North Atlantic. Breeds on Tristan da Cunha and islands off Africa and Australia.

Similar Species. Noticeably smaller than Greater Shearwater, with dark rump and less distinct cap. Manx's Shearwater is larger and cap more extensive.

27. BROAD-BILLED PRION / Petrel Ballena Pico Ancho
Pachyptila vittata desolata   *Plate 5*

Description. 11″ (28 cm); wingspan 22″ (55 cm). Small. Pale blue-gray with lead gray head and nape. White eyebrow and black streak through eye. Distinct black W-shaped marking across upper wing surface. Black terminal tail band. Underparts white. Disproportionately broad heavy black bill, lined with minute platelets. Legs blue-gray.

Behavior. Alone or in flocks that can be very large (recorded in hundreds of thousands at sea). Flight restless and untiring. Called "Right Whale Bird" because, like the mammal, it has a series of plates arranged like baleen along the side of the beak. Floor of mouth can extend to form a pouch; fleshy tongue. When feeding, rests its body lightly on surface of sea, holds its wings just clear of the water, and paddles itself rapidly forward with its feet. As it scurries along, it thrusts its head below the surface and filters minute animal life (cephalopods, pteropods, and crustaceans) from seawater. Sometimes dives briefly. Known to feed alongside whales. Walks awkwardly on land. Dead washups appear on beaches lining open ocean, after bad storms at sea.

Status and Habitat. Occasional nonbreeding visitor. *One washup in Golfo Nuevo, Chubut, September 1986.* Open ocean; shelters in lee of land during storms.

Range. Southern oceans from pack ice to northern limits of cool currents. Breeds on South Georgia and other Antarctic islands.

Similar Species. Hard to distinguish in the field from Slender-billed Prion; but the distinct, broad bill easily differentiates it when observed close up.

28. SLENDER-BILLED PRION / Petrel Ballena Pico Delgado
Pachyptila belcheri   *Plate 5*

Description. 10″ (26 cm); wingspan 20″ (50 cm). Pale blue-gray with darker crown and nape; white eyebrow and underparts. Black W-shaped mark across upperwing surface. Black terminal tail band. Slender black bill, tipped sooty gray (some variation in bill size and length). Legs blue-gray.

Behavior. Flocks at sea have been recorded as enormous and likened to snowflakes. Settles on surface during calm weather; sits with head tucked close to body and easily goes unnoticed. Flight agile and close to waves. Feeds in flocks, mainly at night, on amphipods, small squid, and crustaceans. Dives frequently and comes up again a few lengths ahead. Die-offs at sea during storms produce large washups on coast of Patagonia.

Status and Habitat. Occasional nonbreeding visitor. Very hard to see against the sea due to its coloring and unobtrusive behavior. *One individual sitting on the water, well beyond the surf zone, flew off close to the waves in Golfo San José, Chubut, August 1984. Over 100 dead birds per mile on Península Valdés, Chubut, following a bad storm in June 1981.* Open ocean, occasionally close to land.

Range. Sub-Antarctic zone. Nearest breeding colonies on Falkland Islands (Islas Malvinas), where it arrives in August to September and leaves February to March; leaves and returns to its nest under cover of darkness.

Similar Species. Hard to tell from Broad-billed Prion in the field; the slender bill, particularly noticeable in the hand, is distinctive.

STORM PETRELS / Petreles de las Tormentas
(Family Hydrobatidae)

Small birds with nostrils forming a single, pronounced tube on the top of the beak. Their flight is erratic, close to the water, and they often flutter over the surface like butterflies, "skipping" across the surface with their legs dangling. Pelagic, they are ashore only in the breeding season, arriving and leaving the nest under cover of darkness. Twenty-three species occur worldwide, one of them occasionaly found near the shores of Patagonia.

29. WILSON'S STORM PETREL / Petrel de las Tormentas Común
Oceanites oceanicus *Plate 5*

Description. 6″ (17 cm); wingspan 16″ (40 cm). Small. Dark brown with a distinct white rump and flanks. Diagonal, pale brown, upper-wing band. Bill black. Legs black.

Behavior. Usually in flocks, sometimes spread thinly over many square miles of ocean. Hover-flies close to water; dangles its legs and skips across surface, feeding on crustaceans, small fish, and squid as well as scraps gleaned from the water. In strong winds holds wings out stiffly and digs its webbed feet into sea to anchor itself. Often around ships and in their wake. Occasionally alights on the ocean and dives briefly. If annoyed, ejects a foul-smelling oily fluid from its bill. Normally does not land on shores of Patagonia. Shuffles along on its tarsi on land. At sea, emits soft peeping and rasping sounds.

Status and Habitat. Very occasional nonbreeding visitor in March to April and September to October, during migration. *Several individuals sighted in Golfo San José, Chubut, 1979 (J. Jehl and M. Rumboll); then not recorded until October 1988, when loose flocks of several hundred were observed in calm weather several hundred yards offshore, staying for 2–3 weeks.* Pelagic. Follows cold ocean currents.

Range. Circumpolar in Southern Hemisphere. Extends as far as the North Atlantic. Nearest breeding colonies, islands around Cape Horn and Falkland Islands (Islas Malvinas).

PELECANIFORMES

CORMORANTS / Cormoranes
(Family Phalacrocoracidae)

Long-necked birds with long, slender, hook-tipped beaks. The legs are set far back on the body; most species stand very upright. The feet are webbed. All dive to feed. Flight is heavy and straight with rapid wing beats; one species, the Galapagos Cormorant (*Nannopterum harrisi*) is flightless. A cosmopolitan bird, with 30 species worldwide, it is restricted to littoral or continental waters; 5 species are found in Patagonia.

30. NEOTROPIC (OLIVACEOUS) CORMORANT / Biguá
Phalacrocorax olivaceus *Plate 6*

Description. 29″ (73 cm). Long neck and tail. All black or dark brown. Iris green. Bill bluish horn. *Breeding plumage:* White band at base of gular sack. Tuft of white, postocular filoplumes. *Juvenile:* Dark brown at first, then paler on face and undersides.

Behavior. Alone or in small groups. Shy. Roosts on open beaches, rocks surrounded by water, wrecks, piers, and open, mussel-covered ledges, often together with Kelp Gulls; or on branches over fresh water. Often stands with wings outstretched. Sits low on water with body mostly submerged. Sometimes swims with head under water. Dives last 30 sec to 1 min. When chasing small fish, several individuals swim together, parallel to the shore. Diet includes fish, mollusks, crabs, and algae. Flight low and straight with rapid wing beats. Occasionally takes advantage of upcurrents on cliffs to glide inexpertly. Emits a series of harsh piglike grunting sounds.

Forms breeding colonies with a few dozen to several hundred pairs. Nests on bushtops near the sea, often close to, or mixed with, other breeding seabirds. Several pairs will share a single bush. Begins building large nesting platforms out of twigs in October. During courtship the body is arched so that the head and tail point skyward while the chest is lowered repeatedly. Lays 3 or 4 pale blue eggs. Hatching begins in November; chicks fledge in February and colony is abandoned in March for the winter.

Status and Habitat. Common breeding resident. *Breeding colonies on islets of Complejo Islote Lobos in Río Negro, Isla de Los Pájaros and Punta León in Chubut, and Isla Leones in Ría Santa Cruz.* Seacoasts, rivers, lakes, and marshes within sight of water. Not found on oceanic islands.

Range. Central and South America from southern U.S. to Tierra del Fuego.

31. ROCK CORMORANT / Cormorán Cuello Negro
Phalacrocorax magellanicus   *Plate 6*

Description. 27″ (68 cm). Not as slender as previous species; stands less upright. Black, with lower breast and belly white. Sides of head and neck variably white. Facial skin red. Legs black. *Juvenile:* Brown, with faint outline of adult belly markings, mottled white. Facial skin black.

Behavior. Gregarious. Forms colonies to roost and breed. Flight is straight and level, with rapid wing beats; incapable of quick turns. Flying in wide circles, will investigate boats on the water. Feeds alone or in pairs, in kelp beds, in shallow coastal waters. Diet includes fish. To dive, leaps almost clear of the surface and enters water head first. Produces varied grunting and squealing sounds on the nest. Sounds within a breeding colony produce a continual loud murmur.

Breeds in small colonies. Nests on ledges in steep rocks and cliffs that face the sea. Nests built of seaweed. Pairs bicker and squabble over nesting material, and unguarded nests are plundered mercilessly by neighboring birds. During display neck is thrown back, tail is raised, and a short call is given. Courting pairs greet each other placing their cheeks together and bowing their necks to the ground, first to one side then to the other. Mutual preening and nibbling of head and neck usually follow. Laying begins in November. Lays 3 or 4 chalk-white eggs. Hatched featherless and sightless, chicks are soon covered in dark-brown down, begin fledging in January.

Status and Habitat. Common though very local breeding resident. Forms small rookeries mostly numbering a few hundred pairs or less. Easiest colonies to see in Chubut are at Punta Delgada, Punta Pirámide, and Punta Loma, and from a boat on the Ría Deseado in Santa Cruz. *Overall population estimated at about 7500* *pairs in 65 colonies in Patagonia (P. Yorio et al., 1997).* Coastal waters, rocky shores, and islands. Often found together with other cormorants and frequently breed alongside.

Range. Breeds from Isla de los Pájaros in Península Valdés, Chubut, southward to Tierra del Fuego and up the western coast of South America as far as Corral in Chile; Falkland Islands (Islas Malvinas).

32. GUANAY CORMORANT / Cormorán Guanay
Phalacrocorax bougainvillii   *Plate 6*

Description. 31″ (80 cm). Slightly larger, more slender and elegant than other cormorants; stands very erect. Upperparts and neck black with green and violet sheen. Prominent crest of plumes. Oval chin patch, underparts white. Eye mask red. Orbital skin green. Iris brown. *Nonbreeding:* Crest plumes short or lacking. *Chick:* Very distinctive black and white salt-and-pepper coloring. *Juvenile:* Similar to adult with dull-black upperparts.

Behavior. Very gregarious. Breeds and roosts on shore. Strongest flier of all local cormorants. Feeds on fish. Produces varied, grating sounds and quiet murmurs on the nest.

Forms mixed colonies together with Imperial Cormorant, and holds best nesting positions in center of colony. Colony is usually on a flat surface and has well-defined edges. Nest begins as a scrape and slowly takes the form of a bowl 16″ (40 cm) across as the rim is built up with successive layers of excretion and nesting material. Usually lays 3 pale, chalk-blue eggs. *Two-week-old chicks at Punta Lobería, Chubut, early November 1989.*

Status and Habitat. Rare breeding resident. *Fewer than a hundred breeding pairs have ever been counted in Patagonia; numbers dwindled at Punta Tombo, Chubut, to 9 pairs (P. Yorio et al., 1997) since they were first discovered breeding in early 1970s (F. Erize). Colony at Punta Tombo declined in 1970s possibly as a result of human visitation. Two or 3 pairs breeding, also an equal number of hybrids, with Imperial Cormorants, at Punta León, Chubut, December 1988; 10 pairs at Punta Lobería, Chubut, November 1989.* On coast of Peru some colonies contain over one million birds and are still the basis of the lucrative guano trade. On the Atlantic coast of South America the population is so reduced that it is considered virtually extinct. Coastal waters and islands.

Range. Restricted to coastal Chubut. Breeds on islands off west coast of South America, from Lobos de Tierra in Peru to Mocha Island in Chile. Ranges from Point Pariñas to Corral in Chile.

Similar Species. Differs from smaller, less elegant Rock Cormorant by reduced red skin around eye and well-defined oval white patch on chin.

33. IMPERIAL CORMORANT / Cormorán Imperial (Synonimizes
Blue-eyed Cormorant / **Cormorán Imperial [*Ph. a. atriceps*]**
and King Cormorant / **Cormorán Real [*Ph. a. albiventer*]**)
Phalacrocorax atriceps   *Plate 6*

Description. 29″ (75 cm). *Northern race or King Cormorant (Ph. a. albiventer):* Chin, foreneck and underparts white. White on "cheeks" does not reach up to the eye.

Upperparts black. Prominent crest plumes. Eye ring blue, iris brown. Caruncle yellow. Bill brown. Feet flesh color. *Southern race or Blue-eyed Cormorant (Ph. a. atriceps):* Extensive white on face reaches up to eye. White wing bar and dorsal patch very noticeable in flight. *Nonbreeding of both races:* Caruncle, eye ring, and facial markings duller. Crest lacking; white dorsal patch and wing bar reduced or lacking in southern race. *Juvenile of both races:* Lacks caruncle. Eye ring brown. Upperparts dull, dark brownish gray, lacking white dorsal and wing bars. No crest.

Behavior. Occasionally alone, more commonly in flocks. Gregarious. Birds inhabiting large roosts fly off together in morning and return before sundown. Flight level, with rapid, noisy wing beats; flocks adopt string formation. Kicks along the surface of water a considerable distance to take off. Diet includes fish and crustaceans. Feeds alone or in rafts, particularly when following schools of Argentine anchovy (*Engraulis anchoita*). Sometimes a hundred or more land on water and swim and dive in formation.

In breeding colonies, an incessant coming and going of birds bringing nesting material. Birds wandering through colony are harassed by occupants of neighboring nests. In hot weather, sits with beak open and vibrates extended throat region to thermoregulate. Molting begins early in nesting period. Produces repeated harsh croaking sounds on nest and roost.

Courting pairs put their cheeks together and bow their extended necks low to ground, first to one side then to the other. Mutual preening of head and neck follows.

Breeds in colonies on flat surfaces near shore on islands and points; often mixed with Guanay and Rock Cormorants; with Rockhopper Penguins and Black-browed Albatrosses in the Falkland Islands (Islas Malvinas). Strictly gregarious; seems to breed successfully only when colonies number 100 or more birds. Breeding adults arrive in August. Nests are placed almost within striking distance and form a pattern; outline of colony is well defined. Built of seaweed gathered from ocean bed, nest is a steep-sided bowl cemented with successive layers of droppings. Much thieving and squabbling over nesting material among neighboring birds. Laying begins at end of October. Lays 3—less commonly 2 or 4—white eggs. Incubation lasts 28 days. Dolphin Gulls are swift to snatch eggs from unguarded nests. Skuas and Kelp Gulls also take eggs and chicks, while Snowy Sheathbills eat regurgitated scraps and droppings.

Both parents take turns on the nest. Hatching begins at end of November and peaks in mid-December. When chicks are well developed, both parents forage at sea and return briefly to feed young. Occasionally colonies contain chicks in every stage of development. Fledging begins late December and January; colony deserted in March.

Status and Habitat. King Cormorant (*Ph. a. albiventer*) is a common breeding resident, the most common of all cormorants along coast of Patagonia. *The combined population of both subspecies in Patagonia is estimated at 40,000 pairs (P. Yorio, PCZMP, 1996). Colonies are currently exploited for guano in Chubut and Santa Cruz.*

The breeding colony at Punta Tombo dwindled in the course of 10 years, from a population of more than 3000 breeding pairs to 300, apparently as a result of disturbances produced by people. Breeding colonies also at Punta León and islands off Punta Lobería, Cabo Dos Bahías, Puerto Melo, and Bahía Bustamante. Also Isla Quintano, Monte Loayza, Isla Chata, islands in Bahía Laura, Bahía San Julián, Ría

Santa Cruz, Monte León, and Río Gallegos. Small roosts on outcrops, points, and rocks by the sea; large roosts on mainland on Cabo Blanco, Santa Cruz, and on piers at Comodoro Rivadavia. Blue-eyed Cormorant (*Ph. a. atriceps*) is far less common. Freshwater lakes. Coastal waters. Not sighted beyond 18 miles (30 km) out to sea.

Range. King Cormorant (*Ph. a. albiventer*) breeds from Punta León, Chubut, southward to Tierra del Fuego and Falkland Islands (Islas Malvinas). Part of the population ranges northward as far as province of Buenos Aires in March, returning in September. Blue-eyed Cormorant (*Ph. a. atriceps*) breeds in Santa Cruz, Tierra del Fuego, Antarctica, and on islands in sub-Antarctic. Ranges northward along shores of Patagonia and Chile in March.

34. RED-LEGGED CORMORANT / Cormorán gris
Phalacrocorax gaimardi   Plate 6

Description. 23″ (60 cm). Steel gray with pale speckling on wing coverts. Underparts and patches on sides of the neck white. Beak yellow, base red. Narrow eye ring pale blue, iris green. Legs bright red. *Juvenile:* Gray; lacks white neck patches.

Behavior. Not as gregarious as previous. Flight is low and level, with rapid wing beats and head held straight forward.

Forages alone or in pairs. Sits on water and dives for food. Descends to depths of 24–30 ft (8–10 m). Diet includes Argentine anchovy (*Engraulis anchoita*) and other fish. Produces a high-pitched chirping on the nest.

Pairs of up to 100 or more nest in isolated, inaccessible ledges in cliffs by the sea. Nest is built of seaweed, worm tubes, feathers, etc., gathered from sea bed. Laying begins in October. Two to 4 pale-blue eggs, coated in chalky white. Only two chicks are reared. Breeding season is extended and chicks of different stages can be seen at any one time. *Nests with eggs and no chicks seen at Puerto San Julián, late November 1990.*

Status and Habitat. Common resident near its breeding sites. *Population in Patagonia estimated at 1100 breeding pairs in 1995 (P. Gandini & E. Frere). Breeds on cliffs opposite town of Puerto Deseado; 250 nests counted on islands in Ría Deseado in 1916 (Doello-Jurado, 1917). 625 nests on a cliff face on coast at La Mina, Cabo Curioso, north of Puerto San Julián, Santa Cruz. A few pairs breed on rocky coast at Cabo Blanco, Santa Cruz, and 60 nests on a small offshore rock at Monte Loayza, Santa Cruz (E. Frere & P. Gandini, 1995).* Nonbreeding birds common at mouth of Ría Santa Cruz and along piers at Comodoro Rivadavia. *Two birds sighted at Punta Pirámide, Península Valdés, Chubut, November 1981.* Rocky seashores, coastal islands, cliff faces, ledges, piers, and buoys. Not found far from mainland. Inlets, coastal water as far as shipping lanes; never enters fresh water.

Range. Continental shores from Península Valdés southward around tip of South America and up Pacific coast as far as Guañape Islands in Peru.

ARDEIFORMES

HERONS AND EGRETS / Garzas
(Family Ardeidae)

Slender-bodied birds with long neck and legs. The feet end in 4 toes with rudimentary webbing. Beaks are long, straight, and pointed. Flight is slow, with neck tucked back to form an "S," helping to differentiate the family from ibises and storks, which fly with necks extended. Most are found near water or in moist terrain. Of the 60 species worldwide, 5 are found in eastern Patagonia.

35. COCOI (WHITE-NECKED) HERON / Garza Mora
Ardea cocoi   *Plate 7*

Description. 49″ (125 cm). Large. Black cap and hindcrest. Back and wings gray. Underparts white with black band on chest and belly. Beak yellow.

Behavior. Usually alone. On the ground or in trees. Lifts off with a loud call and flies slowly and majestically. Shy. Produces a loud "sqwok."

Status and Habitat. Rare summer visitor in irrigated fields in river valleys of northern and central Patagonia. *One bird in an open, inundated field near Sarmiento, Chubut, December 1989 (W. Conway & G. Harris).* Freshwater lakes and rivers; rarely on the seacoast.

Range. From province of Buenos Aires northward to Panama. Rarely, south to province of Santa Cruz. No breeding records in eastern Patagonia.

36. COMMON (GREAT) EGRET / Garza Blanca
Casmerodius albus   *Plate 7*

Description. 33.1″ (85 cm). Pure snow white. "Veil" of long, white plumes or "egrets." Bill yellow. Feet and legs black.

Behavior. Usually alone; occasionally in flocks of different sizes. Shy; seldom allows close approach. Conspicuous. Movements slow and deliberate. Awaits prey in shallow water, standing perfectly still with neck outstretched. Darts head into water to capture fish, crustaceans, and amphibians. Springs from where it stands into the air and flies with slow, majestic wing beats. Travels far; young birds have been recorded up to 900 miles (1500 km) from their place of birth.

Courtship behavior is elaborate, with bowing, stretching, ritualized preening and displaying of nuptial "egret" plumes. Produces a harsh croak when on the nest. When alarmed, emits a loud "sqwok" as it lifts into the air.

Colonial. Nests in small colonies on bushes. Builds a breeding platform of twigs in September (in more humid regions, nests in reed beds and trees by the water). Old nests are repaired. Lays 3–5 pale blue eggs in October–early November. *Ten nests in the branches of low dry trees in a gully, with eggs (adults in attendance) at Punta Lobería, Chubut, November 1989.* Both parents care for young. Chicks abandon nest at 4 weeks.

Status and Habitat. Fairly common, breeding resident. Population low; *small colonies recorded at Isla de los Pájaros, Punta Tombo, Punta Clara, Punta Lobería, and Caleta Malaspina, Chubut.* Vulnerable due to easy access to colony sites (coastal breeding colonies should not be approached closely during nesting period). Shallows of freshwater lakes, rivers, irrigated fields, and marshy areas. Seacoasts.

Range. Patagonia to North America. Also in many other parts of the world.

Similar Species. Can be confused with the Snowy or Cattle Egret but has a noticeably larger, yellow beak, black legs, and is less gregarious.

37. BLACK-CROWNED NIGHT-HERON / Garza Bruja
Nycticorax nycticorax   *Plate 7*

Description. 22.2″ (57 cm). Hunched posture with a relatively short "tucked in" neck. Heavy horn-colored bill. Crown and back black. Wings and tail slate gray. Chin and belly whitish flushed with gray. Three long and slender white plumes at nape. Eye red. Legs yellowish green. *Juvenile:* Upperparts buff brown streaked and spotted lighter; underparts pale buff with brown streaks. Eye yellow or orange. Legs dull green.

Behavior. Occurs alone or in small groups. Usually roosts in secluded places during day, becoming active toward evening and night. Inconspicuous. If flushed, flies up suddenly with a startled call. Flight is slow and deliberate. Diet includes fish, crustaceans, and insects. Produces an abrupt, loud "kwock!". Small colonies, often together with other colonial birds. Breeds when food is plentiful. Nests in trees, bushes, reed beds, and seaside cliffs. Builds a nesting platform of twigs. Lays 3–5 pale-blue eggs. Chicks produce a high-pitched call.

Status and Habitat. Common breeding resident. Wet, rocky shores and dark, damp seaside caves exposed at low tide. Also varied, wet, inundated, and irrigated land; trees near water.

Range. Worldwide except in Australia and polar or subpolar regions.

38. SNOWY EGRET / Garcita Blanca
Egretta thula   *Plate 7*

Description. 19.5″ (50 cm). Snow white. Showy, long, white vaporous plumes or "egrets" on head, foreneck, and back, which it displays. Long straight bill and legs black. Feet yellow. *Nonbreeding:* Lacks "egrets."

Behavior. Shy and not readily approachable. Occasionally alone, more often in flocks of 10–30. Roosts in bushes or on ground. The whole flock flies off together. Travels far; individuals recorded 1800 miles (3000 km) from place of birth. Wades in shallows or stands on rocky outcrops and beaches by the sea. Diet includes fish. Usually silent. When alarmed, flies up giving a loud hollow "sqwok."

Status and Habitat. Fairly common, though irregular, visitor on the coast as far as the Strait of Magellan and on inland fresh water from September through March. Shallow freshwater lakes and marshy areas. Rocky shores, reefs, and beaches.

Range. From Patagonia to North America. No breeding records for eastern Patagonia.

Similar Species. Smaller than Great Egret and usually in flocks. Differs from Cattle Egret in having black legs and beak.

39. CATTLE EGRET / Garcita Bueyera
Bubulcus ibis   *Plate 7*

Description. 19.5″ (50 cm). Pure white. Crown, nape, throat, and back flushed with orange-buff. Legs, feet, and thick bill yellow. *Nonbreeding:* White, with no orange flush.

Behavior. In flocks, typically around—even riding on—cattle. Feeds on insects that are disturbed as cattle graze. To a lesser degree, diet includes small aquatic vertebrates and invertebrates.

Status and Habitat. Uncommon, September–March visitor as far as Strait of Magellan. *A single flock of 25 birds on rocky reefs exposed at low tide at Punta Norte, Chubut, January 1978; flock of 10 birds on fence by road south of Trelew, Chubut, also 2 flocks of 10–30 birds sitting on bushes at Punta Tombo, Chubut, March 1990.* Not so water related as other egrets. Open pastures, particularly around cattle. Seashores.

Range. Originally from Africa. Introduced in many parts of the world to control insects in cattle-raising areas; now spreading in most continents. Recorded for the first time in Argentina in province of Santa Fe in 1969; since then has become a common resident or visitor as far as Tierra del Fuego, mostly in places where there are cattle.

Similar Species. Smaller than Great Egret and differs from Snowy Egret in having orange legs and thick yellow beak.

STORKS / Cigueñas
(Family Ciconiidae)

Large, heavily built birds with long legs and necks. With bare facial skin, some species have bare head and neck as well. Beaks are long and strong. Their large wings make for slow, majestic flight, with neck outstretched (unlike herons). Storks are mostly found near fresh water. Of 17 species worldwide, one is found in Patagonia.

40. MAGUARI STORK / Cigueña Americana
Ciconia maguari   *Plate 7*

Description. 54.6″ (140 cm); wingspan 48″ (120 cm). Large and very conspicuous. White, with primaries and secondaries black. Facial skin and legs red. Long, straight, pointed beak gray.

Behavior. Usually alone. Paces slowly about searching for reptiles, frogs, insects, small mammals, birds, etc., on which it feeds. Flight slow and majestic.

Status and Habitat. Uncommon nonbreeding visitor. Several records in farmland near Trelew on the Chubut River valley. Open wet fields, freshwater marsh, and inundated areas.

Range. South America, from northern Patagonia, east of the Andes to Venezuela.

IBISES / Bandurrias y Cuervillos
(Family Threskiornithidae)

Medium-sized birds with long necks and legs. Beaks are long, usually downward curved. Their omnivorous diet includes small vertebrates, invertebrates, and plants. Flight is level, with necks outstretched. Flocks in some species adopt V-shaped formation. Of the 28 species worldwide, 2 are found in eastern Patagonia.

41. BUFF-NECKED IBIS / Bandurria Común
Theristicus caudatus   *Plate 7*

Description. 28.8″ (74 cm). Beak long and downward-curved. Head and neck buff with a gray chest band. Back and wing coverts ash gray; primaries and secondaries black. Facial skin, gular flap, and belly black. Eye red. Legs pink.

Behavior. Usually in flocks, occasionally alone. Walks around prodding ground with beak for invertebrates. When alarmed, extends neck forward and calls. Frequently emits a loud, metallic honk, "Penk." Lifts into the air calling. Migrates north to pampas in March and returns in September.

Colonial. Breeding begins in September, often staggered, and chicks in all stages may be seen at one time. Nests in Andean marshes and on cliff faces. Builds a large platform of twigs. Lays 3 or 4 whitish eggs. *There were 150 active nests dispersed along cliffs facing the sea between Cabo Vírgenes and an area 30 miles (50 km) north of Río Gallegos, Santa Cruz, November 1990.*

Status and Habitat. Common, particularly near Strait of Magellan, where it breeds, and in northeastern Patagonia during spring and fall migration. Open countryside, moist grasslands, and fields.

Range. Southern race from Tierra del Fuego to northern Patagonia, migrates in winter as far as Buenos Aires. *A small flock of 5 adults in an open, irrigated grassy area in Puerto Madryn, Chubut, June 1996.* Northern race from northern Argentina to Colombia.

42. WHITE-FACED IBIS / Cuervillo de Cañada
Plegadis chihi   *Plate 7*

Description. 33″ (85 cm). Long downward-curved beak. Body dark chestnut (appears black at a distance); metallic violet and green sheen on upperparts. Eye red. Bare facial skin, pink. In flight, legs extend beyond tail. *Nonbreeding:* Colors less intense.

Behavior. Usually in flocks, occasionally alone. Groups adopt V-formation in flight. Probes mud and water with beak in search of frogs, snails, spiders, and insects.

Forms colonies in reed beds. Bends or breaks reeds to form a platform. Lays 2 or 3 turquoise eggs.

Status and Habitat. Uncommon, breeding (?) resident. Varied wetlands, open grassy fields, and irrigated farmland. *Lone individuals in irrigated fields near Trelew, January 1984 & September 1989.*

Range. From northern Patagonia, most of Argentina as far as central Brazil and Peru. Accidentally to Tierra del Fuego.

PHOENICOPTERIFORMES

FLAMINGOS / Flamencos
(Family Phoenicopteridae)

Large very long-legged and long-necked waterbirds with bright pink hues. Sexes are similar, though males are slightly larger than females. The beak, bent downward at an angle, is lined internally with platelets that serve to filter minute algae and invertebrates from the water. Three webbed toes point forward and a rudimentary toe points backward. Gregarious. Flies with neck outstretched. Found in shallow open areas of fresh, brackish, or saltwater lakes, and muddy seacoasts. Of the 6 species, one is found in Patagonia.

43. CHILEAN FLAMINGO / Flamenco Austral
Phoenicopterus chilensis   *Plate 7*

Description. 43″ (110 cm). Neck and body pale pink. Wing coverts and axiliaries bright vermilion. Primaries and secondaries black, particularly visible in flight. Eye pale yellow. Large downward-bent bill, black; base yellow. Legs blue with red tarsal joints. *Juvenile:* Washed gray or whitish, variably mottled darker. Wing coverts mottled dark brown, white, or pink. Remiges dark brown or black. Eye brown. Bill and legs dark gray.
Behavior. In flocks of 10–20, sometimes up to several thousands; rarely alone. Stands—often on one foot—or wades slowly in shallow water. Occasionally swims. Feeds on small invertebrates and plankton (see family description). Shy; moves away slowly from approaching observer. Strides across water before taking off. Flies slowly and straight with neck and legs extended. Flocks string out diagonally in flight. From October to December groups of birds gather to display in tight groups, extending their necks skyward and walking slowly together back and forth. Vocal in breeding colonies. In flight or on ground, a soft, gurgling, froglike call.
  Colonial. Breeds on shallow, open, undisturbed, salt lakes or brackish lagoons. A few pairs to several hundred nests placed side by side on low-lying islands and lakeshores. Builds a raised bowl of mud or salt 15″ (40 cm) wide. Breeding begins in mid-October. Lays one, rarely two, white eggs. Chicks leave the nest and gather in crèches that are chaperoned by a few adults. Fledging occurs in February and March; colony is deserted throughout winter.
Status and Habitat. Common, breeding (?) resident. Few known breeding colonies. *Over 3000 birds gathered on sewage ponds outside Trelew, Chubut, between August 1989 and January 1990. Although no breeding records exist for eastern Patago-*

nia, courtship display and nest building on the edges of a Trelew sewage pond were observed in November 1989. Threats include oil ponds, human disturbance of colonies, and natural or human-caused variations of water level on breeding lakes. Open, brackish, or saltwater lakes. Seaside mudflats and open beaches.

Range. From Tierra del Fuego, all Argentina, as far as southern Brazil and Peru. In cold winters, birds move northward; large flocks can be found in northeastern Patagonia between May and September.

ANSERIFORMES

SWANS, GEESE, AND DUCKS / Cisnes, Cauquenes y Patos
(Family Anatidae)

Aquatic birds with wide, flattened bills with a hook at the tip. The short legs have 3 webbed toes facing forward and a short halux. Wings have brilliant speculums. Mostly omnivorous, some are vegetarian, others feed on fish. Specific feeding adaptations include "dabbling" at surface of the water; submerging the head and neck; "upending" so that half of the body is submerged; diving or grazing. Good swimmers and fast fliers, many migrate long distances in spring and autumn. They are mostly gregarious, but pair-off alone during the breeding season. Nests are usually on the ground or in trees, abundantly lined with down. The chicks are nidifugous. Males produce high-pitched whistles and females produce harsh scolding calls. Found in varied freshwater grassy fields and seacoasts. Of 144 species worldwide, 18 are found in eastern Patagonia.

44. BLACK-NECKED SWAN / Cisne de Cuello Negro
Cygnus melancoryphus   *Plate 8*

Description. 46.8″ (120 cm). Large and conspicuous. Very graceful. Pure white with black head and neck. Slender, white "mask." Caruncle and base of beak red. Eye brown. Bill blue gray. Legs pink.

Behavior. In flocks of 5–20, sometimes many more; rarely alone. Often together with Coscoroba Swans and ducks. Swims elegantly. Dabbles, totally submerges its head and neck, or upends to feed on aquatic plants. Runs along water before taking off. Flight is fast and level. Part of population moves north in winter. Usually silent. Alarm call is a high-pitched whistle.

Builds a large nesting platform 5 ft (1.5 m) across in reed beds or among grass near water. Lays as many as 6 whitish eggs. Both adults care for cygnets, which often travel on the back of a parent.

Status and Habitat. Common resident. *Thousands of weak, dying, and dead birds recorded on roads, beaches, and lakes in Patagonia during 1988 and 1989; though never confirmed, the cause was thought to have been disease or drought.* Open, freshwater, or brackish lakes and large ponds. Sheltered areas of coastal ocean water.

Range. From Tierra del Fuego to central Argentina. From March to September, north as far as Paraguay.

45. COSCOROBA SWAN / Cisne Coscoroba
Coscoroba coscoroba   *Plate 8*

Description. 39″ (100 cm). Large and conspicuous, although the smallest of all swans. Considered to be related to tree-ducks. Entirely white with concealed wing tips black (visible in flight). Beak and legs orange red. Eye orange.

Behavior. In flocks of 5–20 or more, rarely alone. Commonly together with previous species and with ducks. Swims elegantly. Totally submerges head to feed on aquatic plants. Occasionally on dry land, near water. Flight is strong, level, and fast. Part of population moves north in winter. The name "cóscoroba" is onomatopoeic of its trumpeting call, higher pitched in the male than the female. Calls when settled and in flight.

Status and Habitat. Uncommon visitor. Population low. Typically on freshwater and brackish lakes. Occasionally sheltered areas of coastal, ocean waters.

Range. Tierra del Fuego to central Argentina. From March to September, north as far as Paraguay.

46. UPLAND GOOSE / Avutarda o Cauquén Común
Chloephaga picta   *Plate 8*

Description. 27.3″ (70 cm). White, heavily barred black on back and flanks. Two subspecies differentiated by more (*C. p. dispar*) or less (*C. p. picta*) black barring on underparts. Bill and legs black. In flight, wings white with black primaries and dark green speculum. *Female:* Head and neck rufous brown; back, chest, and belly heavily barred black and white. Bill black. Legs yellow.

Behavior. In flocks, particularly in wintering range and on migration, often together with Ashy-headed Goose. Very territorial in breeding season, forms pairs or family groups. Strong, fast flight. Migrating flocks adopt V-formations in the sky, and land to rest on seashores and roads. Flight feathers molted in February; birds gather in flocks near inland lakes and swim from danger. Feeds by grazing short grasses. Male produces a rapid succession of harsh whistles, female a loud, scolding "ca-craaa."

Breeding takes place between October and January. Pairs nest alone in open—usually grassy—ground near water, typically small rivers and streams. Lays 4–6 eggs. Female incubates and takes care of chicks while male stands guard on high ground nearby; when threatened he flies up, emitting repeated alarm calls and settles close by, while female unobtrusively escorts her brood to water.

Status and Habitat. Common breeding resident. Though plentiful, population suffering. Nests predated by feral, introduced mink. Widely hunted for sport. Combated by farmers in pasture and wheat-growing areas of the pampas and irrigated valleys of Patagonia.

Open, snow-free fields, valleys, and shallow lake beds covered with short grasses; winters on open moist pampa grasslands.

Range. Southern and western Patagonia; part of population migrates through northeastern Patagonia to south of province of Buenos Aires in April to May and returns in August to September. Resident on Falkland Islands (Islas Malvinas). *Many flocks containing between 10 and 50 birds flying north over Golfo San José, Chubut, between late April and late May 1985.*

Similar Species. Females can be confused with the rare Ruddy-headed Goose (*C. rubidiceps*), which is smaller and more finely barred.

47. ASHY-HEADED GOOSE / Cauquén de Cabeza Gris
Chloephaga poliocephala   *Plate 8*

Description. 21.5″ (55 cm). Smaller than Upland Goose. Head ash gray. Chest and part of back rich chestnut. Rest of underparts white, barred black. Beak black. Legs orange and black. In flight, wings white, with black primaries and dark green speculum.

Behavior. Solitary pairs or family groups during the breeding season from September to March. Flocks in wintering range and on migration, often together with the more numerous Upland Goose (*C. picta*). Migrating birds occasionally land on open grassy fields, roads, and beaches. Grazes short tender grasses. Molt occurs in February, when birds gather near inland lakes in Patagonia. Male produces a short harsh whistle; female's call is a loud, scolding "ca-craa."

Pairs nest alone in boggy areas, grassy forest clearings, and open valley pastures near water. Lays up to 9 white eggs. Female incubates and cares for young. *Nest with eggs near Puerto Deseado in December 1987 (W. Conway & G. Harris). Breeding pairs by rivers and lakes in southeastern Santa Cruz, December 1989 (W. Conway & G. Harris).*

Status and Habitat. Common breeding resident. Not as abundant as Upland Goose; also hunted for sport and combated by farmers in pampas and Patagonia. Open fields and grassy clearings in woods, usually near water; snow-free lowlands; open grasslands of southern pampas. Roadsides and seashores during migration.

Range. Breeds in southern and western Patagonia. In April to May, part of population ranges north through eastern Patagonia to province of Buenos Aires and returns in August to September. Resident on Falkland Islands (Islas Malvinas).

48. RUDDY-HEADED GOOSE / Cauquén Colorado
Chloephaga rubidiceps   *Plate 8*

Description. 19.5″ (50 cm). Smaller than the two preceding species. Head and neck ruddy, forming a clearly defined hood. Fine, black, and buff-white barring on body. Nonbarred undertail coverts rufous. Beak black. Legs orange. In flight, wings white with black primaries and dark green speculum.

Behavior. In pairs. Flocks together with previous two species during migration. Feeds on short grasses. Male produces a high whistle; female, a harsh cackling.

Nests among grasses near water. Laying begins in November; up to 6 white eggs.

Status and Habitat. Rare breeding (?) resident in southeastern Patagonia. Population abundant until mid-1950s, is now very reduced. *One pair near Cabo Virgenes, December 1989 (W. Conway & G. Harris).* Open, usually grass-covered ground, close to water.

Range. Tierra del Fuego and southern Patagonia. In April to May migrates north through northeastern Patagonia as far as the south of province of Buenos Aires. Resident on Falkland Islands (Islas Malvinas).

Similar Species. Differs from larger female Upland Goose in finer barring and more defined head and neck coloring.

49. WHITE-HEADED STEAMER-DUCK / Pato Vapor Cabeza Blanca
Tachyeres leucocephalus   *Plate 9*

Description. 31.2″ (80 cm). Large and thick-set, with heavy bill. Wings short. Whitish head. Body mottled gray; vinaceous on chest. Belly white. Bill orange. *Female:* Similar, with brownish head and white postocular streak. Bill greenish yellow.

Behavior. In pairs, family groups, or—sometimes large—flocks. *Flocks of 50–60 birds at Bahía Bustamante, Chubut, November 1989, and on an island in bottom of Caleta Malaspina, Chubut, December 1991.* Sits on rocky beaches and reefs; hurries to water when threatened. Shy; if undisturbed becomes accustomed to people. Capable of heavy, laborious flight, usually ending with a splash as it lands on water. If threatened at sea, "steams" away along the surface, paddling untidily with its wings. Dives to feed among kelp on mollusks, crustaceans, and fish near sea bed. Breeding pairs strongly territorial and viciously defend their area of ocean. Male produces a loud whistle; the female, a harsh cackle.

Nests alone in secluded spots among bushes on shore. Lays 5–8 cream-colored eggs. Female incubates while male remains close by. *One female on nest inside a bush on tourist trail at Punta Tombo, Chubut, December 1989 (W. Conway & G. Harris).*

Status and Habitat. Common breeding resident. Population numerous but fairly restricted. Best observed at Punta Tombo, Cabo Dos Bahías, and Bahía Bustamante in Chubut. Seacoast, within and a little beyond surf zone; isolated rocky beaches and reefs. *One lone adult on a pond 12 miles (20 km) from sea, December 1989 (W. Conway & G. Harris).*

Range. From Punta Tombo to Comodoro Rivadavia, Chubut.

50. FLYING STEAMER-DUCK / Pato Vapor Volador
Tachyeres patachonicus   *Plate 9*

Description. 26.5″ (68 cm). Heavily built but not as large as the previous species; more "ducklike." Head gray-brown with prominent postocular white stripe. Mottled gray body. Underside white. Beak yellow. Large white speculum. *Female:* similar, with darker head and very distinct postocular stripe. Beak bluish green.

Behavior. In pairs or family groups between September and February. Non-breeding birds form large, loose flocks. *50–60 on coastal, saltwater lagoons near* *mouth of Caleta Valdés, November 1985.* Flies strongly. "Steams" by paddling along surface of water like the previous species. Dives for mollusks and crustaceans. Very territorial; breeding pairs viciously fight others to defend an area of water.

During display male produces a rapid succession of short loud whistles while female produces a harsh cackle; combined voices are reminiscent of the sounds of an old paddle steamer.

Nests alone in secluded places among grasses or bushes near fresh or salt water. Lays 5–9 white eggs. Female incubates while male remains close by.

Status and Habitat. Common breeding resident. Inland, open lakes and ponds, seacoasts. *Single pair in Golfo San José, Chubut, December 1987.*

Range. All Patagonia from Tierra del Fuego to Río Negro. Also southern Chile to Valdivia.

51. CRESTED DUCK / Pato Crestón
Lophonetta specularioides   *Plate 10*

Description. 23.4″ (60 cm). Cap, hindcrest—usually not visible—and back dark brown. Rest of head, neck, and underparts pale brown, mottled darker. Eye red. Secondaries broadly edged white, very noticeable in flight; speculum vinaceous.

Behavior. In pairs, family groups, or flocks of up to 50 birds. Shy. Does not usually mix with other ducks. Strong fast flight. Feeds by upending and diving. Diet includes small invertebrates and algae. Male produces a sharp whistle; female, a harsh nasal call.

Pairs breed alone in secluded places along shores of lakes and ponds near the sea and inland. Nest is thickly lined with down. Lays up to 9 whitish eggs. Incubation lasts 30 days. Both parents care for ducklings.

Status and Habitat. Common breeding resident. One of the most frequently encountered ducks along coast, freshwater lakes and ponds, seashores, and shallow inshore waters.

Range. From Tierra del Fuego, all Patagonia, and north along the Andes as far as Peru.

52. SPECTACLED (BRONZE-WINGED) DUCK / Pato Anteojo
Anas specularis   *Plate 9*

Description. 21.5″ (55 cm). Dark-brown head with distinctive, clearly defined white patches in front of eye and on throat. Back brown. Belly pale brown. Speculum bronze. Beak steel gray. Feet orange.

Behavior. In pairs or small groups. Shy. Does not usually mix with other ducks. Strong flight. Feeds by upending. Female produces a short barking "quack"; male, a loud hissing whistle.

Status and Habitat. Uncommon nonbreeding visitor. Mostly restricted to freshwater lakes, ponds, and rivers in wooded parts of southern Andes; occasionally open lakes on the steppe.

Range. Western Patagonia. Part of population ranges east and north as far as province of Buenos Aires from April to September.

53. WHITE-CHEEKED (BAHAMA) PINTAIL / Pato Gargantillo
Anas bahamensis *Plate 10*

Description. 18.7″ (48 cm). Head brown with well-defined semicircular patch of white on cheek and throat. Back dark brown. Belly buff, spotted brown. Beak blackish, base red. Eye reddish. Tail long and pointed.

Behavior. In pairs or flocks, often with other waterbirds. *50–100 together with flocks of Chilean Flamingos and Wilson's Phalaropes and Common Stilts on a sewage pond with abundant green algae near Trelew, November 1989.* Shy. Fast flight with rapid wing beat. Dabbles for algae and small invertebrates in shallow, fresh, or brackish water. Male produces a clear double whistle; female, a short, low vibrating call (Canevari et al. 1991).

Status and Habitat. Occasional nonbreeding (?) visitor. *50–60 birds on open shallow lake in steppe south of Puerto Madryn, January 1976.* Freshwater lakes and ponds.

Range. From northeastern Chubut, much of South and Central America, to southern USA. Southern populations migrate north between April and August.

54. CINNAMON TEAL / Pato Colorado
Anas cyanoptera *Plate 9*

Description. 17.5″ (45 cm). Head, neck, and body dark reddish chestnut. Eye red or yellow. Bill black. Wing coverts light blue, conspicuous in flight. *Female:* Buff spotted and mottled dark brown.

Behavior. In pairs or small groups, often together with other ducks. Fast flight in tight flocks. Dives frequently to feed. Diet includes plants, larvae, insects, small mollusks, and other invertebrates. Low rattling call in the breeding season (Canevari et al. 1991).

Nest concealed in aquatic vegetation or grass near water. Lays up to 13 cream-colored eggs. Incubation lasts 24–25 days. As with other ducks, after hatching, ducklings are "imprinted" by the mother's appearance and call, and they follow her closely from then on.

Status and Habitat. Uncommon visitor from September to April. Freshwater marshes, lakes, and ponds covered with dense vegetation; inundated, grassy fields.

Range. Patchy. From Tierra del Fuego to southern Peru and Brazil. Also northern South America to western North America.

55. RED SHOVELER / Pato Cuchara
Anas platalea *Plate 9*

Description. 20″ (51 cm). Head pale gray, finely speckled black. Body rufous, spotted black. Eye white. Large, thick bill black. Legs yellow. In flight, upper wing coverts pale blue. *Female:* Pale brown, spotted, and mottled black.

Behavior. In pairs or flocks often together with other ducks. Relatively unafraid. Swims, or waddles through the shallows, bending its neck low to dabble. Also up-ends in deeper water. Diet includes aquatic vegetation and small invertebrates. Produces a repeated low "wheezz."

Nests concealed among grasses near fresh water. Lays as many as 10 cream-colored eggs. Incubation lasts 25 days.

Status and Habitat. Common resident. One of the most abundant ducks, more so between September and April. Open or vegetation-covered shallow lakes, ponds, and rivers. Marshes.

Range. Tierra del Fuego to central Argentina; between March and August ranges north to Peru and Brazil.

56. SOUTHERN WIDGEON / Pato Overo
Anas sibilatrix   *Plate 10*

Description. 19.5″ (50 cm). "Face" white. Rest of head and neck black with green or purple sheen. Upperparts black; feathers edged white. Underparts white, tinged rufous on flanks. Tail black. Eye brown. Bill and legs black. In flight, black and white wing pattern.

Behavior. In pairs or small flocks, often together with other ducks. Shy, feeds at or near surface of water. Diet mainly plant matter. Fast flight. Male produces a musical wheezy whistle, when settled or in flight; female, a nasal call.

Nests concealed in grasses some distance from water. Lays 5–8 cream-colored eggs. Both adults take care of the ducklings.

Status and Habitat. Common from September to March. Freshwater lakes, ponds, and rivers; inundated fields and grassy lakeshores.

Range. From Tierra del Fuego to southern Buenos Aires. Range extends as far as southern Brazil from March to August.

57. SPECKLED TEAL / Pato Barcino
Anas flavirostris   *Plate 10*

Description. 15.6″ (40 cm). Small and stocky. Head and neck gray-brown, finely speckled black. Back dark brown; underparts pale brown, mottled black. Eye brown. Beak yellow; culmen and tip black. Legs blue gray. In flight, secondaries edged buff; speculum black and rust.

Behavior. In pairs or small flocks of 10–20. Not as shy as other ducks. Flies fast in compact flocks. Male produces a high-pitched, bisyllabic whistle; female produces a harsh nasal call.

Beginning in August, nests in hollows of trees, in abandoned nests of other birds, or concealed in grasses near water. Lays 5–8 cream-colored eggs. Both parents take care of ducklings.

Status and Habitat. Common breeding resident. Freshwater lakes, ponds, rivers, and inundated areas. Rocky seashores, beaches, and tidal pools.

Range. Tierra del Fuego, all of Patagonia to central Argentina. Between April and September, north to Paraguay. *A. f. oxyptera* from northwestern Argentina, Andes to Colombia.

Similar Species. Differs from larger Brown Pintail in shorter, thicker neck, dark head, and short tail.

58. SILVER TEAL / Pato Capuchino
Anas versicolor *Plate 10*

Description. 15.6″ (40 cm). Distinct black cap. Rest of head and neck whitish. Body heavily spotted, mottled, and vermiculated black and white. Beak black, base orange. In flight, speculum metallic green, edged white.
Behavior. In pairs or small flocks often together with other ducks. Diet includes aquatic plants, insects, larvae, and other small invertebrates. Male produces a quiet, nasal call; female call is harsh and high.
  Nest concealed among vegetation close to water, well lined with down. Lays up to 9 cream-colored eggs. Both parents incubate and tend ducklings.
Status and Habitat. Uncommon visitor from September to March. Shallow, freshwater lakes, ponds, and inundated areas with abundant vegetation.
Range. From Tierra del Fuego to southern Brazil and Paraguay.

59. BROWN PINTAIL / Pato Maicero
Anas georgica *Plate 10*

Description. 20″ (51 cm). Slender with a relatively long thin neck and pointed tail. Head and neck pale brown, finely speckled darker. Rest of underparts pale brown, spotted, and mottled darker. Upperparts dark brown, feathers edged paler. Eye brown. Beak yellow with culmen and tip black. In flight, greenish black speculum, edged front and back with creamy buff.
Behavior. Solitary, in pairs or flocks, often mixed with other ducks. Shy. Holds head high when alert. Fast flight with rapid wing beats. Dabbles and upends in the water to feed on mollusks and aquatic vegetation. Also feeds on seeds in open grassy fields. Settled or in flight, male produces a low trisyllabic whistle; female, a harsh nasal call.
  Nest is a shallow cup, thickly lined with down, concealed in grass, often far from water. Lays 4–10 eggs. Female incubates and tends ducklings.
Status and Habitat. Common breeding resident. One of the most abundant ducks in Patagonia, particularly between September and March. Varied freshwater lakes, ponds, rivers, irrigated areas, and grassy fields near water. Less common on seacoast.
Range. All southern and central Argentina, and Andes to Colombia. In winter ranges north to southern Brazil.
Similar Species. Differs from smaller Speckled Teal in long slender neck, longer tail, and paler head.

60. ROSY-BILLED POCHARD / Pato Picazo
Netta peposaca *Plate 9*

Description. 21.5″ (55 cm). Head, neck, chest, and back black with violet sheen; flanks ash gray. Beak and caruncle bright pink. Eye red. In flight, broad white wing band. *Female:* Upperparts dark rufous brown; underparts lighter. Undertail coverts white. Beak brownish.

Behavior. In pairs or flocks, often together with other ducks. Fast flight with rapid, noisy wing beats. Feeds at surface, upends or dives; diet includes mainly aquatic plants. Usually silent. Male produces a quiet whistle; female, a harsh nasal call.

Builds a large nest of reeds and twigs concealed within reed beds. Lays up to 16 cream-colored eggs.

Status and Habitat. Common September–March. Freshwater lakes, ponds, and inundated areas with abundant vegetation.

Range. Santa Cruz to central Argentina. Migrates as far as southern Brazil between April and August.

61. LAKE DUCK / Pato Zambullidor Chico
Oxyura vittata   *Plate 9*

Description. 15.6″ (40 cm). Small and toylike. Lower neck, chest, and back rich chestnut. Hood black, ending horizontally on neck. Stiff tail feathers, black. Belly white. Beak sky blue. Eye brown. *Female:* Upperparts mottled and barred brown. Cheek stripe, throat, and underparts whitish. Tail black. Bill brown.

Behavior. In pairs or small flocks, often with other ducks. Holds tail vertical when alert. Dives frequently. Rarely flies during day; does so close to surface and lands a short distance away. Courting male produces high-pitched, drawn-out, drumming call followed by repeated low, hollow sounds.

Builds a small nest among reeds near water level. Lays up to 10 rough-surfaced, relatively large cream-colored eggs.

Status and Habitat. Common breeding resident. *Good sighting opportunities at Trelew sewage pond, Chubut.* Freshwater lakes, ponds, and rivers, in open water and areas partially covered with vegetation.

Range. Tierra del Fuego, most of Argentina to southern Brazil.

FALCONIFORMES

AMERICAN VULTURES / Jotes y Cóndores
(Family Cathartidae)

Large birds of prey—carrion feeders—with bald heads and strong hooked beaks. Their coloring is predominantly black with white markings. They display superb soaring flight. The 7 species are restricted to the New World; one of them is common in this region.

62. TURKEY VULTURE / Jote de Cabeza Colorada
Cathartes aura   *Plate 11*

Description. 21″ (55 cm); wingspan 66″ (170 cm). Black with pale remiges. Head bald, red with yellow nape.

Behavior. Alone or in small loose groups. Soars with wings held above horizontal, tilting and adjusting to catch updrafts. Occasionally beats wings 3 or 4 times in succession. Roosts in cliff faces and elevated structures (lighthouses and beacons). Feeds on carrion, commonly on road kills. Usually silent.

No nesting records for eastern Patagonia, but numbers in breeding season suggest it may breed. Elsewhere nests on ledges in high cliffs. Lays one or 2 whitish eggs.

Status and Habitat. Common breeding (?) visitor near coast of Chubut from early September to April. *35 birds on a tall metal structure west of Istmo Ameghino, Chubut, March 1991.* Varied; open country, forests, and steppe; occasionally sea cliffs.

Range. Much of South America to North America. Southern populations migrate north between April and September.

Similar Species. Black Vulture (not illustrated), found in hilly terrain near Sierra Grande 100 miles north of Península Valdés, differs by dark wings with pale "windows," wings held horizontal, and black head; also beats wings noticeably faster.

OSPREYS / Águilas Pescadoras
(Family Pandionidae)

Eagle-like with relatively long bent wings. Long sharp claws. Flies over water, into which it plunges directly from flight, to capture fish. A single cosmopolitan species.

63. OSPREY / Águila Pescadora o Sangual
Pandion haliaetus

Description. 22″ (56 cm). Head and underparts white with prominent black eyestripe. Upperparts dark brown.

Behavior. Usually alone. Flies slowly over water with occasional glides and hovering pauses. Dives feet first to catch fish. Flies up again, shakes itself briefly in the air, and continues flight. High-pitched whistle.

Status and Habitat. Rare summer nonbreeding visitor. *A single adult, diving for fish near eastern coast of Golfo San José, Chubut, January 1982.* Seacoasts, lakes, and large rivers.

Range. Cosmopolitan. North American migrants range to northern and central Argentina.

EAGLES, HAWKS, AND HARRIERS / Águilas, Aguiluchos y Gavilanes
(Family Accipitridae)

Birds of prey with short, powerful hooked beaks lacking "notched" edges. They have strong, sharp claws, and some species have feathered tarsi. Their wings are broad. Diurnal. Females are slightly larger than males. They are cosmopolitan with 210 species, 5 of which are found in eastern Patagonia.

64. BLACK-CHESTED BUZZARD-EAGLE / Águila Mora o Escudada
Geranoaetus melanoleucus   *Plate 11*

Description. 24″ (60 cm). Large and stocky. Very broad wedge-shaped wings held horizontal in flight. Tail does not extend beyond trailing edge of wings. Head, chest, and upperparts slate gray. Rest of underparts white. Underwing finely barred gray. *Female:* 27″ (70 cm). *Juvenile:* Wings narrower than adult, tail longer, extending beyond trailing edge of wings. Heavily streaked buff, brown, and black.

Behavior. Alone, in pairs, or in family groups. Soars gracefully on updrafts along cliff edges. Partially folds its wings to dive down to ground to capture prey. Diet includes armadillos, birds, and reptiles. Often mobbed by kestrels. Roosts on ledges. Short, high-pitched, scolding whistles, "Chee-chee-chee."

Builds a large nesting platform of twigs on ledges in cliff faces. Lays 2 white eggs. Chicks hatch late November or December, covered in white down. Often one chick larger than the other. Juveniles leave the nest by February.

Status and Habitat. Common breeding resident. Though hunting is illegal, frequently shot when perched on telegraph poles by the roadside. Tall cliffs on the sea. Mountains, foothills, and savanna.

Range. Much of western and southern South America and eastern Brazil.

65. RED-BACKED HAWK / Aguilucho Común o Ñanco
Buteo polyosoma   *Plate 11*

Description. 18″ (45 cm). Usually ash gray above and pure white below. Tail white with black subterminal band. Many variations from basic color pattern: from entirely dark to variably barred and streaked black, gray, or brown below. *Female:* 20″ (52 cm). Back usually rufous. *Juvenile:* Upperparts usually dark brown, underparts buff, streaked, and barred with brown.

Behavior. Alone or in pairs. Fairly unafraid. Sits on telegraph poles and bush tops. Intermittently soars and beats its wings in flight. Occasionally hovers while searching the ground for rodents, small birds, and reptiles upon which it feeds. Shrill "keeeeah-keeeah."

Beginning in September, builds a large nesting platform of twigs on tops of large bushes, 6–9 ft (2–3 m) above ground. Usually lays 2 eggs. *One nest with 4 almost fully fledged chicks on Península Valdés, Chubut, November 1986.*

Status and Habitat. Common breeding resident. Although legally protected and the subject of friendly lore, is often shot when perched on telegraph poles by passing motorists. Open scrub or grass-covered steppe. Open terrain of mountains and foothills to 10,000 ft (3500m).

Range. Patagonia and the Andes as far as Colombia, occasionally northeastern Argentina and eastern Brazil.

66. WHITE-TAILED KITE / Milano Blanco
Elanus leucurus   *Plate 11*

Description. 13″ (34 cm). Long pointed wings. White head with black eye ring. Back pearl gray. "Wrists" and upper wing coverts black.

Behavior. Usually solitary. Flies gracefully, frequently stopping to hover 15–30 ft (5–10 m) above ground on fluttering, upheld wings. Swoops down to capture rodents and reptiles. High whistle ending on rasping, guttural note.

No breeding records in the region. In other parts, builds a small twig nesting platform on top of a bush.

Status and Habitat. Uncommon summer visitor in northeastern Patagonia. *A lone bird hovering by the roadside on the outskirts of Puerto Madryn, Chubut, December 1976.* Range is expanding slowly. Dry open grass and scrub, also scattered trees and open woodland.

Range. Northern Patagonia to southern Brazil; also northern South America.

67. CINEREUS HARRIER / Gavilán Ceniciento
Circus cinereus   Plate 11

Description. 16″ (40 cm). Ash-gray head. White rump. Underparts white, finely barred cinnamon. Eye yellow. In flight, underwing white, with tips and trailing edge black. *Female:* 18″ (45 cm). Upperparts brown. Underparts including underwing surface white, barred brown.

Behavior. Alone or in loose flocks. Soaring flight close to ground, constantly tilting this way and that. Alights to capture rodents and reptiles. Perches on ground or on clumps of grass. Quiet clicking and "keeee" in flight near nest.

Nests on boggy ground in freshwater marshy terrain. *Several dozen pairs beginning to nest in grass-covered marsh area around freshwater springs that flow into Salina Grande on Península Valdés, Chubut, September 1981.* Nest is concealed in the vegetation. Lays 3 or 4 pale-blue eggs.

Status and Habitat. Fairly common breeding resident. Open grass or bush-covered terrain. Marshes.

Range. All Patagonia and the Andean range and foothills as far as Colombia. Less commonly the rest of Argentina as far as southern Brazil.

Similar Species. Female can be confused with female Long-winged Harrier, except is smaller, lacks facial disk, and has barred underparts.

68. LONG-WINGED HARRIER / Gavilán Grande
Circus buffoni   Plate 11

Description. 19″ (50 cm). Large with long wings. Upperparts blackish with noticeable white rump. Black hood with white eyebrow and facial disk. Chest and belly white; underwing barred and flight feathers tipped black. Tail barred. Slender legs and toes, yellow. *Female:* 23″ (60 cm). Hood and upperparts brown. Eyebrow and facial disk whitish. Underparts white, streaked buff. *Dark phase:* Underparts black. Flight feathers and tail barred white.

Behavior. Usually solitary. Soars low over ground tilting this way and that. Feeds on small mammals, birds, and eggs. Habitually silent.

Status and Habitat. Uncommon nonbreeding visitor from September to March. *One adult male on Península Valdés, Chubut, November 1984.* Open grassland, moist pastures, and marshes. Prefers wetter countryside than previous species.

Range. Central and northern Argentina to southern Brazil. Also northern South America. Less commonly ranges through much of the rest of South America.

Similar Species. Female differs from female Cinereus Harrier by larger size, well-marked facial markings, and streaked underparts.

CARACARAS AND FALCONS / Chimangos, Caranchos y Halcones
(Family Falconidae)

Birds of prey with short, hooked beaks with notched edges. In general, wings are narrower and tails longer than in the previous family, and flight is more agile. Legs are unfeathered. Diurnal. Male and female are alike. World-wide distribution of 57 species, 5 of which are found in eastern Patagonia.

69. CHIMANGO CARACARA / Chimango
Milvago chimango   *Plate 12*

Description. 14″ (37 cm). Head and back pale brown; rump cream. Tail relatively long, barred pale brown and cream. Belly cream. Wings faintly barred same color, with pale "windows" at base of primaries.

Behavior. Alone or in loose flocks. Untidy flight. Often alights on the ground. Feeds primarily on carrion but also captures insects and small vertebrates. Vocal; loud "cheeee."

Nests in tops of trees and bushes, at 9–40 ft (3 to 15 m) above ground. Builds a large platform of twigs; nest lined with grass, pieces of wool, rags, paper. Lays 2–4 cream-colored eggs.

Status and Habitat. Common resident near irrigated areas, moist countryside, and in outskirts of urban areas. Uncommon in dry steppe. *Several individuals near springs around Salina Grande and Salina Chica, October 1982. Several birds around garbage tips near Trelew, Chubut, February 1996.* Open grassland, wooded areas, refuse dumps.

Range. All of Argentina, Uruguay, and most of Chile.

70. CRESTED CARACARA / Carancho
Polyborus plancus   *Plate 12*

Description. 21″ (55 cm). Relatively long neck, long legs, and powerful beak. Bare facial skin pink. Cap and crest black. Neck and chest cream, barred black. In flight, conspicuous white "windows" at base of primaries, Tail white with black subterminal band. *Juvenile:* Dark brown; blackish cap. Neck and chest streaked with black. Pale plumaged individuals have been recorded on several occasions in northeastern Patagonia. *Two pure white and one pale individual recorded together at Bahía Bustamante, Chubut, January 1991; also one white individual at Punta Tombo, Chubut, in 1982 (C. Garcia).*

Behavior. Alone or in small loose flocks. Often on ground or fence posts. Feeds primarily on carrion; commonly lands on road kills. Diet also includes small mammals, birds, and reptiles. Loud croaking "raack, raack."

Nests high in trees or tall bushes. Builds a very large nest of twigs and sticks, lined with grass and wool. Lays 2 cream-colored eggs, streaked with rust.

Status and Habitat. Uncommon breeding resident. Open grassland, wooded areas, mountains, and foothills; refuse dumps.

Range. From Tierra del Fuego to southwestern USA.

71. PEREGRINE FALCON / Halcón Peregrino
Falco peregrinus   *Plate 12*

Description. 18″ (47 cm). Characteristic black hood. Upperparts steel gray, underparts streaked buff white and barred with black. In flight, wings pointed with finely barred undersides; wedge-shaped tail. Female slightly larger.

Behavior. Usually alone. Flight swift, with rapid wing beats and short glides often high in the sky. Dives with partially closed wings at speeds estimated around 180 mph (300 kph) to attack birds in flight (pigeons, shorebirds, kestrels, etc.). *One adult chasing flocks of shorebirds on Playa Fracaso Golfo, San José, Chubut, April 1981. Another adult chasing a kestrel on eastern shore of Golfo San José, Chubut, October 1984.* Particularly near nest a sharp repeated "kek-kek-kek."

Breeds on inaccessible ledges of tall cliffs. Nest has little lining. Lays 2–4 cream-colored eggs. *A nest with 2 chicks on cliffs at Punta Pirámide Chubut, December 1987. One adult behaving as though protecting young on Isla Leones, Chubut, February 1986.*

Status and Habitat. Uncommon breeding resident. Although the situation in Patagonia is unknown, in other parts has suffered badly due to uncontrolled use of pesticides, which seriously affect the bird's fertility. Beaches and cliffs on sea-coasts. Open country near rivers and lakes. Large cities.

Range. Tierra del Fuego, Patagonia, and western Argentina. In winter, ranges to northern Argentina and Ecuador along the Andes.

72. APLOMADO FALCON / Halcón Aplomado
Falco femoralis   *Plate 12*

Description. 16″ (40 cm). Slender bodied. Black hood with long buff-white eyebrow. Mustachial streak black. Upperparts steel gray; underparts white to pale rufous, with thick, black barring across belly forming a distinct "waistcoat." Wings pointed. Tail long, banded black and white.

Behavior. Usually alone, occasionally in pairs. Perches on top of bushes, fence posts, or telephone poles. Flies low and fast, occasionally hovering over the ground. Feeds in flight on insects and small birds. Scolding "ee-ee-ee-ee" call.

Uses bush tops, stick nests abandoned by other birds. Lays 1–4 cream-colored eggs with red blotches. *One nest perched on top of a bush with two worried parents circling round, La Anita, Península Valdés, Chubut, November 1988.*

Status and Habitat. Fairly common breeding resident. Dry, open grass and scrubland; open woodland.

Range. From Tierra del Fuego to southwestern USA.

Similar Species. Differs from Peregrine Falcon by noticeably longer tail, rich colored underparts, and dark "waistband."

73. AMERICAN KESTREL / Halconcito Común
Falco sparverius   *Plate 12*

Description. 10″ (25 cm). Small with long tail and pointed wings. Crown gray. Mustachial, postocular, and hindcrown streaks black. Back and tail rufous with black subterminal band. Chest spotted black. *Female:* Back and tail barred black. Chest streaked brown.

Behavior. Usually in pairs. Perches on telephone posts, wires, and tall bushes. Hovers above ground in search of lizards, small birds, insects, and rodents. Mobs larger birds of prey that approach its nest. Shrill "klee-klee-klee."

    Breeds from September to December on high ledges of cliffs. Lays 3–5 white eggs, spotted rust. Chicks are covered in white down. Sometimes 2 broods hatch in one season.

Status and Habitat. Common breeding resident, particularly near cliffs. Outskirts of towns. Open grassland, scrub, and wooded areas. Roadsides.

Range. From Tierra del Fuego, much of South America, to North America.

GRUIFORMES

RAILS, COOTS, etc. / Gallinetas, Gallaretas, etc.
(Family Rallidae)

    Small to medium-sized birds that live in freshwater areas with dense vegetation. Mostly shy and secretive, all have rounded bodies with shortish tails. Rails have longish bills, crakes have short bills; both inhabit thick reed beds. Coots and gallinules are aquatic, have lobed toes, and are excellent swimmers. There are 120 species in the world, 5 of them found in eastern Patagonia.

74. PLUMBEOUS RAIL / Gallineta Común
Pardirallus sanguinolentus   *Plate 13*

Description. 11″ (27 cm). Body appears laterally "compressed." Bill long, slightly down-curved, yellow; blue and red at base. Upperparts brown, underparts dark lead gray. Eye red. Legs pink.

Behavior. Shy and fairly nocturnal, rarely ventures out from under cover of vegetation. Usually heard rather than seen. Walks with tail held upright. Rarely swims or flies. Prefers to run for cover and conceals itself in vegetation. Feeds on insects. Melodious whistle "veedle-day."

    Nests on ground in thick, damp vegetation. Lays 4–6 eggs.

Status and Habitat. Breeding resident. Common but hard to see. Restricted to densely vegetated freshwater areas along Chubut River valley.

Range. From Tierra del Fuego to Peru and southern Brazil.

75. WHITE-WINGED COOT / **Gallareta Chica**
Fulica leucoptera   *Plate 13*

Description. 12″ (30 cm). Mostly slate gray. Rounded frontal shield and beak yellow. Trailing edge of secondaries white.

Behavior. In flocks, sometimes large. Often found together with ducks and other coots. Frequently walks among reeds, though never far from water; swims out into the open. Flies more readily than other coots. Noisy, nasal cackle.

Builds a bulky nest of floating vegetation on water. Lays up to 9 eggs.

Status and Habitat. Common breeding resident. On freshwater lakes and ponds along the Chubut River valley.

Range. From Tierra del Fuego to southern Brazil.

76. RED-GARTERED COOT / **Gallareta de Ligas Rojas**
Fulica armillata   *Plate 13*

Description. 14″ (35 cm). Slightly larger than other coots. Mostly slate gray. Pointed frontal shield and beak yellow; a dark red line separates the shield from the beak. Legs yellow with red tarsal joints.

Behavior. Often in large flocks. Swims in reeds and out into open water. Dives to feed on aquatic vegetation. A loud, nasal cackling reminiscent of laughter. The most vocal of the three coots. If alarmed, it seeks cover in dense reeds. Scuttles across the water. Chases are common.

Builds a large floating nest out of vegetation. Lays up to 7 eggs.

Status and Habitat. Common breeding resident. The most abundant of the three coots. Freshwater lakes and ponds. Chubut River valley. Occasionally on the sea, close to shore.

Range. From Tierra del Fuego to southern Brazil.

77. RED-FRONTED COOT / **Gallareta de Escudete Rojo**
Fulica rufifrons   *Plate 13*

Description. 12″ (32 cm). Mostly slate gray. Longish frontal shield, deep red. Beak yellow.

Behavior. Shy; usually remains close to, or among, the reeds. Swims with tail vertical. Dives frequently.

Builds a large floating nest in the reeds.

Status and Habitat. Common though less abundant than the previous two species throughout its range. Breeding resident in densely vegetated freshwater lakes and ponds along Chubut River valley.

Range. Tierra del Fuego to southern Brazil.

78. SPOT-FLANKED GALLINULE / **Pollona Chica**
Gallinula melanops   *Plate 13*

Description. 8″ (20 cm). Small. Short beak and frontal shield, yellow green. Head and neck lead gray, darker around the beak. Back brown, flanks spotted white. Eye red.

Behavior. Not shy. Usually solitary. Swims nodding its head back and forth. Flicks its tail. Dives frequently. Feeds on aquatic vegetation. Silent.

Builds nest on wet ground close to—but not on—water; concealed and roofed over with vegetation. Lays 4–6 eggs.

Status and Habitat. Uncommon breeding resident in densely vegetated lakes and ponds along Chubut River valley. Freshwater lakes and ponds with abundant vegetation.

Range. From Patagonia to southern Brazil. Also Peru and Colombia.

CHARADRIIFORMES

PAINTED SNIPE / Aguateros
(Family Rostratulidae)

Small and shy sandpiper-like birds with long downward-curved beaks. Wetlands. Of 2 species worldwide, one is recorded for the coast of Patagonia.

79. SOUTH AMERICAN PAINTED SNIPE / Aguatero
Nycticryphes semicollaris   *Plate 13*

Description. 7″ (17 cm). Small. Beak long with tip curved downward. Brown with clearly defined white lower belly. Stripe behind eye, crown and V-shaped line on back, buff white. White spots on wing.

Behavior. Alone or in pairs. Shy and unobtrusive. Silent. Hunched posture; walks and stands with head held low. Flies only if disturbed, and lands a short way off.

Status and Habitat. Accidental. *One vagrant recorded in scrub terrain, Puerto Madryn, Chubut, May 1988.* Inundated fields, marshes, lakes, and ponds with dense vegetation.

Range. Northern Patagonia to southern Brazil.

OYSTERCATCHERS / Ostreros
(Family Haematopodidae)

Pigeon-sized birds with large heads and long, laterally compressed bright red beaks. They are very vocal, with loud piping whistles. Of the 7 species, 3 are found locally.

80. AMERICAN OYSTERCATCHER / Ostrero Común
Haematopus palliatus (ostralegus)   *Plate 14*

Description. 16″ (40 cm). Head and chest black. Back brown, underparts white. Eye yellow, ringed with red. Beak red. In flight, white wing bar. Chick has shorter beak than adult, with black tip.

Behavior. In pairs or family groups; flocks in winter. Not shy, but keeps its distance. Feeds at water's edge. Using its slender, powerful beak, it pries, probes, and levers for mollusks, crabs, shrimps, worms, and insects. At high tide it roosts, often together with gulls and Neotropic Cormorants along top of beaches.

Territorial in breeding season, one pair occupies a section of beach. Long loud piping "wheep"; often a series, in duet. Breeding begins September. Nest an unlined scrape, placed a little above high-tide line. Lays 2–3 heavily mottled brown eggs. Leads intruders away from eggs or small chicks with a crouched walk, sometimes "sitting" on imaginary nest. Usually only one chick is raised at a time. If brood is lost, may lay once or even twice more until January. Chick leaves nest soon after hatching.

Status and Habitat. Common breeding resident. Pebble beaches, reefs, mudflats, and mussel beds. *Single scrapes above high-tide mark on a pebble beach, with eggs or chicks, at Golfo San José, Chubut, December 1981–96.*

Range. Coastline of South America to North America

Similar Species. Differs from Magellanic Oystercatcher in having brown back, red eye ring, and less white in wings.

81. MAGELLANIC OYSTERCATCHER / Ostrero del Sur
Haematopus leucopodus   *Plate 14*

Description. 16″ (40 cm). Black head, chest, and upperparts. Rest of underparts and large wing patch white. Beak bright red, long, and laterally compressed. Eye and eye ring yellow.

Behavior. In pairs or family groups. Nonbreeding birds form large flocks. When inland, feeds on invertebrates pried from loose soil and muddy shores of ponds. On seacoasts, feeds on mollusks and other invertebrates at water's edge of rocky shores, reefs, and mudflats. At high tide, roosts along top of beaches. Runs along ground with beak pointing downward and tail raised. A far-carrying, high, wavering piping, noticeably higher pitched than American Oystercatcher. Also a quick succession of "peeps."

Breeds inland, up to 200 miles (350 km) from sea, on open grassy areas, usually—though not always—near water.

Status and Habitat. Shores of lakes and ponds and open, moist, grassy steppe near fresh water; more common in southern parts of range. Large nonbreeding flocks on seacoast. *50–100 birds on rocky reefs exposed at low tide, Punta Tombo, Chubut, December 1983 (W. Conway & G. Harris). A similar flock on a pebble shore at Monte León, Santa Cruz, December 1989 (W. Conway & G. Harris).*

Range. Breeding range restricted to open Patagonian steppe from Tierra del Fuego and southern Patagonia as far as northwestern Chubut. Falkland Islands (Islas Malvinas). Nonbreeding distribution extends along the coast to Península Valdés.

Similar Species. Differs from American Oystercatcher in black back, yellow eye ring, and more extensive white on wings.

82. BLACKISH OYSTERCATCHER / Ostrero Negro
Haematopus ater   *Plate 14*

Description. 18″ (45 cm). Larger than previous two species; bright red beak slightly shorter. Plumage entirely black, duller on back. Eye yellow, eye ring red.

Behavior. In pairs or family groups. Not shy, particularly when breeding. Stands still or walks quickly away with crouched head, then takes off with a loud call. Feeds on limpets (*Patella sp.*), prying mollusks from rocks with its knifelike beak; also mussels, barnacles, fish, crabs, and gastropods. Not as noisy as the previous two species. Call is a musical, wavering piping.

Makes a shallow unlined scrape in sand or pebbles, on the beach above high tide. Lays two heavily marked, greenish brown eggs, smaller in size but very similar in coloration to those of Kelp Gull. *Scrape containing two eggs, within large colony of Kelp Gulls, and 10 yards from nesting Chilean Skuas on a rocky point, Punta Tombo, Chubut, December 1979 (W. Conway & G. Harris).*

Status and Habitat. Common. Restricted to rocky shores of islands and points along shore. *Single pair on sandy beach among rocks, Punta Conos, Península Valdés, Chubut, March 1981.*

Range. Coastal South America from Tierra del Fuego to Península Valdés along the Atlantic (occasionally to Uruguay) and to Peru on the Pacific.

LAPWINGS AND PLOVERS / Teros y Chorlos
(Family Charadriidae)

Small to medium-sized birds, with rounded bodies and relatively short beaks and legs. The sexes are similar, and they are usually in flocks. In the breeding season, pairs nest alone; some breed in the Southern Hemisphere, others in the northern. Most make short or lengthy migrations. Of the 63 species, 7 are found on the coast of Patagonia.

83. SOUTHERN LAPWING / Tero Común
Vanellus chilensis   *Plate 14*

Description. 14″ (35 cm). Black crest, chest, and "cravat." Back gray-brown with coppery sheen. Eye red. Beak pink. Sharp wing spur. In flight, underwing black and white, tail white with black subterminal band.

Behavior. In pairs or loose flocks. Stands on bare or grassy, open ground. Noisy; circles in flight, calling insistently; strident, high "teedit-teedit."

Nests on ground in small concealed depression in grass. Lays 4 eggs.

Status and Habitat. Common; breeds in pastures, marshes, and irrigated fields along Chubut River and on moist, grass-covered lake beds in the steppe. Often close to farmhouses.

Range. From Tierra del Fuego, most of South America to Panama. *In August, a few pairs arrive and take residence on moist, grassy areas near farm buildings, Punta Delgada, Península Valdés, Chubut, breed, and then leave as summer progresses and lakes and ponds dry up (F. Quiñenao).*

84. GOLDEN PLOVER / Chorlo Dorado
Pluvialis dominica   *Plate 15*

Description. 11″ (28 cm). Brown upperparts, feathers edged lighter. Broad pale eyebrow. Underparts off-white. *Breeding plumage:* Upperparts black mottled yellow; white eyebrow continues down sides; Below black.

Behavior. Alone or in small flocks in open areas. Runs a few paces, then stops and stands very erect. Feeds on seeds. Migrates over 8000 miles (15,000 km) each year. Produces a fluted "peeeu."

Status and Habitat. Occasional nonbreeding visitor. *Single individual in open ground covered with short grasses near coast at Punta Tombo, Chubut, November 1978.*

Range. Breeds in North America and Siberia. From September to March, all of South America to Tierra del Fuego. Some birds winter over.

85. TWO-BANDED PLOVER / Chorlito de Doble Collar
Charadrius falklandicus   *Plate 15*

Description. 6″ (16 cm). Nape rufous; rest of upperparts brown. Underparts white with two distinctive black chestbands. *Nonbreeding and juvenile plumage:* Upperparts brown; underparts white with two chest bands insinuated.

Behavior. In pairs during the breeding season; large flocks in winter, often together with other shorebirds. Makes short runs along sand with head crouched, then stops and stands upright. Stands on one leg turning to face the wind like a windsock; also hops. Feeds at low tide, where mud is wet, on invertebrates. Usually silent. Call is a short "quit quit."

From October to November, nests alone, often well back from shore. Makes a small scrape and lays 3 olivaceous eggs, spotted with brown.

Status and Habitat. Common breeding resident. Flocks all year round; in hundreds April to August, when it often outnumbers all other shorebirds. Seaside beaches and mudflats. Shores of inland lakes and ponds.

Range. Throughout Patagonia; from March to September to northern Argentina.

86. SEMIPALMATED PLOVER / Chorlito Semipalmado
Charadrius semipalmatus   *Plate 15*

Description. 7″ (18 cm). Underparts white with a single pale chest band. Two of the 3 front toes partially webbed, "semipalmated." *Breeding plumage:* White collar and a single distinct black chest band.

Behavior. In small flocks on mudflats, often with other shorebirds. Not shy. Feeds on grass seeds, Nereid worms, flies, small crabs, and mollusks. Sharp "chec."

Status and Habitat. Uncommon nonbreeding visitor. Mudflats on seacoasts. Muddy shores of freshwater lakes and ponds.

Range. Breeds in North America. From September to March, all of South America as far as Patagonia.

87. TAWNY-THROATED DOTTEREL / Chorlo Cabezón
Oreopholus ruficollis   *Plate 14*

Description. 10″ (25 cm). Stands rather upright. Throat tawny. Back heavily streaked black and buff. Black patch on belly. Beak long, black. Chicks have large heads and look toylike.

Behavior. Alone or in small flocks. Not shy but keeps its distance. Stands on embankments. Flight fast. When threatened, chicks "freeze" close to ground and are hard to see. Two or 3 wavering melancholy whistles in flight, "Piuuu-uu."

Nest a shallow unlined scrape. Lays 3 brownish eggs spotted black. Chicks leave nest after hatching.

Status and Habitat. Common from September to March. Not associated with water. Dry, open terrain, grassland or scrubland, and roadsides.

Range. Breeds in Patagonia and western Argentina as far as Ecuador. From April to August, ranges to northern Argentina and Uruguay.

88. RUFOUS-CHESTED DOTTEREL / Chorlo de Pecho Castaño
Eudromias (Zonibyx) modestus   Plate 15

Description. 8″ (20 cm). Chest rufous, outlined black. Eyebrow white. Upperparts brown. Tail dark brown with outer feathers white. *Nonbreeding:* Chest brown, clearly separated from white belly. Eyebrow white.

Behavior. Not shy. In small flocks of 5–20 on beaches above high-tide mark, often some distance from water. Runs a few paces, then pecks at insects on the ground. Calls in flight. Short, melancholy "pirip, pirip, pirip."

Nests from October to January. Makes a shallow scrape on ground, lined with grass. Lays 2, speckled, pale-brown eggs.

Status and Habitat. Common breeding resident in the south, uncommon non-breeding winter visitor in northern Patagonia. *Two flocks of 6–8 birds on a short grass-covered shore of a freshwater pond near Punta León, Chubut, September 1989.* Shores of freshwater lakes, marshes. Seacoasts.

Range. Breeds in Tierra del Fuego and southern Patagonia. From March to September, migrates as far as central Argentina and Uruguay.

89. MAGELLANIC PLOVER / Chorlo de Magallanes
Pluvianellus socialis   *Plate 14*

Description. 7″ (18 cm). Looks like a dove. Gray head, chest, and upperparts. Belly white. Eye red. Legs pink. Wing bar and outer tail feathers white, visible in flight.

Behavior. Alone or in small groups. Walks quickly about, jerking its head rapidly back and forth in dovelike fashion. Flicks stones over with its beak. Wades into tidal pools and treads busily in circles to stir up small organisms upon which it feeds. Flies fast. A low whistle, usually answered by other members of the flock.

Nests from October to December. Makes a shallow scrape among the pebbles on the shores of freshwater lakes. Lays 2 brown, speckled eggs.

Status and Habitat. Scarce. One of the rarest shorebirds. *Five birds on a mudflat together with Red Knots and Hudsonian Godwits, Bahía Fracaso, Península Valdés, Chubut, April 1981. Ten birds with a large flock of Two-banded Plovers feeding on a sandy beach, Puerto Madryn, Chubut, July 1988.* Muddy and pebble shores of inland, freshwater lakes, and ponds on the southern Patagonian steppe.

Range. Breeds in Tierra del Fuego and southern Santa Cruz. *Laguna Los Escarchados, a snow-melt lake in western Santa Cruz (J. Jehl 1976).* From March to September ranges north along the coast as far as Río Negro; accidentally to Buenos Aires.

SANDPIPERS / Chorlos y Vuelvepiedras
(Family Scolopacidae)

Small to medium-sized shorebirds. Most are gregarious and can form flocks of several thousand birds, and many migrate large distances. Of the 82 species, 12 are found on the coast of Patagonia.

90. RUDDY TURNSTONE / Vuelvepiedras Común
Arenaria interpres   *Plate 14*

Description. 8″ (21 cm). Upperparts brown. Head and chest with brown-and-white pattern and markings. Legs bright orange. In flight, upper wing surface black with conspicuous white wing bars; white rump. *Breeding plumage:* Striking brown-and-white pattern on the head and chest. Upperparts rufous. Legs red.
Behavior. In small flocks. Stands on rocky outcrops near the breakers. Named such because of its habit of flicking stones over with its beak to capture small invertebrates. Low "cut-cut-cut."
Status and Habitat. Uncommon summer visitor. *A flock of 30 birds in nonbreeding plumage sitting on a rocky point outcrop by the sea, Punta Tombo, Chubut, December 1983 (W. Conway & G. Harris).*
Range. Breeds in Alaska and Canada. Migrates through South America as far as southern Patagonia between September and March.

91. HUDSONIAN GODWIT / Becasina de Mar
Limosa haemastica   *Plate 15*

Description. 13″ (33 cm). Large, with long neck and legs. Long, slightly upward curved beak. Upperparts gray brown with white rump. Eyebrow and underparts whitish. *Breeding plumage:* Underparts rufous, upperparts streaked blackish. Birds in both plumages can be seen here.
Behavior. In small flocks often together with Red Knots. Shy. Stands at water's edge. Wades in shallows to feed on mollusks, crustaceans, and other invertebrates. Occasionally swims. Usually silent. In flight, calls "twetweet."
Status and Habitat. Common though not very numerous. Muddy shores of lakes, ponds and seacoasts. *Six birds on shores of a sewage pond on outskirts of Trelew, Chubut, November 1989. 84 birds on mudflats, Bahía Fracaso, Península Valdés, Chubut, April 1981.*
Range. Breeds in Alaska and Canada. From September to March, migrates as far as Tierra del Fuego. Some birds winter over.

92. LESSER YELLOWLEGS / Chorlo Menor de Patas Amarillas
Tringa flavipes   *Plate 15*

Description. 9″ (23 cm). Slender, straight black bill. Long yellow legs. Gray-brown upperparts, spotted and streaked white. Underparts white. Chest spotted, dusky.
Behavior. Alone or in flocks, sometimes with South American Stilt. Not shy. In flight, calls "blee-blee."

Status and Habitat. Common along muddy shores of freshwater lakes, ponds, and rivers. *Several lone individuals on the shores of a sewage pond, near Trelew, Chubut, April 1989.*

Range. Breeds in Alaska and Canada. Migrates as far as Tierra del Fuego from September to March.

Similar Species. Similar to the following species but noticeably smaller and has a straight beak.

93. GREATER YELLOWLEGS / Chorlo Mayor de Patas Amarillas
Tringa melanoleuca   *Plate 15*

Description. 11″ (29 cm). Long, slightly upward-curved bill. Long yellow legs. Neck longish. Upperparts brown, streaked and spotted dark brown and white. Pale eyebrow, underparts white; chest streaked dusky.

Behavior. Alone, occasionally in flocks, sometimes together with Lesser Yellowlegs and other shorebirds. Dips head when alarmed. Flies up, calling loud "pleep-pleeep-pleeeep." Feeds on crustaceans and aquatic insects.

Status and Habitat. Common, though less so than the previous species. Always seen near fresh water. Muddy shores of lakes, ponds, and rivers.

Range. Breeds in Alaska and Canada. Migrates as far as Tierra del Fuego from September to March.

Similar Species. Hard to tell apart from Lesser Yellowlegs but noticeably larger and has a longer, slightly upward-bent beak.

94. PECTORAL SANDPIPER / Playerito Pectoral
Calidris melanotos   *Plate 16*

Description. 8″ (20 cm). Relatively large with longish neck. Upperparts spotted dark brown. Breast brown, in sharp contrast to white lower underparts. Legs greenish yellow. In flight, no wing bars; center of rump brown.

Behavior. Usually alone or in loose flocks, sometimes together with other shorebirds. Stands erect in short grass and on open muddy shores. Feeds on insects and aquatic invertebrates. Fast, zigzagging flight. A series of rough "preep" calls.

Status and Habitat. Uncommon visitor between September and April. *A single bird on a mudflat, Riacho San José, Chubut, November 1979.* Mostly wet, short grass near freshwater ponds and lakes, and in flooded fields. Rarely seacoasts.

Range. Breeds in Alaska, Canada, and Siberia. Migrates as far as Tierra del Fuego from September to March.

95. RED KNOT / Chorlo Rojizo
Calidris canutus   *Plate 16*

Description. 9″ (23 cm). Stocky. Neck shortish. Straight black bill. Upperparts gray brown. Pale eyebrow. Underparts white, faintly mottled brown. In flight, faint white wing bar and pale rump. *Breeding plumage:* Eyebrow, sides of head, and underparts brick red. Upperparts mottled buff and dusky.

Behavior. In single flocks from one or two dozen birds to over 3000, sometimes together with other shorebirds, often Hudsonian Godwits. Walks nervously this way and that, rapidly prodding for mollusks and other small invertebrates. Migrating flocks very active, frequently taking off and flying very rapidly in a tight group, turning together this way and that, then resettling. When a flock passes overhead, the rush of beating wings causes a sudden, noisy gust. At high tide, flocks roost along top of beach and wait for sea to recede. *One large flock roosting at night in shallow water, in the center of an inland salt lake, 3 or 4 miles from sea, El Salitral, Península Valdés, Chubut, April 1981.* Soft whistle.

Status and Habitat. Common migrant mid-September to late April. Total population thought to be low, spread over a few large flocks. *2500 birds on an open mudflat, Playa Fracaso, Península Valdés, Chubut, April 1981. 900 birds on an open sandy beach, Playa Flechero, Península Valdés, Chubut, March 1992.* Mudflats on seacoasts.

Range. Breeds in North American tundra. Migrates as far as Tierra del Fuego. *Journeys nearly 20,000 miles every year.* Small flocks winter over.

Similar Species. Sanderlings are smaller and paler. Unlike Sanderlings, several birds in flock are usually in partial breeding plumage, showing a certain amount of rufous.

96. SANDERLING / Chorlito Blanco
Calidris alba   *Plate 16*

Description. 7″ (17 cm). Small shorebird, the palest of all those found locally. Eye and beak very dark. Upperparts pale gray. Underparts, outer tail feathers, and wing bar white. *Breeding plumage: (not recorded in Patagonia):* Head, chest, and back become mottled and streaked rufous.

Behavior. In flocks, often with other shorebirds. At edge of water, chases after retreating waves and feeds on tiny crustaceans and mollusks. Diet also includes isopods and tenebrionid beetles. Sometimes wades in shallows. Flock takes off in unison and flies in a tight group; turning this way and that, the group shows a flash of white underparts one moment and then darker backs the next. Roosts on rocks just above the water. Distinct "tric" call.

Status and Habitat. Common nonbreeding migrant. Flocks between 50 and several hundred, on rocky shores and beaches. Favors rocky points and islands. *A single flock of 80–100 birds on intertidal rocks, Punta Tombo, Chubut, November 1979. A flock of 150–200 birds on a ledge by the sea. Punta Conos, Golfo San José, Chubut, December 1988.* Also found on pebble or sandy beaches and mudflats on seacoasts. Occasionally on the shores of inland lakes.

Range. Breeds in North American tundra. From September to April migrates as far as Tierra del Fuego. Some birds winter over in nonbreeding plumage. *20–30 birds on an open sandy beach together with Magellanic Plovers and a large flock of Two-banded Plovers, Puerto Madryn, Chubut, July 1989.*

97. WHITE-RUMPED SANDPIPER / Chorlito de Rabadilla Blanca
Calidris fuscicollis   *Plate 16*

Description. 7″ (19 cm). Upperparts gray brown, mottled darker. Underparts whitish, breast streaked brown. *In flight:* White rump.

Behavior. From a few individuals to large flocks, often together with other shorebirds. Not shy. Very active; walks rapidly about, pecking at the wet shore. High pitched, thin "jeet."

Status and Habitat. Fairly common nonbreeding migrant on mudflats and rocky seashores, muddy shores of lakes and ponds on the steppe, and along river banks. *One small flock of 12 on intertidal rocks, Punta Tombo, Chubut, December 1976.*

Range. Breeds in Arctic. Found east of the Andes as far as Tierra del Fuego from end of August to April.

Similar Species. Hard to differentiate from Baird's Sandpiper except for white rump, noticeable in flight.

98. SEMIPALMATED SANDPIPER / Chorlito Enano
Calidris pusilla   *Plate 16*

Description. 5″ (12 cm). Very small. Upperparts and sides of chest gray-brown. Eyebrow, cheek and underparts white. Short beak and legs black. Front toes partially webbed.

Behavior. Active and tame. Often in mixed flocks with other small sandpipers. Sharp "chek" call.

Status and Habitat. Occasional nonbreeding visitor. Seashores and lakesides. *One bird at Punta Tombo, Chubut, November 1976.*

Range. Breeds in North American tundra. Migrant as far as northern Patagonia from September to March.

99. BAIRD'S SANDPIPER / Chorlito Unicolor
Calidris bairdii   *Plate 16*

Description. 7.4″ (19 cm). Upperparts brown, feathers edged white, giving a scaly look. Underparts pale-gray buff, breast lightly mottled brown. In flight, center of rump brown.

Behavior. Alone or in small flocks. When not feeding stands still on shore and allows close approach. Often with other shorebirds. Flock flies up together. Emits a sudden "kreep" as it flies off.

Status and Habitat. Common nonbreeding visitor on sandy or pebble beaches, mudflats and rocky shores on coast; also muddy shores of inland lakes and lagoons.

Range. Breeds in Alaska, northern Canada, Greenland and Siberia. Nonbreeding migrant as far as Tierra del Fuego from September to March. Some individuals winter over.

Similar Species. Hard to tell apart from White-rumped Sandpiper except for dark rump visible in flight.

100. WHIMBREL / Chorlo Trinador
Numenius phaeopus   *Plate 15*

Description. 17″ (43 cm). Very long, downward-curved bill. Upperparts gray-brown spotted and streaked pale cream. Whitish underparts streaked gray on neck and upper chest. Long pale eyebrow.

Behavior. Alone or in small flocks. Walks and runs along shore. Feeds on small mollusks, crustaceans, insects, spiders, and other small invertebrates. Flies in compact groups. A rapid string of loud, musical, brief whistles.

Status and Habitat. Uncommon, nonbreeding visitor between September and March, in flooded fields, inland river banks, and lakeshores; mudflats and beaches. *A flock of 20–30 birds on a mudflat on shores of Ría Santa Cruz, near Punta Quilla, Santa Cruz, December 1992 (W. Conway & G. Harris).*

Range. Breeds in Alaska and northern Canada. Migrant to southern Patagonia.

101. COMMON SNIPE / Becasina Común
Gallinago (Capella) gallinago paraguaiae   *Plate 16*

Description. 10″ (26 cm). Very long, straight bill. Stocky with short neck and legs. Eyes placed very high on head. Cryptic coloration. Eye stripe and cheeks buff white. Back brown with white or buff streaks. Chest buff, spotted with black; belly white, barred with brown on flanks. Legs yellowish.

Behavior. Usually alone. Sits still in the grass; hard to see. Prods the moist ground or shallow water for invertebrates. *Almost invariably a drop of water at the tip of its beak (Rumboll).* Active by day or night. Flight rapid and zigzagging. During breeding season, spectacular aerial display with steep dives accompanied by loud buzzing sound, produced by wind rushing through wing feathers. A series of brief notes "yec-yec-yec" in flight.

Nests among grasses usually in a moist field or marsh. Lays 2 or 3 streaked brown eggs.

Status and Habitat. Uncommon breeding resident in wet fields, grassy riversides, marshes, swamps, inundated fields, and moist grassland.

Range. Several subspecies in many parts of world. Throughout South America as far as Tierra del Fuego.

PHALAROPES / Falaropos o Chorlos Nadadores
(Family Phalaropodidae)

Small, sandpiper-like birds with slender, pointed beaks. Their feet are lobed and they swim buoyantly. Gregarious. Of the 3 species, one is found on the coast of Patagonia.

102. WILSON'S PHALAROPE / Falaropo Tricolor
Phalaropus tricolor   *Plate 16*

Description. 9″ (23 cm). Slender bodied with longish neck. Bill straight and slender. Upperparts pale gray, underparts white. *Breeding plumage:* Black stripe through eye and down neck, edged chestnut.

Behavior. In flocks. Swims in the open or wades in the shallows. Sits on water, rapidly turning this way and that, pecking food from the water with a quick stab of the beak. Feeds on crustaceans, aquatic insects, and vegetable matter. Soft squeaky murmur when feeding; the sound emanating from the flock is reminiscent of that produced by a crowd of people talking in the distance.

Status and Habitat. Infrequent, local, nonbreeding visitor on freshwater ponds and lakes *200 or 300 on a sewage pond, feeding near Chilean Flamingos, Common Stilts, and Bahama Pintails, Trelew, Chubut, November 1989.*

Range. Breeds in North America above Arctic Circle. From September to March, migrant as far as Tierra del Fuego.

STILTS / Teros Reales
(Family Recurvirostridae)

Very long-legged waterbirds with long necks and long, slender beaks. Of the 8 species, one is found on the coast of Patagonia.

103. SOUTH AMERICAN STILT / Tero Real
Himantopus melanurus   *Plate 14*

Description. 13″ (34 cm). Crown, hindneck, and back black (brown in female). Forecrown and underparts pure white. Long, straight, and slender beak black. Legs orange.

Behavior. Alone or in small flocks, often together with Greater and Lesser Yellowlegs. Wades in shallows and probes with its long beak. In flight, legs extend well beyond tail. Feeds on aquatic insects and crustaceans. Noisy, insistent "yip, yip," like the barking of a small dog.

Solitary nesting; a small depression on damp ground. Lays 3 or 4 spotted eggs.

Status and Habitat. Common breeding resident. Muddy shores and shallow water of freshwater lakes, ponds, and inundated fields. *Large loose flock on edges of a sewage pond, Trelew, Chubut, November 1989.*

Range. From northern Patagonia to Bolivia and southern Brazil.

SEEDSNIPES / Agachonas
(Family Thinocoridae)

Small, snipe-sized birds with short conical beaks. Females in particular are cryptic. Often in small flocks sitting silent and motionless on the ground, becoming hard to see. They sometimes allow close approach. With quiet gurgling calls the whole flock bursts into flight, which is rapid and shorebird-like. Seedsnipes feed mainly on seeds and leaves of grasses and do so often on roadsides. They are found on the dry steppe or open Andean terrain. This family is restricted to South America; of the 4 species, 2 are found on the coast of continental Patagonia. Both are partially migratory ranging into the pampas in the winter months.

104. LEAST SEEDSNIPE / Agachona de Corbata
Thinocorus rumicivorus   *Plate 16*

Description. 7″ (18 cm). Rounded with short conical beak. Chin white; head and neck gray with noticeable black "cravat." Belly white. Back very speckled brown. Short yellow legs. *Female:* Cryptic coloration. Head, neck, breast, and back very speckled brown and white; belly white.

Behavior. In family groups in breeding season; small flocks of 5–20 birds on migration. When not feeding, sits or stands still and allows close approach. Male usually easier to spot than female. Fast, zigzagging, snipelike flight. Feeds on seeds and grasses. *One parent using broken-wing display to distract attention from chicks, Península Valdés, Chubut, November 1981.* Quiet, piping calls in flight.

Nests in small groups on shores and roadsides. Lays 2–4 eggs in a small scrape on ground. *Family with 3 or more chicks among dry grasses by roadside, Camarones, Chubut, November 1989.*

Status and Habitat. Common breeding resident, particularly in southern parts of Patagonia. Roadsides, lakeshores, and dried ponds with short vegetation. *Several isolated pairs in open country with sparse grasses near Monte Loayza, Santa Cruz, December 1989 (W. Conway & G. Harris).*

Range. Tierra del Fuego to northern Patagonia. From April to September ranges to central Argentina.

105. GRAY-BREASTED SEEDSNIPE / Agachona de Collar
Thinocorus orbignyianus   Plate 16

Description. 8″ (20 cm). White chin edged black, gray breast edged black, rest of underparts white; upperparts very speckled brown. Short yellow legs. *Female:* Upperparts and breast very speckled brown; rest of underparts white.

Behavior. In flocks in open short-grass terrain. Not shy. Stands erect when alert. If threatened, sits still becoming hard to see, even when very close. Feeds on seeds and grasses. Repeated low, monotonous, whistling call, "Puco-puco-puco," by day and night.

Nests on ground in the grass, often close to water. Lays 3 or 4 reddish, speckled eggs.

Status and Habitat. Common breeding resident on grassy areas and roadsides on southern grassy steppes of Santa Cruz and Tierra del Fuego. Also dry, open Andean grassland.

Range. Southern Patagonia and Andes as far as Peru.

Similar Species. Larger than Least Seedsnipe; females very similar, male breast markings distinctive.

SHEATHBILLS / Palomas Antárticas
(Family Chionididae)

All white, rounded, pigeonlike birds, found only along the seacoast. The beak is conical, sheathed in a horny covering at the base. It lacks webbing between the toes. Although it rarely does so, it is able to swim. It is regarded by some to be closely related to the Seedsnipe, and by others to oystercatchers. Two species are restricted to the Southern Hemisphere, one of them found on the coast of Patagonia.

106. SNOWY SHEATHBILL / Paloma Antártica
Chionis alba   Plate 17

Description. 14″ (35 cm). Entirely white. Somewhat pigeonlike, but not related in any way. Conical beak, yellowish, sheathed at base. Facial skin pink. Legs gray. Wings rounded.

Behavior. In loose flocks. Not shy. Walks around bird colonies—particularly cormorants—scavenging eggs, and between breeding and resting pinnipeds searches for scraps in feces or afterbirth of the mammals. Also feeds on mollusks, crustaceans, and fish. Usually silent.

Status and Habitat. Fairly common all year round, almost always associated with colonies of sea lions, elephant seals, and cormorants. Large flocks between April and September. *Over 100 birds in and around a sea lion colony at Punta León, Chubut, July 1988.* Scarce outside colonies along seacoast.

Range. Breeds in Antarctica and islands in the sub-Antarctic. Ranges north along eastern South America to Uruguay.

SKUAS AND JAEGERS / Salteadores y Skúas
(Family Laridae—Subfamily Stercorariinae)

Large, dark, gull-like, pugnacious oceanic birds. The marine version of the bird of prey, they attack smaller or weaker birds or force them to disgorge and release food. Of the 5 species, 2 are found on the coast of Patagonia.

107. ANTARCTIC SKUA / Skúa Antártico
Stercorarius (Catharacta) skua antarctica   *Plate 17*

Description. 21″ (55 cm). All brown, slightly paler below. In flight, noticeable whitish "windows" at base of primaries. *Chilean Skua (S. s. chilensis):* rich cinnamon underparts, with a noticeable cap.

Behavior. Alone, in pairs, or in small loose flocks. Strong swift flight. Pursues terns and gulls till they disgorge or drop food (fish, eggs, etc.), usually catching the stolen goods before it reaches the ground. Commonly displays on the ground, raising its wings high and vocalizing. Attacks people approaching the nest, swooping rapidly and even striking with its feet. Vocal. Harsh, angry call.

Nests fairly high up the beach, often within or near Kelp Gull colonies and close to penguin and cormorant colonies. Usually lays 2 eggs.

Status and Habitat. Common year-round although numbers low along coast. *Antarctic Skuas (S. s. antarctica) near Magellanic Penguin colony at Punta Tombo, Chubut. Several dozen Chilean Skuas (S. s. chilensis), mixed with a large flock of Kelp Gulls feeding on fish scraps in a rubbish dump, Puerto Deseado, Santa Cruz, January 1990.* Seacoasts and ocean, usually close to land.

Range. Antarctic Skua (*S. s. antarctica*) breeds on coast of Patagonia as far as Chubut. *Three pairs with nests at Punta Tombo, Chubut, December 1991.* Chilean Skua (*S. s. chilensis*) breeds on coast of Tierra del Fuego, Santa Cruz, and southern Chile.

108. PARASITIC JAEGER / Salteador Chico
Stercorarius parasiticus   *Plate 17*

Description. 15″ (38 cm). Falconlike pointed wings. *Light phase:* Black cap contrasts with pale throat; often with dark band across upper breast. Belly white. In flight, pale "windows" in wings. Two central tail feathers, slightly longer, not always noticeable. *Dark phase:* Underparts entirely dark. *Juvenile:* Lacks long central tail feathers. Underparts barred.

Behavior. In small loose bands. Agile fast flight. Chases and harries terns in flight until latter disgorge their food, which is caught before reaching the water. Very shy. Lands on water.

Status and Habitat. Common in open ocean and coastal waters; does not fly over shore.

Range. Breeds in high latitudes in Northern Hemisphere. Migrant on these shores from September to April. *Five to 10 birds spread over a wide area, chasing terns in calm weather, in Golfo San José, Chubut, February 1985.*

GULLS AND TERNS / Gaviotas y Gaviotines
(Family Laridae—Subfamilies Larinae and Sterninae)

Large, well-known family of birds, with many species found worldwide. Although mostly oceanic, some gulls and terns occur only associated with fresh water. Of the 48 species worldwide, 11 are found in Patagonia.

109. DOLPHIN GULL / Gaviota Austral
Larus (Leucophaeus) scoresbii   *Plate 17*

Description. 15″ (38 cm). Pale blue-gray with black back. Beak, eye ring, and feet bright red. Eye pale yellow. *In flight:* Upper wing and back black, edged white. *Nonbreeding adult:* Similar, with dark hood. *Juvenile:* Grayish brown with dark hood and blackish subterminal tail band.

Behavior. In small loose flocks. Common marauder around cormorant colonies and in sea lion and elephant seal rookeries. Always on the alert for opportunity to steal cormorant eggs from unguarded nests; also feeds on organic refuse of pinnipeds. High-pitched, piercing "keeck."

Breeds in small, tight colonies unlike those of the more abundant Kelp Gull; on rocky surfaces some way back from shore. Nests are shallow bowls lined with seaweed and grass, placed about 1 ft (30 cm) apart. Lays 2 brown, speckled eggs.

Status and Habitat. Common, but very restricted, year-round, breeding resident. *Total population in Patagonia estimated at 700 pairs in 26 colonies (P. Yorio et al., 1997).* Beaches, rocky islands, and points on seacoasts, in or near Kelp Gull, penguin, and cormorant colonies, and sea lion rookeries.

Range. Southern coast of South America from Península Valdés to Tierra del Fuego and up Pacific coast as far as Chiloe. Small breeding colonies with 20–30 nests at Punta Tombo, Chubut; Isla Puente, Chubut; Isla Chata, Santa Cruz. *25 birds in winter plumage (5 of them banded at Punta Tombo, 60 miles south) in a sea lion colony, Punta León, Chubut, July 1988.*

110. KELP GULL / Gaviota Cocinera
Larus dominicanus   *Plate 17*

Description. 21″ (55 cm). Large. Body white with back and upper wings black; flight feathers edged white. Beak yellow with lower mandible tipped red. Eye ring red. Legs yellowish green. *Juvenile:* Head and back mottled, gray brown; underparts paler. Dark, ill-defined, subterminal tail band maintained until first adult molt at fourth or fifth year. Beak and legs blackish.

Behavior. In flocks, at times up to several thousands, often together with Neotropic Cormorants, terns, and American Oystercatchers. At night returns to roosts, which are same year after year. Shy. Surprising variety of feeding techniques. Lands on water to feed on schools of fish herded to surface by feeding Dusky Dolphins or Imperial Cormorants. Steals eggs and chicks from penguins, cormorants, and terns. Between June and December, lands on backs of Southern Right Whales around Península Valdés, Chubut, to tear off pieces of skin. Also feeds on invertebrates on shore. Carries mussels aloft on updrafts and drops them on beach to crack them open. Shells and hard parts of prey are regurgitated and can be seen on beach in roosting areas. Along with Black-browed Albatross, the most common seabird feeding on by-catch discarded at sea by coastal fishing vessels. Forages in refuse dumps. Emits a rapid "ke-ke-ke-ke-ke." Also "kelp."

Arrival and pairing begins in September to October. Large, dispersed colonies; each nest separated a yard (1 m) or more from the next, usually close to breeding colonies of penguins or cormorants. On open ground or between dispersed bushes. Usually lays two, variably mottled brown, gray or greenish eggs, in a rough scrape on ground. Incubation lasts about 27 days. When chicks hatch they stand around, seeking shade from hot summer sun under rocks or bushes. Breeding in colony is staggered, so that in middle of season (December) some chicks are well grown while others are still incubating. Fledging occurs at 5 or 6 weeks.

Status and Habitat. Very common and conspicuous, year-round breeding resident. Although probably always abundant, refuse dumps now provide a reliable, year-round source of food. *Population in Patagonia estimated at 73,000 pairs in 92 colonies (P. Yorio et al., 1997).* Some colonies show a marked increase in population, which may be negatively affecting other colonial birds. Varied coastal habitats; seldom seen out of sight of land, very common near ports and piers; and on intertidal flats. Also found around lakes, towns, and garbage dumps many miles inland.

Range. Widely distributed along continental and island shores throughout southern oceans. Large colonies include those at Isla de los Pájaros, Punta Tombo, and Punta León in Chubut.

Similar Species. Although larger, birds in final, subadult plumage can be confused with Band-tailed Gull, but black band across end of tail not so well defined and bill tip of latter is distinctive.

111. FRANKLIN'S GULL / Gaviota Pipixcan

Larus pipixcan   *Plate 17*

Description. 13″ (33 cm). Gray-brown half-hood. Back gray. Mantle gray, primaries black with broad white trailing edge and "windows." Beak black. Legs dark gray. *Breeding plumage:* Blackish hood. Beak red. Legs dark reddish gray.

Behavior. In small flocks, sometimes together with other gulls and terns. Rapid "kuk-kuk-kuk."

Status and Habitat. Uncommon nonbreeding visitor. *One sight record on muddy beach in Puerto Madryn, Chubut, January 1985 (C. Kovax).* Mainly shores of freshwater lakes and rivers. Seacoasts.

Range. Breeds in interior of USA and Canada. Migrant from September to April along the Pacific to Tierra del Fuego, and scatteringly east of the Andes.

Similar Species. Smaller and back darker than wintering Brown-hooded Gull; head never as extensively white.

112. OLROG'S OR BAND-TAILED GULL / Gaviota de Olrog, Cola Negra o Simeón

Larus (belcheri) atlanticus   *Plate 17*

Description. 19″ (48 cm). White with black back and distinct, black subterminal band on tail. Upper wing surface black with trailing edge of secondaries white. Beak yellow, tipped black and red. Legs yellow. *Nonbreeding adult:* Similar to breeding plumage, with gray hood.

Behavior. In flocks. Not shy. Diet in some areas composed almost exclusively of crabs; also can include fish, mollusks, and offal. A rapid, repeated, nasal "ke ke keh."

Breeds in compact colonies on islands, often near colonies of other gulls and terns. Nests placed close to one another, unlike those of Kelp Gull. Nests lined with abundant vegetation. Lays 2 or 3 brown, heavily marked eggs. *Colony containing nests with eggs in incubation on sandy beach of an island in Caleta Malaspina, Chubut, late November 1990; and small chicks in mid-January 1991 (P. Yorio & G. Harris).*

Status and Habitat. Local and scarce; mainly restricted to coastal areas with large, intertidal mudflats. *Around 70 pairs nesting in Caleta Malaspina, Chubut, late November 1990. Total population estimated at 2300 pairs in 10 colonies in northern Patagonia (Yorio et al., 1997).*

Range. From southern Brazil to southern Chubut. *Breeding colonies recorded at Isla Puestos, Isla Gama, Isla Arroyo Jabalí, Bahía San Blas, Buenos Aires, November (P. Yorio & G. Harris); Isla Vernaci (Caleta Malaspina, Chubut, January 1991 (P. Yorio & G. Harris); 400 nests at Isla Trinidad and 800 nests at Islote Norte de Isla Morro de Indio, Buenos Aires (P. Yorio et al., 1997).*

Similar Species. Smaller than adult Kelp Gull with distinct band on tail. Subterminal band is diffuse in Kelp Gull in final stage of subadult plumage.

113. BROWN-HOODED GULL / Gaviota Capucha Café

Larus maculipennis   *Plate 17*

Description. 14″ (35 cm). Dark brown—almost black-looking—hood. Upperparts pale gray. Underparts often suffused with pink. Beak and legs red. *Nonbreeding:* Head white with small, dark patch behind eye. Beak red (sometimes grayish). Legs red or grayish red. *Juvenile:* White head with dark patch behind eye. Upper wing surface blackish with distinct white wing bars. Tail with black subterminal band. Beak gray.

Behavior. In flocks. Follows plows, feeding on insects in the disturbed earth. Diet includes mollusks and crustaceans on the seacoast; also steals eggs from other seabirds and visits garbage dumps for scraps. Like the Kelp Gull, it also lands on backs of Southern Right Whales to tear off pieces of skin. Calls, standing with wings slightly open, first bowing its head low, then stretching its neck up. There is usually much squabbling over nest sites in colonies. Rapid "kek-kek-kek" call. Also a scolding "chiar" and a repeated "kip-chiar."

Breeding begins in October on freshwater lakes with abundant vegetation. Breeds in loose colonies varying from a few dozen birds to several hundred. Builds a bulky nest of twigs, on ground or on stumps of grass and low-lying vegetation. Nests placed some distance from one another depending on availability of suitable sites. Mating takes place on nest. Lays 3 or 4 speckled olive brown eggs. Chicks born in November and leave nest in February. *1000–1500 birds and several hundred nests on small islands and bushes surrounded by water in a sewage pond, Trelew, Chubut, November 1989; many nests contained eggs and one had 2 chicks; colony grew to 2300 nests in 1995 (M. Lizurume).*

Status and Habitat. Common, year-round resident. Open fields, freshwater lakes, and rivers. Common on seacoast. Garbage dumps and outskirts of towns.

Range. From Tierra del Fuego to northern Brazil along the Atlantic, and northern Chile on the Pacific.

114. SOUTH-AMERICAN TERN / Gaviotín Sudamericano
Sterna hirundinacea   *Plate 18*

Description. 15″ (38 cm). Long forked tail. Solid black cap. Long, pointed red beak. Dorsally uniform gray; white underparts. Short red legs. *Nonbreeding adult:* Forehead white. Hindcrown flecked black. Beak dull red to black. *Juvenile:* Similar to nonbreeding plumage, with speckled wing coverts. Tail shorter.

Behavior. In flocks, sometimes large. Roosts on beaches and rocky ledges together with other terns, gulls, and shorebirds (Sanderlings and sandpipers). The group often flies up together in a disorderly cloud. Flight is jerky, looking down at water; up and down the coast, within sight of shore. On spotting a fish, it goes into a dive and plunges into water, emerging almost immediately. Feeds on whitebait (cornalitos). Harsh, high-pitched "kip-kip-kip, teear" call in flight.

Nesting begins in November, sometimes together with other terns. Forms large, fairly dense colonies, on tops of beaches or rocky ledges a short way up from water's edge. *500 birds together with a dozen Cayenne Terns on a pebble beach; nests with eggs, Punta Norte, Península Valdés, November 1979 (W. Conway & G. Harris). 250 birds nesting on an elevated sedimentary ledge, eggs beginning to pip, at Punta Conos, Península Valdés, Chubut, December 1990 (W. Conway & G. Harris).* Breeding records also for Caleta Valdés, Punta Pirámide, Punta Loma, and Punta Tombo in Chubut; Monte Loayza in Santa Cruz. Lays 2 brown-speckled eggs in a bowl-shaped scrape. Breeding sites usually vary from one year to the next. Chicks leave the nest after hatching and crèche together on the beach.

Status and Habitat. Common year-round breeding resident. The most abundant tern on these coasts. Vulnerable to disturbance when breeding. *A colony of several hundred birds at Punta Conos, Chubut, was abandoned in the hatching period apparently as a result of disturbance caused by people and dogs in December 1986.* Seacoasts. Forages close to shore.

Range. From Tierra del Fuego up the coast as far as southern Brazil and along the Pacific to Peru.

Similar Species. The Arctic Tern has shorter beak and legs; the Antarctic Tern has gray underparts; the Common Tern has gray "shoulders."

115. COMMON TERN / Gaviotín Golondrina
Sterna hirundo   Plate 18

Description. 12″ (30 cm). Tail forked. Forecrown white, hindcrown flecked black. Mantle gray with dark gray "shoulders." Beak black. Legs red. Edge of outer primaries black. Legs reddish black. Bill black and eyes black. *Breeding plumage:* Totally black cap. Beak red, tipped black.

Behavior. Alone or in flocks, often together with other terns. Flies over open water looking down; dives to catch fish. Harsh, high-pitched "kip-kip-kip, teeear" in flight.

Status and Habitat. Uncommon. *One bird on a pebble beach at Punta Norte, Chubut, February 1980.* Seacoasts and lakes.

Range. Migrant September to April. Breeds extensively in Northern Hemisphere. Found almost worldwide.

Similar Species. Hard to distinguish from similar terns; dark "shoulders" are distinctive.

116. ARCTIC TERN / Gaviotín Ártico
Sterna paradisea   Plate 18

Description. 13″ (33 cm). Underparts pale gray. Forecrown white, hindcrown flecked black. Beak short. Legs noticeably shorter than similar species, red to dull blackish red. *Breeding plumage:* Entirely black cap. Beak and legs bright red.

Behavior. Alone or in flocks, together with other terns and gulls. Feeds on fish, captured by diving directly from flight. Makes the longest-known migration of any bird: an almost 22,000 mile round trip each year, from Arctic to Antarctic. Harsh, high-pitched "kip-kip-kip, teear."

Status and Habitat. Hypothetical (no records). Seacoasts and oceanic islands.

Range. Breeds in high-latitude Northern Hemisphere. Migrates September to April as far as Antarctica along eastern Atlantic; some birds probably migrate along South American shores.

Similar Species. Noticeably shorter legs and beak than South American, Antarctic, and Common Terns.

117. ANTARCTIC TERN / Gaviotín Antártico
Sterna vittata   Plate 18

Description. 13″ (34 cm). Underparts pearl gray. Forecrown white. Hindcrown flecked black. Beak and short legs red to dull blackish red. *Breeding plumage:* Solid black cap. Beak and legs bright red.

Behavior. In flocks, usually together with other terns and gulls. Similar to South American Tern. In Antarctic, feeds on fish and krill by diving and scooping from surface.

Status and Habitat. Uncommon. On beaches, rocky ledges, and coastal mudflats together with other terns. Seacoast.

Range. Breeds on islands in Antarctic. Visits between March and September. Ranges north to Brazil, South Africa, and New Zealand.

Similar Species. Hard to differentiate from previous 3 species. Gray underparts are distinctive.

118. CAYENNE TERN / Gaviotín de Pico Amarillo
Sterna eurygnatha   *Plate 18*

Description. 16″ (41 cm). Relatively large, solid build. Cap and hindcrest black. Long, slender beak yellow. Upperparts pearl gray, underparts white. Forked tail. *Nonbreeding adult:* Hindcrest black, forecrown white.

Behavior. Roosts in flocks, often together with Royal and South American Terns and Brown-hooded Gulls. Flies jerkily back and forth along coast and dives from some height into water to catch fish. Displays by holding itself very upright, erecting its crest, partially opening its wings and raising its tail. Loud harsh "kirr-ick" call.

In large dense colonies, usually together with Royal or South American Terns. Makes small, bowl-shaped nest on bare ground or pebble beach close to sea. Chicks born in November and abandon nest a month later before fledging, gathering on shore in crèches.

Status and Habitat. Fairly common breeding resident. Breeding colonies scarce. *Records include Punta León and islands in Bahía Melo, Chubut.* Mudflats, pebble and sandy beaches, and rocky ledges on seacoasts.

Range. Ranges from Patagonia along the Atlantic to Venezuela.

Similar Species. In the field, very hard to tell apart from Sandwich Tern (*Sterna sandvicensis*). The latter, of doubtful existence on coast of Patagonia, differs only in having black-tipped beak. Both species known to interbreed in parts where ranges overlap.

119. ROYAL TERN / Gaviotín Real
Sterna maxima   *Plate 18*

Description. 18″ (46 cm). Large, relatively stocky tern. Tail forked. Beak heavy, orange red. Black cap and crest. Back silver gray. Underparts white. Legs black. *Nonbreeding adult:* Hindcrown and crest black, forecrown white. Beak duller.

Behavior. Roosts in flocks, together with other terns and gulls. Flies jerkily and fairly high back and forth along shore, and plunges straight into water for fish. Loud harsh "keerree" call.

Forms large dense colonies, often together with other terns, at top of beach or back among the bushes. Nest a small cup in the soil.

Status and Habitat. Spring and summer resident along coastline of Península Valdés. Very few breeding colonies. *A few pairs nesting with South American and*

Cayenne Terns on an island in Cañadon del Puerto, Ría Deseado, Santa Cruz, January 1997 (M. Oliva Day). Regular breeding colony nesting alongside Cayenne Terns at Punta León, Chubut. Coastal pebble and sandy beaches; rocky ledges.

Range. Northern Patagonia to southern North America on the Atlantic; and Peru to Mexico on the Pacific.

SKIMMERS / Rayadores
(Family Laridae—Subfamily Rynchopinae)

Conspicuous, long-winged birds with highly specialized beaks for "skimming" the water in flight, in search of fish on which to feed. Gregarious. Of the 3 species, one is found in Patagonia.

120. BLACK SKIMMER / Rayador
Rynchops nigra

Description. 19″ (49 cm). Large with long wings. Beak long, red with black tip. Lower mandible, compressed laterally, extends well beyond upper mandible. Upperparts black. Underparts white. Short, red legs.

Behavior. In flocks. Flies back and forth over still water with its beak open and lower mandible slicing the surface. Feeds on fish. Barking call and cooing notes.

Status and Habitat. Accidental nonbreeding visitor. Recorded along coast at latitude 45°S, and in Strait of Magellan. *One lone adult on sandy beach in Puerto Madryn, February 1997 (F.P.N.).* Freshwater lakes and ponds; seacoasts.

Range. Breeds from southern USA; Central and South America as far as central Argentina.

COLUMBIFORMES

DOVES / Palomas
(Family Columbidae)

Well-known family of birds that occurs worldwide in a variety of terrestrial habitats. Rounded bodies, smallish heads, and short neck and legs. The beak is short and slender, with a fleshy covering, or cere, at the base. Of the 284 species, 3 are found on the coast of Patagonia.

121. EARED DOVE / Paloma Torcaza
Zenaida auriculata   *Plate 19*

Description. 9″ (22 cm). Upperparts brownish gray. Underparts vinaceous pink. Two black spots on sides of head. Three or 4 black spots on wings. Legs pink. In flight, wedge-shaped tail tipped white, with black subterminal band. *Juvenile:* Speckled and scaly look. No dots on wing.

Behavior. From a few individuals to several hundred, particularly in agricultural areas. In flocks when not breeding. Feeds on ground. Flies fast and straight. Roosts in trees and large shrubs. Not shy. Low-pitched rising "coo."

Nests in trees and bushes. Builds a small stick platform. Lays 2 white eggs.

Status and Habitat. Common breeding resident. Grain fields, farms, towns, wooded areas. Less commonly mixed scrub and grassy areas; sometimes near coast. *One juvenile on rocks by sea at Punta Tombo, Chubut, 1983.*

Range. Throughout South America.

122. PICUI GROUND-DOVE / Torcacita
Columbina picui   *Plate 19*

Description. 6″ (15 cm). Pale gray upperparts. Black and white wing bars. Underparts pinkish white. Tail longish, black with outer feathers white. Legs very short.

Behavior. In small flocks. Often on ground. Walks quickly about, jerking its head rapidly back and forth in typical pigeon fashion. Roosts in trees. Tame. Repeated low "coo-*o*, coo-*o*."

Nests in trees. Builds a small nest platform of twigs.

Status and Habitat. Common resident in wooded areas and farms. Towns. *Small flock of 7–10 birds foraging in grassy verge of a dirt road in fruit orchards, Trelew, Chubut, January 1988.*

Range. Northern Patagonia to Colombia and northern Brazil.

123. ROCK DOVE / Paloma Cacera
Columba livia

Description. 12″ (32 cm). Fairly large. Varied coloring. Typical form is vinaceous gray, with green and mauve sheen on sides of neck; wing bars black and white.

Behavior. Very well known; semidomestic. One of the birds most adapted to urban areas. In flocks, sometimes numerous; on ground, in trees, and on buildings. Low "coo-*oo*-o."

Nests on ledges of buildings, granaries, and in trees.

Status and Habitat. Common in ports, towns, cities, and farmland. Introduced from Eurasia. Population and range expanding.

Range. Almost worldwide.

PSITTACIFORMES

PARAKEETS / Loros
(Family Psittacidae)

Familiar, brightly colored, raucous group of birds. Short, strong, very curved beaks. Legs short, with two outer digits placed backward. Wings long and pointed. Worldwide, with 327 species; two found on coast of Patagonia.

124. BURROWING PARROT / Loro Barranquero
Cyanoliseus patagonus   *Plate 19*

Description. 16″ (42 cm). Long olive tail. Head and chest olivaceous brown. Rest of underparts and rump bright yellow. Red patch in center of belly. Flight feathers dark, with blue sheen. Eye ring white. Eye ivory.

Behavior. Gregarious. In flocks, gather to sit on telephone lines and posts or on exposed branches at tops of trees. Birds take off together and fly rapidly in loose groups. Sometimes many small flocks can be seen at the same time. Feeds on green shoots, seeds, berries, etc., of desert bushes and grain crops. In evening, birds return in flights to roost on cliffs, sailing in to alight by their burrows. Noisy chatter.

Forms colonies, on inaccessible cliff faces, beginning at end of October in Chubut. Each pair digs a deep burrow back into the cliff wall. 2–5 eggs are laid.

Status and Habitat. Local breeding resident. Occasionally in large transient flocks when, if one is seen, many can be expected. *Several flocks, each containing 20–50 individuals, flying by Puerto Madryn, Chubut, April 1997. One flock of 30 birds on large bush by roadside on Península Valdés, Chubut, December 1976.* Breeds in cliffs along the Chubut River valley. Has been combated heavily in the past as a pest species in its principal roosting and nesting sites near Viedma. Open savanna and bush-covered steppe, farmland, steep river banks, and sea cliffs. Sparse wooded areas near rivers.

Range. Central and northern Patagonia from the coast to the Andean foothills. Also western Argentina to Salta. Travels extensively in search of food.

125. MONK PARAKEET / Cotorra
Myiopsitta monachus   *Plate 19*

Description. 7″ (19 cm). Front of head and breast gray. Upperparts green, underparts paler. Flight feathers dark blue. Beak orange-horn.

Behavior. In noisy flocks. Several pairs build a large communal twig nest fairly high in a tree, well anchored to branches and with many entrances. Each nest has its individual entrance. The nest is used in successive years as a roosting and breeding site. Feeds on green shoots, seeds of trees, and crops. Loud, constant chatter, both at rest and in flight.

Breeding begins in October.

Status and Habitat. Uncommon breeding resident. Often kept as a pet. Recent arrival. Fruit orchards, wooded areas, trees in town "plazas." *A small flock in a plantation of trees, Puerto Madryn, Chubut, January 1988.* Associated with the presence of trees; wooded areas, farms.

Range. East of the Andes; northern Patagonia to Bolivia and southern Brazil.

CUCULIFORMES

CUCKOOS / Cuclillos
(Family Cuculidae)

Slender, short-winged, long-tailed birds, with moderately curved beak. Two toes face backward on the perch. Several species are parasitic, laying their eggs in the nests of other birds. Of the 125 species worldwide, one is found on the coast of Patagonia.

126. GUIRA CUCKOO / Pirincho
Guira guira   *Plate 19*

Description. 14″ (36 cm). Untidy crest, cinnamon. Upperparts pale buff, streaked brown; lower back and rump white. Underparts buff. Long tail, tipped white with a wide, subterminal black band. Beak orange.

Behavior. In small flocks. Often fly off one at a time, across open spaces between trees. Flight is straight and slow. Tail moves up and down as counterbalance when sitting. A succession of 5 or 6 loud, harsh whistling calls, descending the scale, "Pyu-pyu-pyu-pyuu-pyu."

Builds a large untidy nest in which several females lay their pale blue eggs. Females incubate eggs and rear the chicks.

Status and Habitat. Fairly common breeding resident. *A small flock in trees in a farm near Trelew, Chubut, January 1985.* Wooded areas, grassy fields, farms.

Range. From northern Patagonia to northeastern Brazil.

STRIGIFORMES

BARN OWLS / Lechuzas de Campanario
(Family Tytonidae)

Slender-bodied, with heart-shaped facial patterns. These owls stand rather upright and, like other owls, swivel the head in what appears to be all directions, to stare. Active by night. Loud call. They nest in trees and large open buildings. Nine species are found throughout the world, one in Patagonia.

127. BARN OWL / Lechuza de Campanario
Tyto alba   *Plate 20*

Description. 14″ (36 cm). Upperparts light tan, suffused with light pearl gray. Whitish underparts, speckled with black. Noticeable heart-shaped facial disks. Legs feathered.

Behavior. Mostly nocturnal or twilight. Catches mice and other small prey. Hard parts of prey are regurgitated and accumulate underneath roosts. Hisses, rough shrieks, or scraping sounds.

Breeds high in rafters of open barns and farm buildings, steeples, and in hollow trees. Lays 3–5 or more white eggs.

Status and Habitat. Uncommon resident. Found in woodlands, savanna, and a variety of semiopen habitats around farmhouses and abandoned buildings. Needs trees for perching.

Range. Virtually worldwide in tropical and temperate areas. Not found in polar regions or on inaccessible islands.

TRUE OWLS / Lechuzas
(Family Strigidae)

Large rounded heads with—in some cases poorly defined—rounded facial disks and no neck. The head is swiveled in almost all directions to stare. Some species have elongated "earlike" feather tufts on top of the head. Flight is heavy and silent on broad rounded wings. Principally nocturnal, some are diurnal. Of 121 species found worldwide 3 are in Patagonia.

128. GREAT HORNED OWL / Ñacurutú
Bubo virginianus   *Plate 20*

Description. 19″ (50 cm). Large. Catlike yellow eyes and "ear tufts." Upperparts mottled brown. Underparts whitish, finely barred brown.

Behavior. Usually in pairs. Nocturnal. Perches in trees, bushes, or on ground. Sits in secluded areas during day, often going unnoticed, except for the excitement displayed by other small birds nearby. Preys on small mammals and birds. Several deep, mellow hoots.

Nests in caves or under cliff ledges and uses large abandoned nests in trees. Lays 2 or 3 eggs.

Status and Habitat. Common breeding resident. *One bird sitting on ground under a cliff ledge near the sea, during midafternoon, near Puerto Pirámides, Chubut, December 1976.* Found in varied habitat, from woodland to bush-covered steppe and highlands. Cliffs.

Range. Tierra del Fuego to northern Canada and Alaska.

129. BURROWING OWL / Lechucita de las Vizcacheras
Athene (Speotyto) cunicularia   *Plate 20*

Description. 10″ (25 cm). Small. Back sandy brown. Head comparatively small. White eyebrows. Wings gray-brown, spotted white. Underparts whitish, barred brown on breast.

Behavior. In pairs or family groups. Diurnal. Stands very upright, usually on ground or fence post close to its burrow. Swivels its head in all directions. When alarmed, bobs up and down. Hovers. Feeds mainly on small rodents and insects. Usually silent, clucks in alarm, calls in flight. A melancholy "cu-cu-ru" call.

Nests in abandoned mara or armadillo burrows in open fields. Lays 4–6 white eggs. Young owlets can be seen in or near their burrows through the summer. Both parents tend the nest.

Status and Habitat. Common resident. Frequent sightings on open grassy areas near Punta Delgada and Caleta Valdés on Península Valdés; also along Chubut River valley. Arid or semiarid, open, grassy fields.

Range. From Tierra del Fuego to western North America.

130. SHORT-EARED OWL / Lechuzón de Campo
Asio flammeus   *Plate 20*

Description. 15″ (38 cm). Large. Rounded head. Pale facial disk, dark around eyes. Very short, closely set "ear tufts." Underparts pale buff, streaked with brown on breast. Wing lining pale buff.

Behavior. Though mostly nocturnal, also active in daytime, particularly in evenings and on cloudy days. Perches on fence posts. Flies low and waveringly over the ground, searching for rodents; hovers. Usually silent. A sharp call, "Kyow!"

Nests on ground; makes a grass-lined depression, concealed in tall grass. Lays 5–7 whitish eggs.

Status and Habitat. Uncommon resident in open, scrub-covered areas. *One road kill on Península Valdés, Chubut, March 1983.* Open grassland, savanna, fields.

Range. From Tierra del Fuego, much of southern and western South America to Canada and Alaska. Also most of the Old World.

CAPRIMULGIFORMES

NIGHTJARS / Atajacaminos
(Family Caprimulgidae)

Large-headed birds, mouths with enormous gapes, and cryptic plumage. They are active by night or twilight. The eyes reflect red when shone by headlights. Silent, irregular flight. During the daytime, they alight on the ground and crouch low. Found throughout the world. Of 67 species, one is found in Patagonia.

131. BAND-WINGED NIGHTJAR / Atajacaminos Común
Caprimulgus longirostris   *Plate 20*

Description. 9″ (22 cm). Rounded wings and longish tail. Mottled gray-brown coloring. White flashes at base of primaries and tips of outer tail feathers. Whitish throat. Cinnamon hind neck, visible at close quarters. *Female:* No white in the tail and flashes in the wing less noticeable.

Behavior. Strictly nocturnal. In small flocks. Sits on ground and flies up to catch insects in flight. Frequently seen flying up in front of a car at night. Eyes shine red in headlights. During the day it usually rests on the ground concealed under a bush. Quiet ventriloquial "chuit" call.

Nests on ground hidden among the grasses. Lays one white egg.

Status and Habitat. Common between September and April. *Five or six birds sitting on a dusty road that winds through scrub, during a calm evening, Península Valdés, Chubut, March 1985.* Roadsides. Varied, grassy clearings, farmland, open hillsides, woodland borders, and mixed bush and grass-covered steppe.

Range. From southern Patagonia to central and northwestern Argentina as far as Venezuela. Southern portions of population move north in May and return in September.

TROCHILIFORMES

HUMMINGBIRDS / Picaflores
(Family Trochilidae)

A large family of small, exclusively American birds, found from Alaska to Tierra del Fuego. They have a darting, buzzing flight, beating their wings at enormous speed; can hold still in the air and even fly backward. Plumage is brilliant, and beak long and slender, often curved downward. Legs are small. There are more than 300 species; one is occasionally found in eastern Patagonia.

132. GREEN-BACKED FIRECROWN / **Picaflor de Cabeza Granate**
Sephanoides sephanoides   *Plate 19*

Description. 3″ (9 cm). Upperparts bronze-green, underparts gray-green. Crown brilliant red when it catches the light. White spot behind eye. *Female:* Lacks red crown.

Behavior. Perches on branches. Flies fast between trees and tall vegetation. Hovers before flowers to feed on nectar and pollen. Repeated, high-pitched, buzzing "zit."

Status and Habitat. Occasional nonbreeding visitor between March and September. In farms and wooded areas along Chubut River valley and sometimes in the steppe. Sub-Andean forests, farms, and flowering scrub.

Range. From Tierra del Fuego northward along the Andes to Mendoza. In winter, some birds migrate eastward as far as the coast.

CORACIIFORMES

KINGFISHERS / Martín Pescadores
(Family Alcedinidae)

Small to medium-sized birds with straight and strong beaks specialized for feeding on arthropods, small reptiles, and fish. Many, but not all, are associated with water. Colorful plumage. Cosmopolitan. Of 86 species, one is found on the coast of Patagonia.

133. RINGED KINGFISHER / Martín Pescador Grande
Ceryle torquata   *Plate 19*

Description. 14″ (36 cm). Head and back pale gray-blue. Wide collar white. Underparts rufous. Underwing white. Beak and legs gray. *Female:* Upper chest gray; underwing rufous.
Behavior. Alone or in family groups. Sits on wires or branches in the open, over water, and hovers above surface. Dives head first into water to catch fish. Produces a loud clicking call.
   Nests in caves, which it digs in river banks. Lays 4 white eggs. Chicks leave nest when one month old.
Status and Habitat. Uncommon resident along Chubut River. Rivers and freshwater ponds.
Range. All of Argentina and much of the rest of South and Central America to Mexico.

PICIFORMES

WOODPECKERS / Pájaro Carpinteros
(Family Picidae)

Mostly tree-climbing, some terrestrial. These birds have short, strong legs with two toes placed backward. Larger woodpeckers have strong chisel-like beaks for chipping at trees. They have long, barbed tongues that can be greatly extended to reach insects deep in the wood. Larger species have stiff tails to assist climbing. Noisy. Represented worldwide with 210 species; one species is found in coastal Patagonia.

134. CHECKERED WOODPECKER / **Carpinterito Bataráz**
Picoides mixtus *Plate 19*

Description. 6″ (15 cm). Small. Upperparts spotted white, tail densely barred. Crown streaked black and white. Patch on hindcrown red. Eyebrow and moustachial stripe white. *Female:* Lacks red patch on hindcrown.
Behavior. Alone or in pairs. Climbs around on smaller branches of trees—not on tree trunks—searching for insects on which to feed. Produces a rapid, loud drumming.
  Nests in holes in trees.
Status and Habitat. Uncommon. In wooded areas along Chubut River valley and near farmhouses on the steppe. Midheight in trees, plantations, farms, and woodland. *One bird in trees in irrigated farmland near Trelew, Chubut, October 1987 (C. Passera).*
Range. From northern Patagonia to central Brazil.

PASSERIFORMES

MINERS, EARTHCREEPERS, etc. / Camineras, Bandurritas, Canasteros, etc.
(Family Furnariidae)

  Small land birds with drab—usually brown—plumages and short rounded wings. Their flight is fairly weak and in some cases almost butterfly-like. Bill without hooked tip. Many species make elaborate and distinctive nests of sticks, mud, etc., and others dig tunnels in embankments. Furnarids produce loud— often tuneless—songs. The family is restricted to South and Central America. There are 218 species, of which 13 are found on the east coast of Patagonia.

135. COMMON MINER / **Caminera Común**
Geositta cunicularia *Plate 21*

Description. 5″ (14 cm). Upperparts pale brown, slightly streaked on crown. Eyebrow pale cream. Bill relatively long and slightly curved downward. Underparts whitish; breast lightly scaled brown. In flight, primaries and secondaries pale rufous; base of outer tail feathers buff; noticeable subterminal band blackish.
Behavior. Terrestrial. Not shy. Conspicuous; stands erect in the open on roads and embankments. Flies up 30–45 ft (10–15 m) into the air repeating a rapid, trilled call, "Wheet-ta-wheet-ta-wheet-ta. . . ."
  Digs a tunnel 3–9 ft (1–3 m) long, in embankments, with a grass-lined chamber at end. Lays 2 or 3 white eggs.
Status and Habitat. Common. Open Andean hillsides, steppe and grassland. *Scat-*

tered individuals on open grasslands with sandy soil embankments. Punta Norte, Penín-sula Valdés, Chubut, September to March.

Range. Tierra del Fuego to northern Argentina and southern Peru. Southern birds move northward in winter.

136. SHORT-BILLED MINER / Caminera de Pico Corto;
Geositta antarctica   *Plate 21*

Description. 6″ (16 cm). Short thick bill, Upperparts pale brown; edges of flight feathers paler. Pale eyebrow. Brownish under eye. Underparts pale buff, slightly streaked brown on chest. In flight, wings brownish; base of outer tail feathers whitish; subterminal band dark brown.

Behavior. Alone or in small flocks. Very terrestrial. Flies low and drops down a little distance away. Produces a repeated "witik witik witik" call (R. Straneck).

Digs a tunnel in a dry embankment for nesting. Lays 3 white eggs.

Status and Habitat. Common resident on steppes with low grass and bare terrain.

Range. South of Santa Cruz and Tierra del Fuego. Between April and August, migrates to central Argentina. South of Chile.

Similar Species. Very similar to the previous species but bill is shorter and, in flight, no rufous in wings. Much less common.

137. SCALE-THROATED EARTHCREEPER / Bandurrita Común
Upucerthia dumetaria   *Plate 21*

Description. 8″ (20 cm). Long, slender, downward-curved bill. Upperparts brown. Eyebrow whitish. Breast pale brown with darker scaling. Belly off-white. In flight, pale cinnamon wing bar; outer rectrices dark brown.

Behavior. Usually alone. Not shy. Mostly on ground; walks around, busily pecking and probing for insects. Also sings from tops of bushes. Repeated loud "qweet."

Digs a tunnel in a soft soil embankment, 3 ft (1 m) or more long, the end of which widens into a nesting chamber lined with grass. Lays 2 or 3 eggs. As in other furnarids, both parents bring food to nest and carry away chick droppings. *Two birds bringing insects and leaving with droppings from a nest in a shallow embank-ment by the roadside on Península Valdés, Chubut, October 1981.*

Status and Habitat. Common breeding resident. Dry bush and grass-covered steppe and Andean hillsides. Roadsides.

Range. Tierra del Fuego, Patagonia, and western Argentina to Peru. In winter, migrates to northern Argentina.

138. BAND-TAILED EARTHCREEPER / Patagón, Turco
Eremobius phoenicurus   *Plate 21*

Description. 6″ (16 cm). Strong beak, very slightly curved downward. Upperparts mouse-brown. Eyebrow white. Underparts pale gray-brown. Tail rufous, tipped black.

Behavior. Tame. Carries its tail vertical; runs and hops along the ground with quick movements, catching insects before they can escape. Flies low and determinedly. Loud "chirrrr!"

Builds a ball-shaped nest out of twigs, 12–20″ (30–50 cm) in diameter, in low thorny bushes. A tunnel entrance leads to a nest chamber lined with feathers. Lays 2–4 white eggs.

Status and Habitat. Common from August to April. In numbers during spring and fall migration. *Several dozen road kills along a 60-mile (100 km) stretch of road between Puerto Madryn and Pirámides, Chubut, April 1984.* Bush and grass-covered steppe from Andean hillsides to coast.

Range. Patagonia. Partially migratory. From April to August, southern birds move north as far as central Argentina.

139. RUFOUS HORNERO / Hornero Común
Furnarius rufus   *Plate 21*

Description. 7″ (18 cm). Beak straight. Upperparts rich rufous, tail reddish. Underparts pale. Chin whitish.

Behavior. Tame and conspicuous. Struts and runs along the damp ground or short grass in search of insects. Produces a series of shrill descending notes, usually sung in duet by the pair.

Builds a soccer-ball-sized nest of mud on posts or branches of trees.

Status and Habitat. Common breeding resident, though restricted to wet grasslands, wooded areas, farms, city parks. Requires mud and trees or posts etc., for nesting. Recent arrival.

Range. Farms along Chubut River valley, and in groves of trees in Puerto Madryn. Northern Patagonia to Brazil.

Note. National bird of Argentina.

140. BAR-WINGED CINCLODES / Remolinera Parda
Cinclodes fuscus   *Plate 21*

Description. 6″ (16 cm). Upperparts and sides of head brown. Noticeable white eyebrow and malar stripe. Underparts pale brown. Outer tail feathers tipped pale. In flight, ochre wing bar.

Behavior. Terrestrial; occasionally on posts or bushes. Does not raise tail. Runs and walks along ground. Usually forages alone. Gleans ground and grass for moths, beetles, larvae, and worms. Tame. Usually silent. Stands on hillocks and flutters its wings uttering an extended, shrill "tetet't't't't't."

Nests in cracks and holes dug in ground.

Status and Habitat. Common though not abundant in southern parts September to March. Wintering birds in northern Patagonia. Moist shores of lagoons, open areas, bush-covered terrain, highlands.

Range. Tierra del Fuego, Patagonia, and western Argentina to Colombia. In winter, migrates to northern Argentina.

141. WREN-LIKE RUSHBIRD / Junquero
Phleocryptes melanops *Plate 21*

Description. 5″ (13 cm). Small. Crown and eye stripe dark brown, spotted black. White eyebrow. Back heavily streaked black, white, and gray. Wings cinnamon and blackish. Short tail, dark brown. Underparts whitish.

Behavior. Tame. Usually heard before it is seen; appears briefly from time to time in exposed places. Actively climbs around among emergent vegetation, close to water surface, gleaning for insects. Constant loud ticking sound as of two stones tapped together.

Builds a small cup fixed to the reeds.

Status and Habitat. Common in dense reed beds.

Range. Chubut River valley; Sarmiento. Tierra del Fuego to southern Brazil and Peru.

142. PLAIN-MANTLED TIT-SPINETAIL / Coludito Cola Negra
Leptasthenura aegithaloides *Plate 21*

Description. 6″ (16 cm). Wren-sized with short beak. Very long, pointed tail feathers, dark brown. Crown cinnamon, streaked with black. Eyebrow white. Back gray-brown. Underparts whitish.

Behavior. Found alone or in pairs. With active nervous movements, searches for insects among branches of bushes. Will perch briefly on exposed branches. Not shy. Makes a remarkably loud sound for its small size. High-pitched cricketlike "zzeeezezezeet," sometimes a scolding, continuous, high "prrrr."

Nests in holes in cliffs and embankments. Lines nest with grass and feathers. Lays 2 or 3 small white eggs. Young fledge and leave the nest within 3 weeks of hatching. Often hatches 2 clutches a season.

Status and Habitat. Common breeding resident in bush-covered plains, embankments.

Range. Throughout Patagonia and northwestern Argentina as far as Peru.

143. LESSER CANASTERO / Canastero Coludo
Asthenes pyrrholeuca *Plate 21*

Description. 6″ (15 cm). Mouse-brown upperparts. Eyebrow and underparts whitish. Tail long, rufous with blackish center. Beak straight and slender. Some individuals have orange chin patches.

Behavior. Fairly shy; spends most of time inside bushes, searching branches for insects. Flies quickly and irregularly with short wing bursts from one bush to another, holding tail slightly cocked. When disturbed disappears immediately from sight among branches. Rarely perches on exposed branches. Not terrestrial. In breeding season produces a shrill "twee-deedeet," also a sharp contact call, "qweet."

The nest, usually concealed in the middle of a green bush, is a small elongated bowl of twigs 8″ (20 cm) in diameter. Its wide, rounded opening faces upward or slightly off to one side. Lays 3 white eggs. Both parents spend the day feeding chicks. Fledging occurs within a few weeks.

Status and Habitat. One of most common canasteros in northeastern Patagonia. Mainly bush-covered steppe. Also brush near fresh water.

Range. Patagonia and western Argentina. In winter, ranges northward to central Argentina.

144. PATAGONIAN CANASTERO / Canastero Patagónico
Asthenes patagonica   *Plate 21*

Description. 6″ (15 cm). Crown and back mouse-brown. Sides of head and breast gray. Belly pale cinnamon. Tail shorter than previous species, mostly black. Beak short and small. Inconspicuous black streaking on chin.

Behavior. Tame. Frequently runs along the ground with tail cocked; also actively forages among branches of bushes and briefly appears on exposed perches on top. Feeds on insects. Silent when close to nest. Sharp contact call "Qweet."

Builds very noticeable, soccer-ball-sized twig nest, usually on exposed, dry branch near top of a prickly Piquillín (*Condalia microphylla*) bush. Entrance to nest is through a short, round tunnel made of thorny twigs. Lays 3 or 4 white eggs. Both parents care for young. New nests are built each season. The grass snake (*Phylodrias* sp.) has been recorded feeding on eggs and chicks in the nest.

Status and Habitat. Common breeding resident in scrub-covered areas. *Recorded all year round in Península Valdés and Punta Tombo, Chubut.* The conspicuous nest is indicative of bird's presence in an area. Bush-covered steppe.

Range. Restricted to northern Patagonia.

145. CORDILLERAN CANASTERO / Canastero Pálido
Asthenes modesta   *Plate 21*

Description. 6″ (15 cm). Crown and back gray-brown. Eyebrow, throat, and underparts whitish. Tail fairly long, two central feathers longest, each feather blackish brown, edged pale. Orange chinpatch bordered black.

Behavior. Forages alone. Carries tail slightly cocked. Mainly in bushes; briefly sits on exposed branches; also runs along ground. Sharp "peet." Also a continual, scolding, shrill "tirrrr."

Nests in holes in trees, bushes, and on ground. Lays 2–4 whitish eggs.

Status and Habitat. Scarce in bush-covered steppe. Sightings at Punta Tombo, Chubut. More common in hilly country.

Range. Patagonia and western Argentina to Peru.

Similar Species. Not as ruddy colored as Lesser Canastero. Tail feathers somewhat pointed and individually edged pale brown.

146. AUSTRAL CANASTERO / Canastero Manchado Chico
Asthenes anthoides   *Plate 21*

Description. 6″ (16 cm). Upperparts buff, streaked with dark brown. White eyebrow. Underparts pale buff; chin patch rufous; throat streaked and dotted black. Cinnamon patch on wings. Tail short with pointed feathers, dusky, edged white. In flight, cinnamon wing bar.

Behavior. Alone or in pairs, on ground or in low bushes. Often holds its tail upright. Occasionally perches briefly on tops of bushes and fence posts.

Status and Habitat. Rare and local. Declining possibly because of habitat destruction through overgrazing by sheep. Andean foothills and moist sub-Antarctic steppe.

Range. Tierra del Fuego to Neuquén. Punta Dungeness at mouth of Strait of Magellan (Ridgely and Tudor 1994).

147. WHITE-THROATED CACHALOTE / Coperote o Cachalote Pardo
Pseudoseisura gutturalis   *Plate 21*

Description. 8″ (21 cm). Short hindcrest. Upperparts uniform mouse-brown. Underparts pale brown with noticeable white chin patch outlined black. Beak strong and straight.

Behavior. Shy. In pairs or family groups. Often heard before it is seen. When excited it erects its short crest. Found on ground or in bushes where it perches on exposed branches. Feeds on lizards, insects. Produces a shrill, Hornero-like call.

Builds a very large nest of twigs, over 3 ft (1 m) in diameter, often occupying the entire bush. A long tunnel leads to nest chamber, which is lined with feathers and grasses. Same nest is sometimes used in successive seasons, although often several half-made or abandoned nests are found in bushes in vicinity of active nest. Lays 4 white eggs.

Status and Habitat. Scarce. *One active nest in Punta Tombo December (Conway 1964). Two birds calling near a large nest in a molle bush (Schinus polygamus), in an area dominated by creosote bush (Larrea divaricata) near Route 3 behind Puerto Madryn, December 1983.* Dry, bush-covered steppe and Andean hillsides.

Range. Northern Patagonia and western Argentina.

TYRANT FLYCATCHERS / Gauchos, Monjitas, etc.
(Family Tyrannidae)

Large family, many with striking colors. Beaks are strong, with hooked tips surrounded basally by hairlike vibrissae. Often aggressive. Agile flight. Many catch insects on the wing. Restricted to the Americas. Many are migratory. Of 380 species, 14 are found in coastal Patagonia.

148. GRAY-BELLIED SHRIKE-TYRANT / Gaucho Común
Agriornis microptera   *Plate 22*

Description. 9″ (23 cm). Mockingbird-sized but more compact. Crown and back gray brown. Eyebrow white. Wing feathers edged pale. Throat white, heavily streaked black. Rest of underparts pale brown. Slender white edge to outer tail feathers. Strong, straight hook-tipped beak dark brown. Lower mandible orange.

Behavior. Usually alone. Perches on exposed branches on top of bushes. Flies straight and low from one bush to another. Runs along ground picking up insects. Occasionally flies up to catch insects on the wing. Usually silent. Produces high-pitched whistle in breeding season.

Builds a large nest of twigs, placed in a bush, 3 ft (1 m) or more above ground. Eggs are white, stained brown near the pointed end. *One nest in a Piquillín bush (Condalia microphylla) contained 3 eggs on Península Valdés, Chubut (R. Straneck). A chick demanded food from parent, Estancia La Anita, Península Valdés, Chubut, mid-December 1990.*

Status and Habitat. Fairly common, particularly from early September to late June. Bush-covered steppe and Andean hillsides.

Range. Patagonia and northwestern Argentina to Peru. In winter, ranges north and east to southern Brazil.

149. CHOCOLATE-VENTED TYRANT / Gaucho Chocolate
Neoxolmis rufiventris   *Plate 22*

Description. 9″ (23 cm). Mockingbird-sized. Beak straight, black. Blackish face; rest of head, neck, and back gray. Belly rufous. In flight, mantle gray, edged white; primaries black, secondaries rufous.

Behavior. Shy. In small loose flocks. Stands very straight on ground out in open, or on mounds, nervously flicking wings and tail. Flight fast with irregular wing beats. Usually silent. Call is a musical, wheezy whistle produced at dawn and dusk during breeding.

Builds bowl-shaped nest on ground, lined with grasses and feathers. Lays 2 or 3 eggs which are white, slightly stained brown around the rounded end.

Status and Habitat. Fairly common from September to March. Open grass and scrub-covered steppe. Regular roadside visitor, during spring and fall migration, on Península Valdés and Punta Tombo.

Range. All of Patagonia. Ranges north to southern Brazil in winter.

150. MOUSE-BROWN MONJITA / Monjita Parda
Agriornis (Xolmis) murina   *Plate 22*

Description. 6″ (16 cm). Crown and back gray-brown. Eyebrow white. Flight feathers edged white. Throat white with notable black streaks. Below creamy white.

Behavior. Usually forages alone. Stands erect. Makes short sprints along ground chasing insects; stops, cocks head to one side to inspect surroundings. Also perches on tops of bushes. Usually silent. Occasional high-pitched whistle-like call.

Status and Habitat. Scarce breeding (?) visitor in Península Valdés, Chubut, from September to March. Dry bush-covered steppe.

Range. Northern Patagonia. In winter ranges northward to Paraguay and Bolivia.

Similar Species. Smaller than the Gray-bellied Shrike-Tyrant, with smaller beak and buff-colored flanks.

151. RUSTY-BACKED MONJITA / Monjita Castaña
Neoxolmis (Xolmis) rubetra   *Plate 22*

Description. 7″ (18 cm). Crown and back orange rufous with prominent white eyebrow and cheek. Underparts white; breast narrowly streaked black. Straight black beak. Tail black, outer rectrices edges white. *In flight:* Upper wings patterned rufous and black, under wing coverts pale rust. *Juvenile:* Upperparts dull rust brown, underparts whitish.

Behavior. In flocks in spring; alone or in pairs in summer. Perches on exposed branches of bushes; also on ground. Stands rather upright. Usually silent.

Fledglings in an open grassy field near Punta Norte, Chubut, December 1984.

Status and Habitat. Scarce. Bush-covered steppe or grassland. Conspicuous from September to March in creosote bush (*Larrea* sp.) areas and Piquillín (*Condalia microphylla*) and Quilimbai (*Chuquiraga avellanedae*) bush areas on Península Valdés, Chubut.

Range. Northern Patagonia. Ranges to northern Argentina in winter.

152. DARK-FACED GROUND-TYRANT / Dormilona Cara Negra
Muscisaxicola macloviana   *Plate 22*

Description. 6″ (15 cm). Small and slender. Face black. Crown dark brown. Back gray. Tail black. Underparts white. Beak straight and black.

Behavior. Alone or in flocks. Not shy. Nervously flicks tail and wings. Runs along sand and on dry kelp along tops of beaches, catching invertebrates. Flies close to ground, flitting its wings, which are often suspended against the wind. In large loose flocks on migration in April and August. Usually silent. Call is a discreet "zilip," produced in flight.

Nests in holes in the ground on Andean slopes.

Status and Habitat. Common. Beaches and cliffs; open hillsides and high Andean slopes with sparse grasses. Tops of beaches and cliff faces on seacoasts of Península Valdés from June to September.

Range. Western Tierra del Fuego and Patagonia. In winter, ranges throughout Patagonia to central Argentina and north as far as Peru.

153. RUFOUS-BACKED NEGRITO / Sobrepuesto
Lessonia rufa   *Plate 22*

Description. 4″ (11 cm). Small. All black with rufous back. Short beak. *Female:* Crown brown; eye stripe and cheek white. Back rufous. Underparts pale brown.

Behavior. In pairs or flocks. Stands on rocks, small mounds, and low bushes, nervously flicking tail and wings. Very active. Makes short, low flights; also sprints a few paces along ground, then stops and faces the wind. Feeds on insects. In loose flocks from March to September. Usually silent. Male makes a thin whistle in flight.

Constructs a small nest of grass and feathers. Lays 3 or 4 eggs. *One nest with 3 chicks on a small cliff ledge a few yards above high tide mark, east coast of Golfo San José, Chubut, December 1986.*

Status and Habitat. Very common. One of the most familiar small birds on the moist shores of lagoons and beaches. Humid ground by roadsides. Coasts.

Range. Tierra del Fuego, Patagonia, and Altiplano. Between March and September, the southern population ranges northward to Brazil.

154. WHITE-WINGED BLACK-TYRANT / Viudita Común
Knipolegus aterrimus   *Plate 22*

Description. 5″ (13 cm). Back dark brown. Head and underparts shiny black. Beak steel gray, darker at tip. In flight wings black with noticeable white wing bars. Tail and rump black. *Female:* gray-brown upperparts; rump bright cinammon, noticeable in flight. Underparts pale buff. Wing bars cinnamon.

Behavior. Solitary and shy. Agile flight. Sits on exposed branches of bushes and on rocky outcrops. Flies up to catch insects on the wing.

Status and Habitat. Uncommon breeding resident. *One adult flying around in the gullies leading down to the sea at Punta León, Chubut, November 1988.*

Range. Chubut and Río Negro through central Argentina, Andes of Bolivia and Peru. An isolated population in eastern Brazil.

155. SPECTACLED TYRANT / Pico de Plata
Hymenops perspicillata   *Plate 23*

Description. 5″ (13 cm). Black with yellow beak and eye ring. Primaries white, very evident in flight. *Female:* Inconspicuous. Upperparts brown, streaked black. Underparts pale, streaked brown. Rufous wing bar visible in flight. Beak and eye ring similar to male.

Behavior. Male very conspicuous. On ground, or perches on posts and exposed bushes. Captures insects on the wing. Flies 20 to 30 ft (7 or 10 m) into the air, emits a clicking sound at top of the arc, and returns to same perch.

Nests in clumps of grass or reeds. Makes a small cup and lays up to 3 eggs.

Status and Habitat. Fairly common, summer resident near marshes, reed beds, and rivers. Irrigated fields and pastures. *A male doing display flights from a perch on the top of a bush in a field on a farm near Trelew, Chubut, January 1982.*

Range. From northern Patagonia to northern Argentina; between April and August, to central Brazil.

156. GREAT KISKADEE / Benteveo
Pitangus sulphuratus   *Plate 23*

Description. 8″ (22 cm). Strong, hook-tipped, black beak. Black cap with conspicuous white eyebrow. Hidden crown red. Upperparts brown. White throat fading to yellow on lower underparts.

Behavior. Alone or in pairs. Noisy. Conspicuous. Perches on exposed branches. Catches insects in flight or on ground. Hovers and feeds off surface of fresh water. Shrill "kiskad-*e* ee."

Builds a rounded, untidy nest in trees or bushes. Lays up to 5 eggs. *A pair on a nest in pine trees on the waterfront in Puerto Madryn, Chubut, December 1991 (K. Conway).* Nests in trees of farms in Chubut River valley.

Status and Habitat. Fairly common breeding resident. Varied: rivers, fields, gardens, and parks.

Range. Northern Patagonia to southern North America. *A lone bird calling from a telephone wire in an open yard in Puerto Madryn, Chubut, June 1992.*

157. FORK-TAILED FLYCATCHER / Tijereta
Tyrannus savana   Plate 23

Description. 15″ (38 cm). Black cap. Hidden crown yellow. Upperparts gray. Underparts white. Long, forked tail black. *Female:* Tail half the length.

Behavior. Scattered individuals or in flocks. Captures insects in flight. Sits on fence wires and exposed perches. Twitters in flight. Builds a small nest.

Status and Habitat. Scarce summer visitor. Dry, scrub-covered plains; savanna, forest clearings, and open fields. *Several individuals on telephone wires in Puerto Madryn, Chubut, January 1990.*

Range. Northern Patagonia to North America. Southern population migrates north in winter.

158. WHITE-CRESTED TYRANNULET / Piojito Vientre Amarillo
Serpophaga subcristata   Plate 23

Description. 3″ (9 cm). Very small. Crown and back olivaceous gray. Small pale eyebrow. Hidden crown white. Below pale gray, turning to yellowish on lower belly. Pale wing bars. Tail brown.

Behavior. Active; perches and flits among smaller branches. Varied, low-pitched calls.

Status and Habitat. Scarce. *One bird sitting in branches of a Tamarisk (Tamarix gallica) in a farm near Trelew, Chubut, January 1982.* Wooded areas, savanna, farms.

Range. Northern Patagonia to central Brazil.

159. WARBLING DORADITO / Doradito Común
Pseudocolopteryx flaviventris   Plate 23

Description. 4″ (10 cm). Small. Crown and slight crest rufous. Rest of upperparts brown. Underparts yellow. Wing bars rufous.

Behavior. Usually alone or in pairs. Active. Shy. Hides among reeds and hard to see. Usually together with Many-colored Rush-Tyrant. Calls "chek-chek-chekchik."

Nests in wetland vegetation. Builds a small cup of grasses, lined with soft material. Lays 4 eggs.

Status and Habitat. Restricted to reed beds and brush near fresh water along lower Chubut River valley.

Range. Northern Patagonia to southern Brazil.

PLATES

PLATE 1

RHEAS; TINAMOUS / Ñandues; Perdices y Martinetas

DARWIN'S RHEA / Choique o Ñandú Petizo 1
Pterocnemia pennata
1a Adult Very large. Long neck and legs. No tail. Body feathers gray to pale brownish, tipped with white.

1b Juvenile Uniform gray at one month.

DARWIN'S TINAMOU / Perdíz Chica Pálida 2
Nothura darwinii
2 Adult Small. No crest. Rounded body with no tail. Very short legs. Crown and neck pale buff, spotted dark brown. Back streaked and barred with white and brown.

PATAGONIAN TINAMOU / Keú Patagónico 4
Tinamotis ingoufi
3 Adult Long neck, rounded body and short legs. No crest. Three long white stripes on sides of head. Rest of body buff, heavily barred and spotted brown.

ELEGANT CRESTED-TINAMOU / Martineta o Copetona Común 3
Eudromia elegans
4a Adult Long neck. Noticeable crest. Long white eyebrow and cheek stripe. Body streaked and barred dark brown. Legs very short.

4b Juvenile Pale gray streaked and barred darker. Crest.

PLATE 2

PENGUINS; GREBES / Pingüinos; Macaes

MAGELLANIC PENGUIN / Pingüino de Magallanes 5
Spheniscus magellanicus
1a Adult Black bands on head and sides. Belly white.

1b First year Pearl gray upperparts. Pale face and belly. No bands.

KING PENGUIN / Pingüino Rey 6
Aptenodytes patagonicus
2 Adult Comparatively large and heavy. Back gray. Orange and yellow auricular patch. Chest flushed yellow. Belly white.

ROCKHOPPER PENGUIN / Pingüino de Penacho Amarillo 8
Eudyptes chrysocome
3 Adult Comparatively small and stocky. Head and back black. Golden "eyebrows" and side plumes. Beak red.

PIED-BILLED GREBE / Macá de Pico Grueso 14
Podilymbus podiceps
4a Breeding Head and back gray brown. Throat and band on bill black. Belly pale gray.

4b Nonbreeding No bill band. Throat whitish.

SILVERY GREBE / Macá Plateado 11
Podiceps occipitalis
5 Adult Back gray. Nape and hindneck black. Foreneck and belly pure white. Eye red. Post-ocular plumes yellow.

GREAT GREBE / Macá Grande 13
Podiceps major
6a Breeding Long slender neck and beak. Sides of neck rufous. Head gray; hindneck, short crest, and back black.

6b Nonbreeding Upperparts brownish. Sides of neck whitish.

WHITE-TUFTED GREBE / Macá Común 10
Podiceps rolland
7a Breeding Short crest. Upperparts black. Sides of head white. Underparts rufous. Eye red.

7b Nonbreeding Neck and underparts whitish. Back brown.

HOODED GREBE / Macá Tobiano 12
Podiceps gallardoi
8 Adult Distinct hood, hindneck, and back black. White forehead. Orange crest. Sides of neck and belly white.

1a

1b

2

3

4b

4a

5

6b

8

7a

7b

6a

g.Harris
1997

PLATE 3

RARE PENGUINS, ALBATROSSES, AND PETRELS / Pingüinos, Albatros y Petreles Raros

MACARONI PENGUIN / Pingüino de Penacho Anaranjado 7
Eudyptes chrysolophus
1 Adult Head and back black. Crown of orange plumes on forehead and above eyes. Belly white. Beak thick and reddish.

GENTOO PENGUIN / Pingüino de Pico Rojo 9
Pygoscelis papua
2 Adult Head and back black, with white band across crown. Belly white. Beak orange red.

WANDERING ALBATROSS / Albatros Errante 15
Diomedea exulans
3 Adult Upper wing black, varyingly marked white from base outward (in old birds only tips and trailing edges black). Outer tail feathers usually black. Bill yellow.

ROYAL ALBATROSS / Albatros Real 16
Diomedea epomophora
4 Adult Upper wing black, varyingly white on leading edge (only tips and trailing edges black in old birds). Outer tail black. Black line on cutting edge of upper mandible.

GRAY-HEADED ALBATROSS / Albatros de Cabeza Gris 18
Diomedea chrysostoma
5 Adult Head and neck bluish gray. Upper wing and back black. Rump and belly white. Tail band black.

GRAY PETREL (PEDIUNKER) / Petrel Gris 23
Procellaria (Adamastor) cinerea
6 Adult Head and back ash gray. Chin and belly white. Underwing and tail pale gray.

3

PLATE 4

ALBATROSSES; PETRELS / Albatros; Petreles

BLACK-BROWED ALBATROSS / Albatros
Chico o de Ceja Negra 17
Diomedea melanophrys
1 Adult Large. Upper wing and terminal tail band black. Eyebrow black.

SOUTHERN GIANT PETREL / Petrel
Gigante del Sur 19
Macronectes giganteus
2a Adult Large. Long wings, often held crooked. Body variably gray. Head, neck white.

2b Juvenile Dark brown.

WHITE-CHINNED PETREL
(SHOEMAKER) / Petrel Negro 22
Procellaria aequinoctialis
3 Adult Resembles a small albatross. Dark brown except for white chin patch. Smaller, wings straighter, and neck shorter than Giant Petrel.

SOUTHERN FULMAR / Petrel Plateado 20
Fulmarus glacialoides
4 Adult Upper wings pale gray with distinct white "windows" at base of primaries. Head and belly white.

4

1

1

1

2a

2b

2b

3

4

G. Harris

PLATE 5

PETRELS, PRIONS, AND SHEARWATERS; STORM PETRELS / Petreles; Petreles de las Tormentas

CAPE PETREL / **Petrel Damero, del Cabo o Pintado 21**
Daption capense
1 Adult Striking black and white markings on the wings distinctive. White rump. Terminal tail band black.

BROAD-BILLED PRION / **Petrel Ballena Pico Ancho 27**
Pachyptila vittata desolata
2 Adult Head slate gray. Eyebrow white. Pale blue-gray with a dinstinct dark "W" on the upper wing in flight. Broad, heavy bill.

SLENDER-BILLED PRION / **Petrel Ballena Pico Delgado 28**
Pachyptila belcheri
3 Adult Size and color like Broad-billed Prion but head pale blue-gray. Bill very slender (evident in the hand).

GREATER SHEARWATER / **Pardela de Cabeza Negra 24**
Puffinus gravis
4 Adult Distinct black cap. Back dark gray. Rump white, Tail black.

LITTLE SHEARWATER / **Pardela Chica 26**
Puffinus assimilis elegans
5 Adult Small. Hood black extending well below the eye. Back, rump, and tail black. Chin and belly white.

SOOTY SHEARWATER / **Pardela Oscura 25**
Puffinus griseus
6 Adult Long slender wings. Overall brown. Pale underwings visible in flight.

WILSON'S STORM PETREL / **Petrel de las Tormentas Común 29**
Oceanites oceanicus
7 Adult Small. Overall dark brown with very noticeable white rump. Pale brown upper wing converts.

G. Harris
'87

PLATE 6

CORMORANTS / Cormoranes

IMPERIAL CORMORANT / Cormorán
Imperial 33
Phalacrocorax atriceps
1a Northern race or King Cormorant *(Ph. a. albiventer)* White on face less extensive. Lacks dorsal white patch, and white wing bar less conspicuous or lacking.

1b Southern race or Blue-eyed Cormorant *(Ph. a. atriceps)* Upperparts and crest black. Foreneck and belly white extending high up the cheek. White dorsal patch and wing bar in breeding plumage.

ROCK CORMORANT / Cormorán de
Cuello Negro 31
Phalacrocorax magellanicus
2 Adult Neck black to upper chest; often flecked white. Belly white, Facial skin at base of beak and around eye red.

GUANAY CORMORANT / Cormorán
Guanay 32
Phalacrocorax bougainvillii
3 Adult Larger and more slender than other cormorants. Crest, neck, and back black. Oval chin patch, chest and belly white. Eye ring red.

RED-LEGGED CORMORANT / Cormorán
Gris 34
Phalacrocorax gaimardi
4 Adult Steel gray upperparts. Belly and oval patch on side of neck white. Legs and base of beak bright red.

NEOTROPIC (OLIVACEOUS)
CORMORANT / Biguá 30
Phalacrocorax olivaceus
5a Breeding Slender; long tail. Entirely black, except postocular plumes and band at base of lower mandible white.

5b Nonbreeding Lacks white blumes on head.

1a

1a

1b

1b

1b

2

2

3

3

3

4

4

5b

5a

5a

g. Harris

PLATE 7

EGRETS AND HERONS; STORKS; IBISES; FLAMINGOS / Garzas; Cigueñas; Cuervillos y Bandurrias; Flamencos

CATTLE EGRET / Garcita Bueyera 39
Bubulcus ibis
1 Breeding Pure white, with crown, nape, throat, and back flushed with orange-buff. Bill, legs, and feet yellow.

COMMON (GREAT) EGRET / Garza Blanca 36
Casmerodius albus
2 Breeding Large. Pure white. Long "egrets." Bill yellow. Feet and legs black.

COCOI (WHITE-NECKED) HERON / Garza Mora 35
Ardea cocoi
3 Adult Large. Back and wings gray. Cap and hind crest black. Underparts white with black band across chest and belly. Beak yellow.

SNOWY EGRET / Garcita Blanca 38
Egretta thula
4 Breeding Pure white with "egrets." Bill and legs black. Feet yellow.

BLACK-CROWNED NIGHT-HERON / Garza Bruja 37
Nycticorax nycticorax
5a Adult Crown and back black. Wings and tail gray. Underparts whitish flushed gray. Eye red.
5b Juvenile Spotted and streaked brown and buff.

MAGUARI STORK / Cigueña Americana 40
Ciconia maguari
6 Adult Large and very conspicuous. White with flight feathers black. Legs red. Long, straight, pointed beak gray.

WHITE-FACED IBIS / Cuervillo de Cañada 42
Plegadis chihi
7 Adult Beak long and downward-curved. Dark chestnut head and neck, with metallic violet and green sheen on upperparts.

BUFF-NECKED IBIS / Bandurria Común 41
Theristicus caudatus
8 Adult Beak long and downward-curved. Head and neck buff. Gray chest band. Back and wing coverts ash gray. Belly black. Facial skin black. Legs pink.

CHILEAN FLAMINGO / Flamenco Austral 43
Phoenicopterus chilensis
9 Adult Head, neck, and body pink. Wing coverts and axiliaries vermilion. Primaries and secondaries black. Legs bluish with red joints.

PLATE 8

SWANS AND GEESE / Cisnes y Cauquenes

BLACK-NECKED SWAN / Cisne de Cuello Negro 44
Cygnus melancoryphus
1 Adult Large, conspicuous, and graceful. Pure white with black head and neck. Caruncle and base of beak red.

UPLAND GOOSE / Avutarda o Cauquén Común 46
Chloephaga picta
2a Male, white form White, heavily barred black on back and flanks.

2b Male, dark form Similar but chest also heavily barred black.

2c Female Head and neck rufous brown. Chest and belly heavily barred black. Legs yellow.

ASHY-HEADED GOOSE / Cauquén de Cabeza Gris 47
Chloephaga poliocephala
3 Adult Head ash gray. Chest and part of back rich chestnut. Rest of underparts white, barred black.

RUDDY-HEADED GOOSE / Cauquén Colorado 48
Chloephaga rubidiceps
4 Adult Smaller than female Upland Goose. Clearly defined ruddy head and neck. Fine, black and buff white barring on body. Undertail coverts rufous.

COSCOROBA SWAN / Cisne Coscoroba 45
Coscoroba coscoroba
5 Adult Large and conspicuous. White. Beak and legs orange red. Wing tips black, visible in flight.

G. Harris

PLATE 9

DUCKS / Patos

CINNAMON TEAL / Pato Colorado 54
Anas cyanoptera
1a Male Dark reddish chestnut. Wing coverts pale blue.

1b Female Buff, spotted and mottled dark brown.

LAKE DUCK / Pato Zambullidor Chico 61
Oxyura vittata
2a Male Small. Chest and back rich chestnut. Hood and stiff tail black. Beak sky blue.

2b Female Mottled and barred brown. Cheek stripe and throat whitish.

SPECTACLED (BRONZE-WINGED) DUCK / Pato Anteojo 52
Anas specularis
3 Adult Dark-brown head with well-defined white patches in front of eye and on throat. Back brown. Bronze speculum.

RED SHOVELER / Pato Cuchara 55
Anas platalea
4a Male Head pale gray, finely speckled black. Large, thick bill black. Body rufous, spotted black. Wing coverts pale blue.

4b Female Pale brown, mottled black.

ROSY-BILLED POCHARD / Pato Picazo 60
Netta peposaca
5a Male Black with violet sheen. Flanks ash gray. Eye red. Beak and caruncle pink.

5b Female Dark rust brown, lighter below. Undertail coverts white. No caruncle.

FLYING STEAMER-DUCK / Pato Vapor Volador 50
Tachyeres patachonicus
6a Male Similar to White-headed Steamer-Duck though slighter. Head gray-brown with white postocular stripe. Beak yellow, tipped dark.

6b Female Beak blue-green.

WHITE-HEADED STEAMER-DUCK / Pato Vapor Cabeza Blanca 49
Tachyeres leucocephalus
7a Male Large and thick-set. Heavy orange bill. Head whitish. Body mottled gray; vinaceous on chest. Belly white.

7b Female Head brownish. Postocular streak white. Bill greenish yellow.

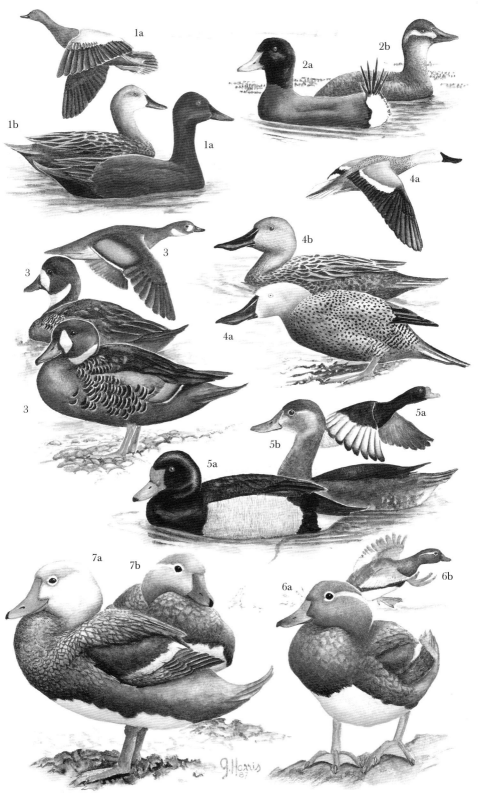

PLATE 10

DUCKS / Patos

SPECKLED TEAL / Pato Barcino 57
Anas flavirostris
1 Adult Relatively small and stocky. Head and neck gray-brown, finely speckled black. Back dark brown. Beak yellow.

SILVER TEAL / Pato Capuchino 58
Anas vesicolor
2 Adult Distinct black cap contrasts with pale "cheeks." Beak black, base orange. In flight, speculum metallic green, edged white.

**WHITE-CHEEKED (BAHAMA) PINTAIL /
Pato Gargantillo 53**
Anas bahamensis
3 Adult Head brown with well-defined semicircular patch of white on cheek and throat. Beak blackish, base red.

BROWN PINTAIL / Pato Maicero 59
Anas georgica
4 Adult Slender. Neck long and thin. Tail long and pointed. Head and neck pale brown, finely speckled darker. Bill yellow; culmen and tip black.

SOUTHERN WIDGEON / Pato Overo 56
Anas sibilatrix
5 Adult Head and neck black with white "face." Feathers of upperparts edged white. Belly white. Rufous on flanks. White wing bars in flight.

CRESTED DUCK / Pato Crestón 51
Lophonetta specularioides
6 Adult Cap and inconspicuous hindcrest dark brown. Face, neck, and underparts pale gray-brown. Chest mottled. In flight, secondaries broadly edged white; speculum vinaceous.

PLATE 11

AMERICAN VULTURES; EAGLES, HAWKS, AND HARRIERS / Jotes y Cóndores; Águilas, Aguiluchos y Gavilanes

TURKEY VULTURE / Jote de Cabeza Colorada 62
Cathartes aura
1 Adult Black with broad pale band on tip and trailing edge of wings. Soars with wings held in an open "V."

BLACK-CHESTED BUZZARD-EAGLE / Águila Mora o Escudada 64
Geranoaetus melanoleucus
2a Adult Wedge-shaped in flight. Chest dark gray. Belly white.

2b Juvenile Tail longer. Chest mottled black and brown.

WHITE-TAILED KITE / Milano Blanco 66
Elanus leucurus
3 Adult White with black eye stripe. Back pearl gray with black "wrists." Hovers.

RED-BACKED HAWK / Aguilucho Común o Ñanco 65
Buteo polyosoma
4a Male Head and back gray. Belly white. Tail band black.

4b Female Larger. Back rufous.

4c Juvenile Underparts streaked buff and brown.

4d Cinnamon phase Underparts cinnamon.

4e Dark phase Underparts dark brown.

LONG-WINGED HARRIER / Gavilán Grande 68
Circus buffoni
5a Male Long wings. Hood and upperparts blackish with white rump and facial "disk." Underparts white.

5b Female Upperparts brown. Belly white and buff.

CINEREUS HARRIER / Gavilán Ceniciento 67
Circus cinereus
6a Male Head and back gray. Belly cinnamon. Rump white. Underwing white with edge and tip black.

6b Female Head and back brown. Underwing barred brown.

1

1

1

2a

2a

2a

2b

3

3

3

4a

4b

4c

4b

4a

4d

4a

4e

4a

5b

5b

5b

5a

6a

6a

6a

6b

g. Harris

PLATE 12

CARACARAS AND FALCONS / Chimangos, Caranchos y Halcones

CHIMANGO CARACARA / **Chimango 69**
Milvago chimango
1 Adult Pale brown. Tail and wings faintly barred. Rump and base of primaries cream. Untidy flight.

CRESTED CARACARA / **Carancho 70**
Polyborus plancus
2a Adult Noticeable cap black. Neck and chest cream faintly barred black. Back and belly black.

2b Juvenile Brown. Neck streaked with cream.

APLOMADO FALCON / **Halcón Aplomado 72**
Falco femoralis
3 Adult Slender. Hood and mustache black. Eyebrow white. Black "waistcoat." Long tail, barred black and white. Lower abdomen pale rufous.

PEREGRINE FALCON / **Halcón Peregrino 71**
Falco peregrinus
4 Adult Pointed wings. Hood black. Back gray. Underparts cream, barred black. Rapid wing beats; glides.

AMERICAN KESTREL / **Halconcito Común 73**
Falco sparverius
5a Male Mustache, eye stripe, and nape black. Back and tail rufous, subterminal band black. Belly spotted black.

5b Female Back and tail barred. Belly streaked brown.

12

PLATE 13

COOTS, RAILS, ETC. / Gallaretas, Gallinetas, etc.

RED-GARTERED COOT / **Gallareta de Ligas Rojas 76**
Fulica armillata
1 Adult Slate gray. Pointed frontal shield and beak yellow, separated by a dark red line. Legs yellow with a red "knee."

WHITE-WINGED COOT / **Gallareta Chica 75**
Fulica leucoptera
2 Adult Slate gray. Rounded frontal shield and beak yellow. Trailing edge of secondaries white.

RED-FRONTED COOT / **Gallareta de Escudete Rojo 77**
Fulica rufifrons
3 Adult Slate gray. Longish frontal shield deep red. Beak yellow.

SPOT-FLANKED GALLINULE / **Pollona Chica 78**
Gallinula melanops
4 Adult Small. Short beak and frontal shield yellow green. Head and neck lead gray, darker around the beak. Back brown, flanks spotted white. Eye red.

PLUMBEOUS RAIL / **Gallineta Común 74**
Pardirallus sanguinolentus
5 Adult Bill long, slightly decurved, blue and red at base. Upperparts brown, below dark lead gray. Eye red. Legs pink.

SOUTH AMERICAN PAINTED SNIPE / **Aguatero 79**
Nycticryphes semicollaris
6 Adult Small. Beak long with downward curved tip. Upperparts dark brown, with crown stripe, eyebrow, and band on back buff white.

G. Harris

PLATE 14

OYSTERCATCHERS; STILTS; LAPWINGS AND PLOVERS / Ostreros; Teros Reales;
Teros y Chorlos

**AMERICAN OYSTERCATCHER / Ostrero
Común 80**
Haematopus palliatus (ostralegus)
1 Adult Back brown. Eye yellow, eye ring red.
Beak long, red. In flight, white wing bar.

**MAGELLANIC OYSTERCATCHER / Ostrero
del Sur 81**
Haematopus leucopodus
2 Adult Back black. Eye and eye ring yellow.
Beak long, bright red. In flight, large white wing
patches.

**BLACKISH OYSTERCATCHER / Ostrero
Negro 82**
Haematopus ater
3 Adult Entirely black, duller on back. Beak
bright red. Eye yellow, eye ring red.

**TAWNY-THROATED DOTTEREL / Chorlo
Cabezón 87**
Oreopholus ruficollis
4 Adult Stands upright. Throat tawny. Back
heavily streaked black and buff. Black patch on
belly.

SOUTH AMERICAN STILT / Tero Real 103
Himantopus melanurus
5 Adult Upperparts black (or brown in female). Forecrown and underparts pure white.
Beak long straight and slender, black. Legs
orange.

**RUDDY TURNSTONE / Vuelvepiedras
Común 90**
Arenaria interpres
6a Nonbreeding Brown and white markings on
head and chest. Legs orange.

6b Breeding Black and white markings on
head and chest.

**MAGELLANIC PLOVER / Chorlo de
Magallanes 89**
Pluvianellus socialis
7 Adult Dovelike. Gray. Eye red. Legs pink. In
flight, wing bar and outer tail feathers white.

SOUTHERN LAPWING / Tero Común 83
Vanellus chilensis
8 Adult Crest, chest, and "cravat" black. Back
gray-brown with coppery sheen. Wing pattern
black and white. Subterminal tail band black.

PLATE 15

PLOVERS; SANDPIPERS / Chorlos

GOLDEN PLOVER / **Chorlo Dorado 84**
Pluvialis dominica
1a Nonbreeding Broad pale eyebrow. Below off-white.

1b Breeding Upperparts black mottled yellow. Below black.

RUFOUS-CHESTED DOTTEREL / **Chorlo de Pecho Castaño 88**
Eudromias (Zonibyx) modestus
2a Breeding Rufous chest, outlined black. White eyebrow.

2b Nonbreeding Chest brown; belly white. White eyebrow.

SEMIPALMATED PLOVER / **Chorlito Semipalmado 86**
Charadrius semipalmatus
3a Nonbreeding Collar and nape white. Single chest band pale brown.

3b Breeding Line through crown and eye and single chest band black.

TWO-BANDED PLOVER / **Chorlito de Doble Collar 85**
Charadrius falklandicus
4a Breeding Two black chest bands. Nape rufous.

4b Nonbreeding Upperparts brown. Below white with two chest bands insinuated.

HUDSONIAN GODWIT / **Becasina de Mar 91**
Limosa haemastica
5a Nonbreeding Long neck and legs. Slightly upcurved beak. Back gray brown with white rump. Eyebrow whitish.

5b Breeding Underparts rufous.

LESSER YELLOWLEGS / **Chorlo Menor de Patas Amarillas 92**
Tringa flavipes
6 Adult Straight black bill shorter than that of Greater Yellowlegs. Long yellow legs. Back gray-brown streaked and spotted white.

GREATER YELLOWLEGS / **Chorlo Mayor de Patas Amarillas 93**
Tringa melanoleuca
7 Adult Slightly upcurved bill, longer than that of Lesser Yellowlegs. Long yellow legs. Back dark brown streaked and spotted white.

WHIMBREL / **Chorlo Trinador 100**
Numenius phaeopus
8 Adult Very long downward-curved beak. Pale eyebrow. Upperparts gray-brown and cream. Belly whitish.

J. Harris
97

PLATE 16

SANDERLINGS, KNOTS, AND SANDPIPERS; PHALAROPES; SNIPES; SEEDSNIPES / Chorlos; Falaropos o Chorlos Nadadores; Becasinas; Agachonas

SANDERLING / **Chorlito Blanco 96**
Calidris alba
1a Nonbreeding Small. Back pale gray. Belly white. Eye, beak, and legs black.

1b Breeding Head, chest, and back mottled and streaked rufous.

RED KNOT / **Chorlo Rojizo 95**
Calidris canutus
2a Nonbreeding Upperparts gray-brown. Noticeable white eyebrow. Belly mottled whitish.

2b Breeding Eyebrow, sides of head, and belly rufous. Back buff and dusky.

BAIRD'S SANDPIPER / **Chorlito Unicolor 99**
Calidris bairdii
3 Adult Upperparts brown. Eyebrow white. Belly white; breast lightly mottled brown. In flight, center of rump brown.

WHITE-RUMPED SANDPIPER / **Chorlito de Rabadilla Blanca 97**
Calidris fuscicollis
4 Adult Upperparts gray-brown (rufous in breeding plumage). Belly white; breast streaked brown. In flight, rump white.

PECTORAL SANDPIPER / **Playerito Pectoral 94**
Calidris melanotos
5 Adult Upperparts spotted dark brown. Breast brown; belly white. No wing bars. Center of rump brown.

SEMIPALMATED SANDPIPER / **Chorlito Enano 98**
Calidris pusilla
6 Adult Very small. Upperparts and sides of chest gray-brown. Eyebrow, cheek, and underparts white. Beak short. Legs black.

WILSON'S PHALAROPE / **Falaropo Tricolor 102**
Phalaropus tricolor
7 Nonbreeding Slender. Long neck and straight beak. Back pale gray, belly white. Eyebrow white. *Breeding:* Black and chestnut down sides of neck.

COMMON SNIPE / **Becasina Común 101**
Gallinago (Capella) gallinago paraguaiae
8 Adult Very long, straight bill. Eye stripe and cheek pale buff. Back mottled brown, black, and white. Belly buff, spotted black.

LEAST SEEDSNIPE / **Agachona de Corbata 104**
Thinocorus rumicivorus
9a Male Head and neck gray. Black "cravat." Back speckled brown.

9b Female Head, breast, and back speckled brown and white. Belly white.

GRAY-BREASTED SEEDSNIPE / **Agachona de Collar 105**
Thinocorus orbignyianus
10 Male Chin white-edged black. Neck and chest gray. Belly white. *Female:* Similar to female Least Seedsnipe but larger.

PLATE 17

GULLS; JAEGERS AND SKUAS; SHEATHBILLS / Gaviotas; Salteadores y Skúas; Palomas Antárticas

DOLPHIN GULL / Gaviota Austral 109
Larus (Leucophaeus) scoresbii
1a Breeding Pale blue-gray body. Black back. Beak, eye ring, and feet red.

1b Nonbreeding Dark hood.

1c Juvenile Gray-brown. Hood and tail band dark brown.

KELP GULL / Gaviota Cocinera 110
Larus dominicanus
2a Adult Back and upper wings black, edged white. Beak yellow.

2b Juvenile Mottled gray-brown, paler below. Tail with subterminal black band. Beak and legs blackish.

FRANKLIN'S GULL / Gaviota Pipixcan 111
Larus pipixcan
3 Nonbreeding Smaller than Brown-hooded Gull. Back dark gray. Gray-brown half-hood. Beak black. Legs dark gray.

OLROG'S OR BAND-TAILED GULL / Gaviota de Olrog, Cola Negra o Simeón 112
Larus (belcheri) atlanticus
4a Breeding Similar to adult Kelp Gull but smaller. Beak tipped black and red. Black band on tail.

4b Nonbreeding Gray hood.

BROWN-HOODED GULL / Gaviota Capucha Café 113
Larus maculipennis
5a Breeding Dark brown hood. Back pale gray. Belly often suffused with pink. Beak and legs red.

5b Nonbreeding White head with small dark patch behind eye. Beak and legs red.

PARASITIC JAEGER / Salteador Chico 108
Stercorarius parasiticus
6a Light phase Pointed wings. Black cap. Belly whitish. In flight, pale "windows" in wings. Central tail feathers slightly longer, hard to see.

6b Dark phase All of underparts dark gray brown.

SNOWY SHEATHBILL / Paloma Antártica 106
Chionis alba
7 Adult Pigeonlike. Entirely white. Short, conical beak, yellowish. Legs gray. Wings rounded.

ANTARCTIC SKUA / Skúa Antártico parda 107
Stercorarius (Catharacta) skua antarctica
8a Common race *(S. skua antartica)* Head and back brown, pale below. Pale "windows" in wings.

8b Chilean race *(S. skua chilensis)* Distinct cap. Underparts cinnamon.

TERNS / Gaviotines

SOUTH AMERICAN TERN / Gaviotín Sudamericano 114
Sterna hirundinacea
1a Breeding Solid black cap. Long, pointed red beak. Back uniform gray. Belly white. Legs red.

1b Nonbreeding Hindcrown flecked black. Beak variably black to dull red.

ANTARCTIC TERN / Gaviotín Antártico 117
Sterna vittata
2a Nonbreeding Underparts pearl gray. Hindcrown flecked black. Relatively short beak and legs, red to blackish.

2b Breeding Solid black cap. Beak and legs bright red.

ARCTIC TERN / Gaviotín Ártico 116
Sterna paradisea
3a Nonbreeding Underparts pale gray. Hindcrown flecked black. Legs very short; beak and legs dull red to blackish.

3b Breeding Solid black cap. Beak and legs bright red.

COMMON TERN / Gaviotín Golondrina 115
Sterna hirundo
4a Nonbreeding Hindcrown flecked black. Mantle gray, dark "shoulders." Beak black, legs red. Outer primary black.

4b Breeding Solid black cap. Beak red, tipped black.

CAYENNE TERN / Gaviotín de Pico Amarillo 118
Sterna eurygnatha
5a Breeding Cap and hindcrest solid black. Long, slender beak, yellow. Back pearl gray; belly white.

5b Nonbreeding Hindcrest black; forecrown white.

ROYAL TERN / Gaviotín Real 119
Sterna maxima
6a Breeding Beak orange red. Cap and crest black. Back silver gray. Belly white. Legs black.

6b Nonbreeding Hindcrown and crest black; forecrown white. Beak duller.

18

G. Harris

PLATE 19

DOVES; HUMMINGBIRDS; CUCKOOS; PARAKEETS; WOODPECKERS;
KINGFISHERS / Palomas; Picaflores; Cuclillos; Loros; Pájaro Carpinteros;
Martín Pescadores

PICUI GROUND-DOVE / Torcacita 122
Columbina picui
1 Adult Pale gray upperparts. Black and white
wing bars. Underparts pinkish white. Tail long,
black with outer feathers white.

EARED DOVE / Paloma Torcaza 121
Zenaida auriculata
2 Adult Brownish gray, underparts vinaceous
pink. Auricular spots black. Black spots on
wings. Legs pink. Tail tipped white, with black
subterminal band.

GREEN-BACKED FIRECROWN / Picaflor de Cabeza Granate 132
Sephanoides sephanoides
3 Male Upperparts bronze green, below gray-
green. Crown brilliant red. White spot behind
eye.

GUIRA CUCKOO / Pirincho 126
Guira guira
4 Adult Untidy crest cinnamon. Streaked appearance. Rump white. Long tail, tipped white;
wide subterminal black band.

BURROWING PARROT / Loro Barranquero 124
Cyanoliseus patagonus
5 Adult Long olive tail. Head and chest olive
brown. Belly bright yellow with red patch in
center. Flight feathers dark with blue sheen.

MONK PARAKEET / Cotorra 125
Myiopsitta monachus
6 Adult Front of head and breast gray. Rest
green, paler on underparts. Flight feathers dark
blue. Beak orange-horn.

CHECKERED WOODPECKER / Carpinterito Bataráz 134
Picoides mixtus
7 Male Small. Upperparts spotted white.
Crown streaked black and white; hindcrown
red.

RINGED KINGFISHER / Martín Pescador Grande 133
Ceryle torquata
8a Male Head and back pale blue-gray. White
collar. Breast and belly rufous.

8b Female Breast gray. "Necklace" white.

PLATE 20

TRUE OWLS; BARN OWLS; NIGHTJARS / Lechuzas; Lechuzas de Campanario; Atajacaminos

GREAT HORNED OWL / Ñacurutú 128
Bubo virginianus
1 Adult Very large. Catlike eyes and "ears tufts." Underparts finely barred.

BARN OWL / **Lechuza de Campanario 127**
Tyto alba
2 Adult Large, heart-shaped facial disks. Whitish underparts.

SHORT-EARED OWL / **Lechuzón de Campo 130**
Asio flammeus
3 Adult Well-defined, pale facial disk, dark around the eyes. Short—barely noticeable— "ear tufts." Underparts pale buff. Breast streaked brown.

BURROWING OWL / **Lechucita de las Vizcacheras 129**
Athene (Speotyto) cunicularia
4 Adult Relatively small. Pale sandy brown. White eyebrows. Underparts whitish, barred brown.

BAND-WINGED NIGHTJAR / **Atajacaminos Común 131**
Caprimulgus longirostris
5 Adult Rounded wings and long tail. White flashes on underside of wings and outer tail feathers. Whitish throat.

g Harris '85

PLATE 21

CANASTEROS, MINERS, ETC. / Canasteros, Camineras, etc.

PLAIN-MANTLED TIT-SPINETAIL / Coludito Cola Negra 142
Leptasthenura aegithaloides
1 Adult Wren-sized. Two very long, pointed tail feathers. Crown cinnamon, streaked with black.

LESSER CANASTERO / Canastero Coludo 143
Asthenes pyrrholeuca
2 Adult Mouse-brown above, paler below. Pale eyebrow. Long tail, rufous with blackish central feathers.

CORDILLERAN CANASTERO / Canastero Pálido 145
Asthenes modesta
3 Adult Upperparts gray-brown. Eyebrow and underparts whitish. Tail long, central feathers longest, blackish brown, edged whitish.

PATAGONIAN CANASTERO / Canastero Patagónico 144
Asthenes patagonica
4 Adult Beak short. Sides of head and breast gray; belly pale cinnamon. Tail relatively short and usually cocked, mostly black.

AUSTRAL CANASTERO / Canastero Manchado Chico 146
Asthenes anthoides
5 Adult Upperparts buff, streaked dark brown. Cinnamon shoulder and bar in flight.

WHITE-THROATED CACHALOTE / Coperote o Cachalote Pardo 147
Pseudoseisura gutturalis
6 Adult Mouse-brown, pale below. White chin patch outlined black. Beak strong and straight.

BAND-TAILED EARTHCREEPER / Patagón, Turco 138
Eremobius phoenicurus
7 Adult Back mouse-brown, underparts paler. Eyebrow white. Tail rufous, tipped black. Strong beak, slightly curved downward.

RUFOUS HORNERO / Hornero Común 139
Furnarius rufus
8 Adult Upperparts rufous. Tail reddish. Underparts pale. Chin whitish.

SCALE-THROATED EARTHCREEPER / Bandurrita Común 137
Upucerthia dumetaria
9 Adult Long, slender, downward-curved beak. White eyebrow; breast scaled. In flight, pale cinnamon wing bar, outer tail feathers dark brown.

WREN-LIKE RUSHBIRD / Junquero 141
Phleocryptes melanops
10 Adult Crown dark brown, spotted black. White eyebrow. Back heavily streaked black, white, and gray. Wings cinnamon and blackish. Short tail.

BAR-WINGED CINCLODES / Remolinera Parda 140
Cinclodes fuscus
11 Adult Upperparts and sides of head dark brown with well-marked white eyebrow and malar stripe. In flight, noticeable ochre wing bar.

COMMON MINER / Caminera Común 135
Geositta cunicularia
12 Adult Back pale brown. Eyebrow pale. Breast lightly scaled brown. In flight, wing band pale rufous; base of outer rectrices pale buff, subterminal band blackish.

SHORT-BILLED MINER / Caminera de Pico Corto 136
Geositta antarctica
13 Adult Short thick bill. Pale eyebrow. In flight, wings brown (not pale rufous), and tail whitish rather than buff at base.

PLATE 22

TYRANT FLYCATCHERS / Monjitas, Dormilonas, etc.

**WHITE-WINGED BLACK-TYRANT / Viudita
Común 154**
Knipolegus aterrimus
1a Male Black with white wing bars, noticeable
in flight.

1b Female Brown with bright cinnamon rufous
rump. Double wing bars buff.

**RUSTY-BACKED MONJITA / Monjita
Castaña 151**
Neoxolmis (Xolmis) rubetra
2 Adult Upperparts rufous. White eyebrow. Tail
black with white outer edges. Wings patterned
rufous, black, and white.

**GRAY-BELLIED SHRIKE-TYRANT / Gaucho
Común 148**
Agriornis microptera
3 Adult Upperparts brown. Pale eyebrow.
Throat white, heavily streaked black. Belly pale
brown. Strong, hook-tipped beak, lower
mandible orange.

**MOUSE-BROWN MONJITA / Monjita
Parda 150**
Agriornis (Xolmis) murina
4 Adult Upperparts gray-brown; eyebrow white.
Flight feathers edged white. Throat white,
streaked with black.

**DARK-FACED GROUND-TYRANT /
Dormilona Cara Negra 152**
Muscisaxicola macloviana
5 Adult Small. Face black. Crown dark brown.
Rest of upperparts gray. Underparts white.

**CHOCOLATE-VENTED TYRANT / Gaucho
Chocolate 149**
Neoxolmis rufiventris
6 Adult Blackish face. Back gray. Belly rufous.
In flight, wings patterned black, white, and ru-
fous.

**RUFOUS-BACKED NEGRITO /
Sobrepuesto 153**
Lessonia rufa
7a Male Small. Black with rufous back.

7b Female Upperparts brown with rufous back.
Below pale brown.

PLATE 23

FLYCATCHERS / Tyranidos

FORK-TAILED FLYCATCHER / Tijereta 157
Tyrannus savana
1 Male Black cap. Hidden crown yellow. Upperparts gray. Belly white. Long forked tail black.

SPECTACLED TYRANT / Pico de Plata 155
Hymenops perspicillata
2a Male All black with yellow beak and eye ring. In flight, a flash of white primaries.

2b Female Upperparts brown, streaked black. Rufous flight feathers.

GREAT KISKADEE / Benteveo 156
Pitangus sulphuratus
3 Adult Strong, straight black beak. Black cap with conspicuous white eyebrow. Upperparts brown. Throat white fading to yellow on belly.

WHITE-CRESTED TYRANNULET / Piojito Vientre Amarillo 158
Serpophaga subcristata
4 Adult Very small. Upperparts olivaceous gray with small pale eyebrow. Below pale gray, turning to yellowish on lower belly. Pale wing bars.

TUFTED TIT-TYRANT / Torito Pico Negro 161
Anairetes parulus
5 Adult Very small. Noticeable, erect crest plumes black. Eye pale. Upperparts brown; belly pale yellow, streaked brown.

WARBLING DORADITO / Doradito Común 159
Pseudocolopteryx flaviventris
6 Adult Very small. Crown and slight crest rufous. Upperparts brown. Underparts yellow. Wing bars rufous.

MANY-COLORED RUSH-TYRANT / Siete Colores de Laguna 160
Tachuris rubrigastra
7 Adult Very small. Brightly colored. Olive green and white. Center of crown and undertail coverts red. Underparts bright yellow.

PLATE 24

SWALLOWS; WRENS; MOCKINGBIRDS / Golondrinas; Ratonas; Calandrias

CHILEAN SWALLOW / Golondrina Azul 162
Tachycineta leucopyga
1 Adult Upperparts dark shiny blue. Underparts and rump white.

SOUTHERN MARTIN / Golondrina Negra 163
Progne elegans
2a Male Entirely black with a purple shine.

2b Female Underparts gray flecked with black.

BLUE-AND-WHITE SWALLOW / Golondrina Barranquera 164
Notiochelidon cyanoleuca
3 Adult Upperparts (including rump) blue black. Underparts white.

BARN SWALLOW / Golondrina Tijereta 165
Hirundo rustica
4 Adult Long forked tail; white band on underside. Upperparts blue black. Chin cinnamon. Belly pale buff.

HOUSE WREN / Ratona Común 167
Troglodytes aedon
5 Adult Very small. Brown, lightly barred darker on wings and tail. Eye stripe and underparts pale buff.

GRASS WREN / Ratona Aperdizada 166
Cistothorus platensis
6 Adult Very small. Carries tail cocked. Upperparts brown, very streaked white and black. Below buff.

WHITE-BANDED MOCKINGBIRD / Calandria de Tres Colas 169
Mimus triurus
7 Adult Upperparts gray-brown, rump rufous. Eyebrow whitish. In flight, striking black and white design.

PATAGONIAN MOCKINGBIRD / Calandria Gris 168
Mimus patagonicus
8 Adult Upperparts uniform mouse-gray. Eyebrow whitish. Wing bars white. Tail black, tipped white.

G. Harris
87

PLATE 25

THRUSHES; PIPITS; COWBIRDS, BLACKBIRDS; WEAVER FINCHES / Zorzales; Cachirlas; Tordos y Pecho Colorados; Gorriones

AUSTRAL THRUSH / Zorzal Patagónico 170
Turdus falklandii
1 Adult Head and back brown. Pale eye ring. Throat white, streaked black. Underside cream. Beak yellowish orange.

CORRENDERA PIPIT / Cachirla Común 171
Anthus correndera
2a New plumage Back streaked black with two white lines. Underparts whitish, heavily streaked black and buff on chest and sides.

2b Worn plumage Markings on chest and back less defined.

SHINY COWBIRD / Tordo Renegrido o Común 172
Molothrus bonariensis
3a Male Overall black with sheen. Beak strong and conical.

3b Female Entirely gray-brown, paler on underside.

HOUSE SPARROW / Gorrión 185
Passer domesticus
4a Male Nape and wings chestnut with black markings. Black "bib."

4b Female Back brown with black markings. White wing bar. Belly pale gray.

BAY-WINGED COWBIRD / Músico o Tordo Mulato 173
Molothrus badius
5 Adult Brownish gray with black mask. Wing feathers rufous, noticeable when sitting and in flight.

YELLOW-WINGED BLACKBIRD / Varillero Ala Amarilla 174
Agelaius thilius
6a Male Black with yellow "shoulders" very visible in flight.

6b Female Brown, streaked black. "Yellow shoulders."

LONG-TAILED MEADOWLARK / Pecho Colorado Grande 175
Sturnella loyca
7a Male Underparts and front edge of wings red. Underwings silvery.

7b Female Eyebrow and chin white. Center of belly tinged red.

PLATE 26

FINCHES; SISKINS / Mistos, Yales, Fringilos; Cabecita Negras

RUFOUS-COLLARED SPARROW /
Chingolo 183
Zonotrichia (Junco) capensis
1a Adult Small. Short crest. Head gray, black, and white. Rufous collar.

1b Juvenile Brown and gray, heavily streaked black.

MOURNING SIERRA-FINCH / Yal
Negro 180
Phrygilus fruticeti
2a Male Dark gray. Bib black. Beak orange yellow.

2b Female Gray, streaked black. Eyebrow and mustache white. Cheeks brown.

2c Juvenile Very streaked gray.

CARBON SIERRA-FINCH / Yal
Negro Chico 181
Phrygilus carbonarius
3a Male Slender. Black looking. Beak golden yellow.

3b Female Mouse-brown, with pale eyebrow. Breast streaked brown.

BLACK-THROATED FINCH / Yal de Ceja
Blanca 182
Melanodera melanodera
4a Male Eyebrow and malar stripe white. Black bib. Underparts and wing markings yellow.

4b Female Dull. Yellow in wings less pronounced.

GRAY-HOODED SIERRA-FINCH / Yal
Amarillo 179
Phrygilus gayi
5a Male Hood, wings, and tail gray. Back olivaceous yellow. Belly yellow.

5b Female Hood streaked black and white. Chin streaked brown. Back olive, belly caramel.

COMMON DIUCA-FINCH / Diuca
Común 178
Diuca diuca
6a Adult Gray. White chin and belly. Thigh rufous. Outer tail white.

6b Juvenile Paler and browner; markings less defined.

PATAGONIAN YELLOW-FINCH / Misto
Patagónico 176
Sicalis lebruni
7a Male Back uniform gray. Yellow wash on forecrown, cheeks, and belly.

7b Female Pale gray. Belly lightly flushed yellow in center.

BLACK-CHINNED SISKIN / Cabecita Negra
de Corbata 184
Spinus (Carduelis) barbata
8a Male Back olive brown. Belly pale yellow. Crown and chin black. Wing bar yellow.

8b Female Dull brown. Belly washed yellow.

GRASSLAND YELLOW-FINCH / Misto
Común 177
Sicalis luteola
9a Male Back brown, streaked darker. Underparts yellow.

9b Female Breast dull brown. Belly and flanks washed pale brown.

PLATE 27

MARAS AND CAVIES; OPOSSUMS; TUCO-TUCOS / Maras y Cuises; Marmosas; Tuco-Tucos

MARA OR PATAGONIAN HARE / Mara o Liebre Patagónica 207

Dolichotis patagonum

1a Adult Large. Square head; big eyes and ears. Rich rust brown, darker on back and rump. White "miniskirt."

1b Juvenile White "miniskirt" present at early age.

PATAGONIAN LESSER CAVY / Cuís Chico 206

Microcavia australis

2a Adult Rounded body; large head and no tail. Eyes large; ears not prominent. Gray-brown, underparts and feet paler.

2b Juvenile Smaller, with similar coloring.

PATAGONIAN OPOSSUM / Comadrejita Patagónica 186

Lestodelphys halli

3 Adult Larger than Dwarf Mouse-Opossum. Long muzzle. Tail often fattened near base. Eye ring black. Chestnut stain on throat and chest.

DWARF MOUSE-OPOSSUM / Marmosa Común 187

Thylamys (Marmosa) pusilla

4 Adult Mouse-sized. Pointed snout. Big eyes and large ears. Black eye ring. Tail often fattened near base. Upperparts gray-brown; belly pure white.

MAGELLAN'S TUCO-TUCO / Tuco-Tuco Magallánico 209

Ctenomys magellanicus

5a Adult Robust. Short "sawn-off" tail. Eyes set very high. Small ears. Gray-brown to pale sandy color.

5b Juvenile Dark brown or gray.

1a

1a

1b

2a

2b

3

4

5a

5b

PLATE 28

NEW WORLD MICE AND RATS / Ratones Cricétidos

PAMPAS FIELD MOUSE / Ratón Pajizo 195
Akodon molinae
1 Adult Small. Ears small. Tail relatively short.
Head and back yellowish brown, belly pale gray.

WHITE-EARED VESPER-MOUSE / Laucha Bimaculada 197
Calomys musculinus
2 Adult Very small. Tail same length as body.
Head and back pale brown or ochre. Belly white.

COMMON LEAF-EARED MOUSE / Rata Orejuda Común 201
Graomys griseoflavus
3 Adult Large; large ears and big eyes. Tail very long. Head and back grayish brown; underparts white, yellowish on flanks and throat.

HIGHLAND DESERT MOUSE / Laucha Colilarga Bayo 198
Eligmodontia typus
4 Adult Small with large ears. Tail long. Head and back ochre brown. Belly white.

RABBIT RAT / Rata Conejo 202
Reithrodon physodes (auritus)
5 Adult Large head with large, oval-shaped ears. Tail relatively short. Above gray-brown, richer on sides. Underparts white.

PLATE 29

KILLER WHALES AND OCEANIC DOLPHINS / Orcas y Delfines

KILLER WHALE / Orca 217
Orcinus orca
1 Male Largest dolphin. Very tall dorsal fin. Black with white patch behind eye and on belly. Gray saddle. *Female and juvenile:* Smaller with curved dorsal fin.

DUSKY DOLPHIN OR FITZ ROY'S DOLPHIN / Delfín Oscuro o de Fitz Roy 220
Lagenorhynchus obscurus
2 Adult Slender. Dark beak. Sickle-shaped dorsal fin. Steel gray with a conspicuous, pale "fork" extending forward and up from lower belly.

BOTTLE-NOSED DOLPHIN / Tonina Común 224
Tursiops truncatus gephyreus
3 Adult Distinct beak. Well-defined "melon." Sickle-shaped dorsal fin. Dark gray upperparts, paler below.

COMMERSON'S DOLPHIN / Tonina Overa 222
Cephalorhynchus commersonii
4 Adult Small and stocky. Rounded dorsal fin. Black, with distinct white "shawl."

PLATE 30

BALEEN WHALES / Ballenas

HUMPBACK WHALE / Yubarta o Ballena Jorobada 232

Megaptera novaeangliae

1 Adult Large. Low dorsal fin. Flippers very long, white. Upperparts dark gray. White patch on belly.

SOUTHERN RIGHT WHALE / Ballena Franca Austral 233

Eubalaena australis

2 Adult Large and robust. Blunt head with very curved mouth line. No dorsal fin. Callosities on head. Body usually black with a white blaze on belly.

SEI WHALE / Ballena Sei o Rorcual Mediano 230

Balaenoptera borealis

3 Adult Large and streamlined. Prominent curved dorsal fin. Head with single dorsal ridge. Upperparts dark gray. Underparts white.

PYGMY RIGHT WHALE / Ballena Franca Pigmea 234

Caperea marginata

4 Adult Relatively small and slender. Head smaller in relation to body than Right Whale; mouth line less curved. Prominent falcate dorsal fin. Upperparts gray

FIN WHALE / Rorcual Común 229

Balaenoptera physalus

5 Adult Very large and streamlined. Dorsal fin larger than Blue Whale. Head more slender and pointed. Upperparts dark gray. Right lower lip and underparts white.

BLUE WHALE / Ballena Azul 228

Balaenoptera musculus

6 Adult Very large and streamlined. Dorsal fin small and placed very far back. Head broad. Bluish gray, mottled paler.

MINKE WHALE / Ballena Minke o Rorcual Menor 231

Balaenoptera acutorostrata

7 Adult Relatively small and streamlined. Head slender and pointed. Tall, curved dorsal fin. Upperparts dark gray or black. Usually has a white patch on flippers.

PLATE 31

GUANACO; FOXES; CATS / Guanaco; Zorros; Gatos

GUANACO / Guanaco 246
Lama guanicoe
1 Adult Large, conspicuous and graceful. Upperparts rich rust; undersides white. Head, forehead, and muzzle gray.

COLPEO FOX / Zorro Colorado 235
Dusicyon culpaeus magellanicus
2 Adult Relatively large and thick-set compared to Argentine Gray Fox. Yellowish underfur with black guard hairs on back. Head, legs, and tail tawny.

ARGENTINE GRAY FOX / Zorro Gris 236
Dusicyon griseus
3 Adult Small, slight build. Large ears and very pointed muzzle. Coat gray with yellowish underfur. Legs, head, and tail pale tawny.

GEOFFROY'S CAT / Gato Montés 241
Felis geoffroyi
4 Adult Slender body and head. Tail thinner and longer than Pampas Cat. Upperparts pale sandy gray, paler below, with conspicuous black spots.

PAMPAS CAT / Gato del Pajonal 240
Felis colocolo
5 Adult Small and robust; thick legs and tail. Slightly mottled, sandy colored coat. Black stripes at the back of the front legs.

PLATE 32

WEASELS AND GRISONS; SKUNKS; ARMADILLOS / Hurones; Zorrinos; Piches y Peludos

PATAGONIAN WEASEL / Huroncito 237
Lyncodon patagonicus
1 Adult Small and slender. Much smaller than Little Grison. Top of head white.

LITTLE GRISON / Hurón Menor 238
Galictis cuja
2 Adult Slender. Forehead and two stripes down sides of neck white. Constant, nervous, quick movements when hunting.

PATAGONIAN SKUNK / Zorrino Patagónico 239
Conepatus humboldti
3 Adult Coat black, brown, or reddish. Tail relatively short. Two white stripes, one on each side of forehead and down the back.

PICHI / Piche Patagónico 192
Zaedyus pichiy
4 Adult Smaller and more rounded than the Larger Hairy Armadillo. Ears extend beyond carapace. Dark gray scales, edged pale horn.

LARGER HAIRY ARMADILLO / Peludo 191
Chaetophractus villosus
5 Adult Larger than the Pichi; carapace more "flattened." Ears do not extend beyond carapace. Sandy gray to rust brown.

PLATE 33

TRUE SEALS; SEA LIONS AND FUR SEALS / Focas y Elefantes Marinos; Lobos Marinos

SOUTHERN ELEPHANT SEAL / Elefante Marino del Sur 245

Mirounga leonina

1a Male Very large. No external ears. Enlarged proboscis. Body blue-gray to pale yellowish.

1b Female Much smaller. Lacks proboscis. Body gray to pale fawn.

1c Subadult male Steel gray when freshly molted.

1d Nursing pup All black from birth to weaning.

1e Weaned pup Silver gray from one month to one year.

SOUTH AMERICAN SEA LION / Lobo Marino del Sur 243

Otaria flavescens (byronia)

2a Male Visible external ears. Short rounded muzzle. Thickened neck and conspicuous mane. Body rich chestnut brown. Mane often pale.

2b Female Smaller. Graceful. Pale rust brown to ochre.

2c Pup All black at birth through first month.

SOUTH AMERICAN FUR SEAL / Lobo Marino de Dos Pelos 244

Arctocephalus australis

3a Male Longish external ears. Muzzle moderately long and pointed. Thick neck. Body dark gray to brown, underparts paler, often yellow rust.

3b Female Smaller. Graceful. Coat gray-brown.

160. MANY-COLORED RUSH-TYRANT / Siete Colores de Laguna
Tachuris rubigastra   *Plate 23*

Description. 4″ (10 cm). Small. Head black with yellow eyebrow. Center of crown and undertail coverts red. Back olive green. Wing streak and outer tail feathers white. Underparts bright yellow.

Behavior. Conspicuous and fairly tame. Climbs and flits among reeds capturing small insects. Repeated, pleasant metallic call.

Weaves pieces of dry reeds together to make a perfect, small cone-shaped nest, attached to a single upright reed. Lays 3 yellowish eggs.

Status and Habitat. Fairly common breeding resident in reed beds along Chubut River valley and Sarmiento.

Range. Central Patagonia to central Brazil and Ecuador.

161. TUFTED TIT-TYRANT / Torito Pico Negro
Anairetes parulus   *Plate 23*

Description. 4″ (10 cm). Very small. Noticeable black, erect crest plumes. Eye pale. Upperparts brown. Underparts pale yellow streaked brown.

Behavior. Tame. Usually alone. Perches briefly on branches; sometimes on exposed parts of bushes. Active inside bushes searching for insects. Calls when moving around vegetation. Quiet, cricketlike "zzweedeedee."

Builds a small, cup-shaped nest in bushes. Lays 3, very small cream-colored eggs.

Status and Habitat. Common breeding resident. Bush-covered steppe and Andean hillsides. Forests.

Range. From Tierra del Fuego, Patagonia, and western Argentina as far as Colombia.

SWALLOWS / Golondrinas
(Family Hirundinidae)

Slender birds with short necks and feet. Their wings are long and pointed and their flight is agile, with much gliding. They gather in flocks, often sitting on high wires. Usually migratory. Of 79 species found worldwide, 4 occur in coastal Patagonia.

162. CHILEAN SWALLOW / Golondrina Azul
Tachycineta leucopyga   *Plate 24*

Description. 5″ (13 cm). Upperparts dark shiny blue. Underparts and rump white. Tail and flight feathers black.

Behavior. In flocks. Flies low over open damp ground catching insects. Also, in flight, picks insects off bushes. Sometimes alights on ground.

Commonly nests under eaves of houses. Lays 3–5 eggs.

Status and Habitat. Fairly common visitor, especially April to August, in fields along Chubut River valley. Moist, grass-covered steppe near water. Forests.

Range. Tierra del Fuego and Patagonia.

163. SOUTHERN MARTIN / Golondrina Negra
Progne elegans *Plate 24*

Description. 8″ (20 cm). Relatively large. Entirely black with purple shine on head and back. *Female:* Upperparts similar to male, underparts gray, flecked with black.
Behavior. In flocks. *Active:* Flies back and forth in front of seaside cliffs and perches nervously on elevated structures (beacons). Drinks water in flight, scooping it from surface of inland lagoons. Produces a loud twitter.
　　Nests under ledges and eaves of houses. Lays 3 or 4 white eggs.
Status and Habitat. Common from early September to March. Common along shore, especially near cliffs around Península Valdés. Cliffs, hillsides, savanna, and towns. *Eaves of houses in Puerto Madryn, Chubut.*
Range. Northern Patagonia. Ranges as far as Peru between April and August.

164. BLUE-AND-WHITE SWALLOW / Golondrina Barranquera
Notiochelidon cyanoleuca *Plate 24*

Description. 7″ (18 cm). Upperparts (including rump) blue-black. Underparts white. Flight feathers and tail black.
Behavior. Tame. In flocks. Flies back and forth, low over the beaches capturing insects, also fairly high in the sky and over open steppe and embankments. *Several birds flying up and down a dip in a pebble beach at Punta Norte, Chubut, March 1983.* Makes loud buzzing and twittering sounds.
　　Nests in colonies in eaves, cliffs, and embankments. Lays 2–4 eggs.
Status and Habitat. Common September to April resident near the coast. Forest clearings, towns, steppe, cliffs, and beaches.
Range. Tierra del Fuego, Patagonia, and western Argentina to Colombia. In winter, southern populations range to northern South America.

165. BARN SWALLOW / Golondrina Tijereta
Hirundo rustica *Plate 24*

Description. 6″ (16 cm). Long, forked tail, shorter and ragged in some individuals. Upper-parts blue-black. Forehead and throat chestnut. Belly pale buff. White band on undertail.
Behavior. Alone or in small groups. *One bird flying around cliffs facing the sea, Golfo San José, Chubut, December 1991 (W. Conway & G. Harris).* Rapid, graceful flight, sometimes swooping close to ground, others circling high.
Status and Habitat. Uncommon, nonbreeding migrant between September and March. Varied terrain.
Range. Almost worldwide distribution. Breeds in North America and Eurasia.

WRENS / Ratonas
(Family Troglodytidae)

　　Small, rounded, thin-billed birds that often carry their tails cocked. Some species are commonly found around human dwellings. Many sing loudly. Mostly New World birds (one species in the Old World). Of the 59 species, 2 occur on the coast of Patagonia.

166. GRASS WREN / **Ratona Aperdizada**
Cistothorus platensis *Plate 24*

Description. 4″ (10 cm). Upperparts brown, very streaked white and black. Wings and tail barred brown and buff. Eyebrow and underparts buff. Legs orange.
Behavior. In small flocks. Inconspicuous, usually hidden in sedge grass or tangles of scrub. Carries tail cocked. Occasionally perches briefly in tops of grasses and sings. Produces trills and a buzzing "chirr. . . ."
Builds a large, ball-like nest on or near ground concealed in grass.
Status and Habitat. Uncommon. Marshy or sedgy areas and open grass near water.
Range. Tierra del Fuego to central Brazil and western South America to North America.

167. HOUSE WREN / **Ratona Común**
Troglodytes aedon *Plate 24*

Description. 4.5″ (11 cm). Upperparts brown, lightly barred darker on wings and tail. Eye stripe and underparts pale buff.
Behavior. Alone or in pairs. Not shy. Active; hops and flits around between trees and bushes. Often perches briefly in exposed places. Has a repeated, loud, pleasant trilling song.
Rounded nest in trees, bushes, buildings, or on the ground.
Status and Habitat. Common, particularly in farms, wooded parks, and towns. Varied open, semiopen areas and forests.
Range. Tierra del Fuego to Canada.

MOCKINGBIRDS / Calandrias
(Family Mimidae)

Slender, drab-colored birds with fairly long tails, well known as songsters. Though they are mostly insectivorous, they will eat fruit and other food occasionally. Found only in the New World. Of the 31 species, 2 occur on the coast of Patagonia.

168. PATAGONIAN MOCKINGBIRD / **Calandria Gris**
Mimus patagonicus *Plate 24*

Description. 9″ (22 cm). Upperparts uniform mouse-gray. Underparts pale gray brown. Eyebrow whitish. Wing bars white. Tail black, tipped white.
Behavior. Cocky, conspicuous, and tame. Terrestrial; chases after insects. Perches on exposed branches and posts and sings. Varied and tuneful song often continued for lengthy periods.
Builds nest of twigs lined with soft materials, in bushes. Lays 3–6 eggs.
Status and Habitat. Common breeding resident. Scrub-covered steppe and around farm buildings.
Range. All of Patagonia and western Argentina as far as the "Altiplano." Southernmost populations range northward April to September.

169. WHITE-BANDED MOCKINGBIRD / Calandria de Tres Colas
Mimus triurus *Plate 24*

Description. 9″ (22 cm). Head and back gray-brown, rump rufous. Eyebrow and underparts pale; flanks buff. In flight, primaries black, secondaries and mantle white; center of tail black, outer rectrices white.
Behavior. Shy. Alone or in family groups. Perches on exposed branches of bushes. Song is varied and musical.
   Builds a nest of twigs and grass, concealed in a bush. Lays 3 or 4 pale blue eggs with brown smudges.
Status and Habitat. Uncommon visitor from September to April. *One individual recorded on Península Valdés at Punta Norte, Chubut, November 1976, and another at Estancia La Anita, Península Valdés, Chubut, November 1983.* Savanna, bush-covered steppe, and open farmland.
Range. Northern Patagonia to southern Brazil.

THRUSHES / Zorzales
(Family Turdidae)

   A well-known family of land birds with many different species throughout the world. Thrushes have rounded bodies and straight beaks. When perched, they often let their wings sag and they flick their tails. Terrestrial as well as arboreal, thrushes are often heard rather than seen. Their songs are often melodious and repetitive. Males begin singing at the start of the breeding season, and to many people a thrush's song is the first sign of spring. There are 303 species in the world, one of which is found on the coast of Patagonia.

170. AUSTRAL THRUSH / Zorzal Patagónico
Turdus falklandii *Plate 25*

Description. 9.5″ (24 cm). Head and back dark brown. Eye ring pale. Throat white, streaked black; rest of underparts cream (spotted with brown in juvenile). Beak and legs yellowish orange.
Behavior. Found on ground or in dense tree canopy. Calls are varied and include a monotonous, reedlike whistle.
Status and Habitat. Uncommon near the coast. *One individual in a city park in Comodoro Rivadavia Chubut, November 1976.* Wooded areas including urban parkland and farms.
Range. Andean Tierra del Fuego and Patagonia.

PIPITS / Cachirlas
(Family Motacillidae)

   Family of sparrow-sized birds with pointed beaks and long hind claws. The brown or buff-colored plumage is often streaked with black. Different species are hard to tell apart in the field. Terrestrial and fairly unafraid, pipits nest on the ground. They are found worldwide. Of the 54 species, one is found on the east coast of Patagonia.

171. CORRENDERA PIPIT / **Cachirla Común**
Anthus correndera   *Plate 25*

Description. 5.5″ (14 cm). Upperparts buff streaked with black; 2 white lines down the back. Eyebrow white. Underparts whitish, heavily streaked buff, and black on chest and sides. Hindclaw very long and straight. Outer rectrices white.
Behavior. Terrestrial. When displaying during the breeding season, sings and flies high in the sky, almost disappearing from view before gliding back down to the ground. High twittering song.
    Builds a small nest on ground, lined with grass. Lays 4 eggs.
Status and Habitat. Common resident. Open grassland, pastures, and scrub desert.
Range. Tierra del Fuego to Peru.

COWBIRDS, BLACKBIRDS, AND MEADOWLARKS
/ Tordos, Varilleros y Pecho Colorados
(Family Emberizidae—Subfamily Icterinae)

Strikingly colored birds with straight sharp conical beaks. Most species are sexually dimorphic. In general, blackbirds are active, noisy, and gregarious. Many of them make hanging, basketlike nests, some breed colonially. Some species are parasitic, laying their eggs in other birds' nests and leaving them to the care of the foster parents: when the blackbird chick hatches, it competes aggressively for food, even pushing other eggs and chicks out of the nest. Of the 94 species, 4 are found on the coast of Patagonia.

172. SHINY COWBIRD / **Tordo Renegrido o Común**
Molothrus bonariensis   *Plate 25*

Description. 7.5 ″ (19 cm). Overall shiny indigo-black. Beak strong and conical. *Female:* Entirely gray-brown, paler on underside.
Behavior. Usually in flocks, sometimes large, on ground or in trees and bushes. Song of male is a pleasant watery warbling.
    Parasitic breeder. Common foster parents (see introduction to the family) are Rufous-collared Sparrows (*Zonotrichia capensis.*) These small finches can often be seen trying to feed young cowbirds, which are many times their size.
Status and Habitat. Common in farmland and urban areas; rarely in bush-covered and open steppe.
Range. From central Patagonia, much of Argentina, and South America to Panama.

173. BAY-WINGED COWBIRD / **Músico o Tordo Mulato**
Molothrus badius   *Plate 25*

Description. 7″ (18 cm). Body entirely brownish gray; black mask. Wing feathers brown with rufous edges. Rufous in wings noticeable when sitting and in flight. Strong conical beak.

Behavior. In groups, often together with previous species. All the birds in a flock sing a simultaneous confusion of songs.

Builds an open twig nest or takes possession of nests of other birds. Lays 5 eggs.

Status and Habitat. Common resident. *A flock of 15 birds foraging on the ground in an irrigated field near Trelew, Chubut, December 1976.* Farmland and parks.

Range. Northern Patagonia, central and northern Argentina, Uruguay, Brazil, Paraguay, and Bolivia.

174. YELLOW-WINGED BLACKBIRD / Varillero Ala Amarilla
Agelaius thilius   Plate 25

Description. 6.5″ (17 cm). Black with yellow "shoulders" visible both when sitting and in flight. Underparts and tail dark grayish brown. *Female:* Brown, streaked black. White eyebrow; yellow "shoulders." Long, pointed beak.

Behavior. In small flocks. Fairly conspicuous; flies out of reed beds and drops down nearby. Forages among reeds or scrub and on the ground. Has a varied gurgling song.

Breeds in colonies in reed beds or nearby brush. Nest is basket shaped and fixed to several upright reeds. Lays up to 4 eggs.

Status and Habitat. Common resident. *Several individuals in the reeds along the edge of an irrigation ditch near Trelew, Chubut, November 1976.* Reeds and tall grasses near freshwater lagoons and ditches.

Range. Much of Argentina to Peru.

175. LONG-TAILED MEADOWLARK / Pecho Colorado Grande
Sturnella loyca   Plate 25

Description. 8.5″ (22 cm). Long, pointed beak. Upperparts gray-brown with black markings. Eyebrow red and white. Much of underparts and front edge of wings red. In flight, undersides of wings silvery. *Female:* Eyebrow and chin white. Center of belly tinged red.

Behavior. Usually in pairs or family groups. In winter, congregates in large flocks. Found on ground or perched on tops of bushes and posts. Produces loud, wheezy calls and chirps, "Zeet-zeet-tooweezeee."

Nests on ground, concealed in tall grass. Nest is fairly large and loose, built of grass and twigs. Lays 3 or 4 eggs.

Status and Habitat. Abundant resident. One of the most common land birds of the region. Moist to dry bush- and grass-covered steppe and Andean hillsides.

Range. Tierra del Fuego, Patagonia to central Argentina, and northwest to Jujuy.

FINCHES / Mistos, Yales, etc.
(Family Emberizidae—Subfamily Emberizinae)

Large, well-known family found almost all over the world. These gregarious songbirds have short, conical bills for seed eating; some are frugivorous. Of the 410 species, 8 are found on the eastern coast of Patagonia.

176. PATAGONIAN YELLOW-FINCH / Misto Patagónico
Sicalis lebruni   *Plate 26*

Description. 5″ (13 cm). Upperparts uniform gray, flushed diffuse yellow on fore-crown, cheeks, and underparts. Wings grayish brown. *Female:* Entirely uniform gray, paler underparts, lightly flushed yellow in the center of belly.
Behavior. In pairs or flocks. Active and fairly shy. Perches on the ground or on bushes and cliffs. Loud and varied, canary-like song.
    Nests in crevices and holes in cliffs and embankments.
Status and Habitat. Common breeding resident. September to March, near cliffs along seacoast and embankments, water holes. In winter, in large flocks in open grass and bush-covered steppe.
Range. Tierra del Fuego, Patagonia, and Sierra de la Ventana.

177. GRASSLAND YELLOW-FINCH / Misto Común
Sicalis luteola   *Plate 26*

Description. 5″ (12 cm). Beak very short and conical. Upperparts brown, streaked darker. Underparts yellow. *Female:* Breast dull pale brown; belly and flanks washed with pale yellow.
Behavior. In flocks, sometimes large. Terrestrial. Flock flies off together. The call is a loud "zi-ziss."
    Nests on ground.
Status and Habitat. April to August, forms large flocks. *A flock of 20–30 birds seen feeding on new grass by the road on Península Valdés, Chubut, June 1982.* Grassland, savanna, and open fields; roadsides.
Range. From central Patagonia to Central America.

178. COMMON DIUCA-FINCH / Diuca Común
Diuca diuca   *Plate 26*

Description. 5.5″ (14 cm). Gray upperparts and chest with well-defined white chin. Belly white. Patch on thigh rufous. Tips of outer tail feathers white. *Juvenile:* Paler and browner, with adult markings less defined.
Behavior. In flocks. Terrestrial as well as in bushes; often perches on exposed branch to sing. Fairly tame. Pleasant, watery, gurgled song.
    Builds a stick nest lined with soft materials, in a bush. Lays 2–4 eggs.
Status and Habitat. Common breeding resident from September to March. Grass and bush-covered steppe and Andean hillsides, fields.
Range. Southern Patagonia to central Argentina and northwest as far as Jujuy. In winter, southern populations range northward.

179. GRAY-HOODED SIERRA-FINCH / Yal Amarillo
Phrygilus gayi   *Plate 26*

Description. 6″ (15 cm). Gray hood, wings, and tail. Back olivaceous, and underparts yellow. *Female:* Hood streaked black and white. Chin streaked brown. Upperparts olivaceous, underparts caramel.

Behavior. In flocks. Conspicuous and fairly tame. Terrestrial and in bushes. Pleasant song and a metallic contact call.

Nests in bushes close to or on ground, well concealed by vegetation. The nest is large and lined with soft material. Lays 2–5 eggs.

Status and Habitat. Common near the coast of Santa Cruz. Uncommon visitor on the seashore of Chubut and Río Negro. *One bird at Punta Tombo, Chubut, November 1981; another in open bush-covered steppe on the outskirts of Puerto Madryn, October 1984.* Andean woodland; occasionally in bush-covered steppe at sea level.

Range. Tierra del Fuego, Patagonia, and western Argentina to Peru.

180. MOURNING SIERRA-FINCH / Yal Negro
Phrygilus fruticeti   *Plate 26*

Description. 6″ (15 cm). Mostly dark gray. Bib black. Beak orange yellow. White wing bars. *Female:* Gray, upperparts streaked black. Eyebrow and mustachial streak white; sides of face brown. *Juvenile:* Heavily streaked black.

Behavior. In flocks, on the ground or in bushes. Male perches, often hunched, on exposed branches at top of bushes as he calls. Sallies out in nuptial flight, rising straight into the air, then calling, glides on stiff wings back to same perch. From August to February, produces a high-pitched "chweeeee-chweedldeet." Contact call is a short "chip."

Builds a lax nest of grasses in the lower branches of bushes. Lays 2 or 3 eggs.

Status and Habitat. Common, year-round resident principally in the coastal areas. *Abundant in Piquillín (Condalia microphylla) and Hume (Suaeda divaricata) bush areas in Chubut.* Bush-covered steppe and Andean hillsides.

Range. Patagonia and western Argentina to Peru.

Similar species. Larger and stockier than Carbon Sierra-Finch

181. CARBON SIERRA-FINCH / Yal Negro Chico
Phrygilus carbonarius   *Plate 26*

Description. 5″ (13 cm). Slender. Very dark gray with black underparts; wings dark brown. Beak golden yellow. *Female:* Mouse-brown; pale eyebrow. Breast streaked brown

Behavior. In pairs. Terrestrial and in bushes. Nuptial flight similar to previous species. Call reminiscent of previous species but distinctly higher pitched.

Status and Habitat. Uncommon. *A family of 3 birds in "Creosote" (Suaeda divaricata) bush area 10 miles (15 km) west of Puerto Madryn, Chubut, January 1984; one bird at Punta Tombo, Chubut, December 1988.* Bush-covered steppe.

Range. Northern Patagonia to Mendoza. April to September, ranges as far as northern Argentina.

Similar species. Differs from more common and larger Mourning Sierra-Finch in having a more slender body; golden beak of male in more striking contrast with blackish body. Female paler.

182. BLACK-THROATED FINCH / **Yal de Ceja Blanca**
Melanodera melanodera   *Plate 26*

Description. 5.5″ (14 cm). Head gray. Eyebrow and mustachial streak white. Black throat. Upperparts olivaceous. Underparts washed with yellow. Yellow edges to flight feathers very noticeable in flight. *Female:* Throat pale yellow. Upperparts brown and yellowish white and wing feathers edged whitish.

Behavior. Alone or in small dispersed flocks. Between April and September, gathers in large flocks. Very terrestrial although also sits on posts and branches. Feeds on fruit and seeds it finds on ground. Song is short and musical.

    Nests on ground, hidden among bushes. Lays 3 or 4 pale turquoise eggs.

Status and Habitat. Common resident in low grassland and areas with "mata negra" (*Junellia tridens*). Roadsides, embankments, and beaches. *Solitary birds and small flocks on the roadsides between Río Gallegos and Cabo Vírgenes, Santa Cruz, November 1994, and Río Gallegos and Río Turbio, Santa Cruz, December 1995.*

Range. Southern Santa Cruz and Tierra del Fuego. South of Chile.

183. RUFOUS-COLLARED SPARROW / **Chingolo**
Zonotrichia (Junco) capensis   *Plate 26*

Description. 5″ (12 cm). Sparrow-like but smaller. Short crest. Markings on head gray, black, and white. Rufous collar. *Juvenile:* Upperparts brown and gray. Underparts pale, heavily streaked black.

Behavior. Friendly and conspicuous. Song is a distinctive, loud, trilled warble. Calls have distinct geographical differences.

    Nests in bushes, trees, grasses, and concealed on ground. Builds small cup of grass and soft materials. Lays 3–5 eggs.

Status and Habitat. Very common breeding resident. One of the most abundant birds in Patagonia. Found in varied habitats: open areas, woodland, bush-covered steppe, parks.

Range. Tierra del Fuego, all South America to southern Mexico.

SISKINS / Cabecita Negras
(Family Fringillidae)

    Small birds with conical beaks. Closely related to the previous family, they are gregarious, with varied thin, trilled voices. Of the 112 species, one is found on the coast of Patagonia.

184. BLACK-CHINNED SISKIN / **Cabecita Negra de Corbata**
Spinus (Carduelis) barbata   *Plate 26*

Description. 5″ (12 cm). Upperparts olive brown. Sides of head and underparts pale yellow. Crown and chin black. Wing bars bright yellow (visible when perched and in flight). *Female:* Duller, underparts faintly washed yellow. Wing bars bright yellow.

Behavior. In small flocks, forages on ground and in trees. Produces a thin trill.

Nests in branches of trees. Builds an open cup of grass and moss, lined with feathers. Lays 3–6 eggs.

Status and Habitat. Common particularly during spring and fall migrations. *A flock of 15–20 birds on dry thistle stems in the Chubut River valley below Dique Ameghino, Chubut, February 1982; a flock of 10 in elm trees and on the ground nearby in Puerto Madryn, Chubut, May 1985.* Southern Andean forests. Trees in urban areas.

Range. Southern Andean forests, foothills, and trees in the steppe.

WEAVER FINCHES / Gorriones
(Family Ploceidae)

Small birds with conical beaks very similar to the finches. They weave elaborate nests, and are found mainly in the Old World. Of the 156 species, one is found on the coast of Patagonia, introduced from Europe.

185. HOUSE SPARROW / Gorrión
Passer domesticus   *Plate 25*

Description. 5″ (13 cm). Nape and wings chestnut with black markings. White wing bar. Black "bib." *Female:* Upperparts brown with black markings on back and white wing bar. Underparts sandy.

Behavior. Very well known. Gregarious, opportunistic; found in urban areas and near human dwellings. Very noisy and not shy. Terrestrial; also in trees and city buildings. Voice is a harsh chirping.

Nests in eaves of buildings.

Status and Habitat. Abundant breeding resident. Introduced from Europe. Common in towns and farms. Mainly associated with human dwellings, is rarely seen in uninhabited parts.

Range. Argentina and much of South America as well as other continents. Almost cosmopolitan.

MAMMALS / Mamíferos

(Class Mammalia)

Animals with backbones. Warm-blooded, bodies insulated with hair. Females have mammary glands to nurse their young. Most present-day mammals produce placentas during gestation and give birth to live young. Humans are placental mammals; marsupials are mammals that, during gestation, do not produce placentas; and platypus and echidnas are a small group of egg-laying mammals.

(Order Marsupialia)

Marsupials have very short gestation periods of 12–28 days. The young are very poorly developed at birth. Attached to one of the mother's mammary glands, which are often—but not always—situated in a pouch, they continue to grow.

OPOSSUMS / Marmosas
(Family Didelphidae)

Relatives of kangaroos and wombats, opossums are now by far the most abundant marsupials in South America. Most have a short and dense coat, in some species with long guard hairs. Coloring ranges from white or cream to brown and black; several species have facial masks. Most have litters of 8 or more young at a time and many species do not have a pouch. Instead, newborn young are protected by a small fold of abdominal skin. Among the earliest groups of mammals, the first marsupials were discovered on late Cretaceous deposits in North America; they inhabited the land over 65 million years ago, before the existence of such varied, present-day mammals as whales, bats, and horses. There are 76 species of South American opossums, of which 2 are found in coastal Patagonia.

186. PATAGONIAN OPOSSUM / Comadrejita Patagónica
Lestodelphys halli   *Plate 27*

Description. Body 6″ (15 cm); tail 4″ (10 cm). Upperparts mouse-gray. Underparts cream to white, with chestnut stain on throat and chest. Elongated muzzle. Eye patch black. Large ears. Fat is stored in the tail, thickening it considerably, particularly at the base.

Behavior. Little known. Feeds on small rodents. *Catches and eats mice in captivity (O. Pearson). Recorded among cavy burrows (Cavia sp.). Male caught in Lihué Calel, La Pampa, had the remains of small mammal fur in its stomach, December 1986 (O. Pearson).*

Status and Habitat. Rare. Most records are from remains found on the dry steppe in the regurgitated pellets of owls. Arid scrub and grasslands. *One adult at dusk in a bush-covered area at Monte León, Santa Cruz, February 1986 (M. Oliva Day).*

Range. Central to northern Patagonia and including La Pampa. *Recorded on coast of Chubut (Bahía San Jorge).*

Similar Species. Larger than the following species, with shorter tail, larger feet, and longer claws; muzzle shorter.

187. DWARF MOUSE-OPOSSUM / Marmosa Común
Thylamys (Marmosa) pusilla   *Plate 27*

Description. Body 4″ (10 cm). Tail 4.5″ (11 cm). Small and mouselike, with a pointed snout, big eyes, and large ears. Tail often noticeably thickened, particularly near base. Fine, soft body fur. Upperparts gray-brown, fading to ochre on sides. Underparts and feet pure white. Eyes surrounded by conspicuous black markings. Feet small.

Behavior. Usually alone. Mainly nocturnal and secretive. Forages on ground and in bushes for insects, small vertebrates, small birds' eggs, and fruit. Hunts with quick, agile movements. Usually silent. Makes a nest of mosses and leaves inside small holes and caves in the ground. Gestation lasts 12–14 days. Does not have a pouch. Newly born offspring cling to fur and mammary glands of the mother.

Status and Habitat. Uncommon resident. Rarely seen in daytime. *Lone individuals recorded in dry areas covered with Piquillín and Quillimbai bushes, Península Valdés, Chubut, April 1981 and September 1984.* Arid bush-covered areas.

Range. North and central Argentina, southwestern Bolivia, and Paraguay.

BATS / QUIRÓPTEROS O MURCIÉLAGOS

(Order Chiroptera)

Bats are the only vertebrates besides birds capable of sustained flight. Gregarious.

The flight-enabling membrane (or patagium) of bats extends between the digits, arms, and legs. Although the general wing pattern is the same, there are considerable differences in shape among the various species. The legs are generally weak, although some species can crawl and even jump. When roosting, bats typically hang upside down. Many hibernate during winter, and body temperature drops to save energy.

Most produce calls above human hearing range—ultrasounds—and echolocate to navigate, feed, and find their roosts. However, some rely principally on eyesight. Many species capture insects in flight. Some feed on fruit, others on fish, or they capture their prey on the ground. One species, the common vampire, found in Central America and northern South America, feeds by sipping blood from wounds it inflicts, mainly in cattle.

Bats are found all over the world and in all habitats except for polar regions. On many islands such as New Zealand and Hawaii, they are the only indigenous mammals. Three species have been recorded in coastal Patagonia.

FREE-TAILED BATS / Murciélagos Cola de Ratón o Molosos
(Family Molossidae)

Bats with long tails extending beyond the tail membrane. They feed on insects which they catch in flight. Some species roost in small groups; others form immensely large colonies. There are 91 species in the world; one is found in eastern Patagonia.

188. MEXICAN FREE-TAILED BAT / Moloso Común
Tadarida brasiliensis

Description. Body 2.5″ (6.5 cm); wingspan 10″ (25 cm) The size of a small mouse. Fur of upperparts dark brown and underparts paler. Eyes small. Ears almost meet at top of head. Wings dark. Tail extends beyond tail membrane.

Behavior. Alone or in loose flocks. Active during twilight and at night. Captures insects in flight. Will crawl on level surfaces, using the small claws on its wings to clamber back up to its perch. Produces metallic clicks to echolocate prey. Migrates over 800 miles (1300 km) from summer to winter sites. Does not hibernate. Breeds and roosts in colonies, usually in caves, hollow trees, and buildings.

Status and Habitat. Fairly common. Varied habitats; savanna, forests, and wide river valleys; towns and cities. *One adult was found on a seaside street in Puerto Madryn, Chubut, October 1994.*

Range. From northern Patagonia, much of South America to southwestern USA, Antilles, and Bahamas.

COMMON OR VESPER BATS / Murciélagos Chicos
(Family Vespertilionidae)

Pleasant-looking bats. The tail does not extend beyond the tail membrane. Mainly insectivorous. Some roost alone, others form colonies of over a million animals. Found worldwide except for polar regions. Of the 319 species, 2 are found in eastern Patagonia.

189. LESSER LARGE-EARED BAT / Murciélago Orejón Chico
Histiotus montanus

Description. Body 2.5″ (6 cm); wingspan 9.5″ (24 cm). Tail does not extend beyond the edge of the tail membrane, and the membrane itself is triangular shape. Body covered in dense gray to pale brown, longish fur. Wings gray. Large ears, same color as wings. Ears do not meet at top of head.

Behavior. Often alone. Nocturnal. Agile but slow flight. Searches for insects on the wing. Produces metallic clicks. Hidden during daytime. Roosts in small colonies, inside caves, in cliffs, and on roofs of buildings. Hibernates in winter. Is able to crawl, using feet and wings. Usually gives birth to a single offspring.

Status and Habitat. Common resident. Occasionally seen at dusk, foraging for insects around buildings on the Patagonian steppe. *Recorded on warm evenings from September to April on the eastern shore of Golfo San José, Chubut.* Forests, wooded areas, and bush-covered steppe to seacoast. Buildings.

Range. Patagonia to southern Brazil and along the west coast to Ecuador.

190. ARGENTINE MOUSE-EARED BAT / Murciélago Común
Myotis levis

Description. Body 2″ (5 cm); wingspan 8.75″ (22 cm). Small. Tail does not extend beyond edge of tail membrane, and the membrane itself is almost triangular in shape. Body fur pale to dark brown. Wings pale brown. Ears short and triangular.

Behavior. Hidden during the day. Becomes active at dusk and during the night. Flies with rapid changes of direction as it chases insects. Produces metallic clicks. Roosts and breeds under roofs of houses. Hibernates in winter.

Status and Habitat. Fairly common and widespread. Varied; savanna, wooded areas, highlands; towns.

Range. From Tierra del Fuego over most of Argentina, Uruguay, Paraguay, and southern Brazil.

EDENTATES / EDENTADOS

(Order Edentata)

A small group with a variety of unique forms that include the anteaters, sloths, and armadillos. "Edentate," meaning "no teeth," is in fact misleading. The only member of the order that lacks teeth altogether is the anteater. Although they do not have incisors, canines, and premolars, the remaining members—armadillos and sloths—have simple molars that grow throughout life. Edentates have large claws for climbing, feeding, or burrowing.

ARMADILLOS / Peludos y Piches
(Family Dasypodidae)

Terrestrial, burrowing edentates, characterized by a bony shell or carapace. All have strong claws for burrowing and foraging. Each jaw is lined with simple molars; and they have a toothless gap in the front of the mouth. The family evolved in South America and is almost restricted to this continent. There are 20 species, 2 of which occur in eastern Patagonia.

191. LARGER HAIRY ARMADILLO / Peludo
Chaetophractus villosus   *Plate 32*

Description. Body 14″ (36 cm). Tail 5.75″ (15 cm). Upperparts covered with small rectangular scutes distributed in bands, forming a rounded, pale gray to rust brown carapace. Eight of the central bands are articulated. Long hairs protrude between the scutes, forming a thin cover. Scutes also circle the tail in bands. A tough frontal plate covers top of head. Underparts pinkish gray to yellowish, sparsely covered with long hairs. Powerful legs armed with large claws. Male slightly larger than female. Penis visible on ventral surface of male, and two pectoral mammary teats visible in female.

Behavior. Alone or in small groups. Shy. Principally nocturnal, though often active during day. Eyesight poor but sense of smell well developed. Omnivorous; feeds on live and dead animal and vegetable matter. Skillful burrower; builds complex networks of tunnels covering several yards and having several entrances. Agile, escapes from danger at a brisk trot, taking cover under bushes, in holes, or by burrowing. Silent. Where unmolested, it may become remarkably tame and bold around houses in the "campo," especially where it is fed. Has been known to live over 15 years in captivity.

Usually gives birth in spring, to 2—less commonly one or 3—young, which are reared inside the burrow till several months old.

Status and Habitat. Common resident. Varied habitats depending on available food (human refuse, edible waste, and carrion) and soft terrain for digging. Open fields, steppe, wooded areas, savanna, often near farmhouses.

Range. Patagonia and central Argentina to Paraguay and Chile. *Introduced by lighthouse keepers before 1970s on Isla Leones, Chubut.*

Similar Species. Larger and heavier than the following species; horny plates, of carapace and frontal plate, less defined; ears relatively larger.

192. PICHI / Piche Patagónico
Zaedyus pichiy   *Plate 32*

Description. Body 9″ (23 cm); tail 4″ (10 cm). Upperparts covered with small, rectangular, clearly defined scutes, with black centers and pale cream contours. These are arranged in bands to form a very rounded carapace. Eight of the central bands are articulated. Scutes along edges of carapace are a pale horn color, in contrast with the back. Sparse hairs grow from spaces between scutes. Top of head covered with scutes forming a frontal plate. Short ears barely protrude from edge of plate. Underparts soft and pinkish, sparsely covered with hairs. Strong legs with long claws.

Behavior. Solitary. Shy. Active during day, rarely at night. Trots about the desert, occasionally stopping to sniff at ground and dig. Superb burrower. Digs shallow burrows when foraging. Deeper burrows, up to 8 ft (2.6 m) long and 5 ft (1.6 m) below surface are used as refuges. Feeds primarily on spiders, insects, and vegetable matter, including bulbs, and beans and pods of "Algarrobillo" bushes. Silent. In winter goes into a torpor.

Young born in January and February. Litter size usually 2 but ranges from one to 3.

Status and Habitat. Fairly common resident. Seen during warm weather from September to April, on roadsides and dry, open, grass-covered to bushy steppe. Stays away from human dwellings and rubbish dumps.

Range. Central and southern Argentina to Strait of Magellan. *Introduced by lighthouse keepers before 1970s on Isla Tova, Chubut.*

Similar Species. Smaller and lighter than previous species; ears smaller; scales on carapace more clearly marked, and those along the edge of the carapace distinctly horn colored.

LAGOMORPHS / LAGOMORFOS

(Order Lagomorpha)

Small to large mammals with soft dense fur. Eyes are placed very high on the head. Ears are large; tail is short. Unlike rodents, hares, rabbits, and pikas, they have two pairs of constantly growing incisors instead of only one pair. Herbivorous.

HARES / Liebres
(Family Leporidae)

A well-known family which includes hares and rabbits and lives in close association with man. They are cosmopolitan except in the Antarctic and parts of the Amazon. One species has been introduced in eastern Patagonia.

193. EUROPEAN HARE / Liebre Europea
Lepus europaeus

Description. Body 25″ (60 cm); tail 2.75″ (6 cm). Ears long and slender. Eyes large. Upperparts yellowish brown; underparts white. Tail short. Forefeet have 5 toes; hindfeet 4 toes.

Behavior. Usually alone. Shy. Mainly nocturnal although also active during day. Swift runner. Feeds on grasses, shoots, seeds, and other vegetable matter. Produces a "foot thump" when alarmed. Will scream if hurt or captured. Does not dig a burrow, but uses a shallow scrape usually concealed at base of a bush or clump of grass, to rest and bear young. Young leverets are covered with fur at birth and can open their eyes immediately.

Status and Habitat. Common resident in cultivated fields and moist grasslands. Less common in open, arid steppe.

Range. Introduced from Europe in 1888 in Rosario, Santa Fe. Extended from there throughout Argentina.

Similar Species. Smaller and lighter than the mara, with longer ears; lacks mara's dark rump and white "miniskirt."

RODENTS / ROEDORES

(Order Rodentia)

Most rodents are squat, compact animals with short legs and a tail. The sexes look alike. Nearly 40% of all mammal species are rodents. They are a highly successful group, found in a wide range of habitats throughout the world. Each jaw has a single pair of large, constantly growing incisors. The lips can be drawn in, behind the incisors, so that the animals can gnaw with their mouths closed.

NEW WORLD MICE AND RATS / Ratones Cricétidos
(Family Muridae: Cricetidae, subfamily Hesperomyinae)

These small rodents are found throughout North and South America, in virtually every habitat except for polar regions. Of the 366 species, 9 are found in eastern Patagonia.

194. PATAGONIAN FIELD MOUSE / Ratón Patagónico
Akodon iniscatus (nucus)

Description. Body 3.5″ (9 cm); tail 2″ (5 cm). Small. Ears small and rounded. Tail relatively short. Upperparts brownish gray; distinctive white patch below the eye not always present. Belly pale gray.
Behavior. Alone or in dispersed groups. Fairly diurnal.
Status and Habitat. Records for bush-covered steppe around Puerto Madryn and Punta Norte, Chubut. Occasional population blooms. Temperate, dry, bush-covered steppe.
Range. Central and northern Patagonia.

195. PAMPAS FIELD MOUSE / Ratón Pajizo
Akodon molinae   *Plate 28*

Description. Body 3.25″ (8.5 cm); tail 2.5″ (6.5 cm). Small. Tail relatively short. Ears small. Upperparts yellowish brown, below pale gray.
Behavior. Alone or in dispersed groups. Forages on ground; feeds on vegetable matter. Principally active at night.
Status and Habitat. Records around Puerto Madryn, Chubut. Population blooms when food is abundant. Grassy areas and mixed, bush-covered steppe.
Range. Northeastern Patagonia to eastern and central Argentina.

196. BAY-TIPPED FIELD MOUSE / Ratón Hocico Bayo
Akodon xanthorinus

Description. Body 3.5″ (9 cm); tail 2″ (5 cm). Tail relatively short. Upperparts bay brown; underparts gray. Face, tail, and legs pale rufous.

Behavior. Feeds mainly on plant material. Nests in concealed places.
Status and Habitat. Open grasslands, savanna, and scrub steppe.
Range. All of Argentine Patagonia.

197. WHITE-EARED VESPER-MOUSE / Laucha Bimaculada
Calomys musculinus   *Plate 28*

Description. Body 2.75″ (7 cm); tail 2.75″ (7 cm). Very small. Upperparts ochre chestnut; underparts white. Sometimes has white tufts behind ears, only noticeable in the hand.
Behavior. Usually on ground, but also climbs bushes. Feeds mainly on plant material. Nests in concealed places. Occasionally in houses.
Status and Habitat. At times found inside houses on farms or on outskirts of villages and towns. Open grasslands, savanna, and scrub steppe.
Range. Northern and central Argentina to northeastern Patagonia.
Note. Is a reservoir of Rickettsial disease (*fiebre hemorragica*) in some areas.

198. HIGHLAND DESERT MOUSE / Laucha Colilarga Bayo
Eligmodontia typus   *Plate 28*

Description. Body 3.5″ (9 cm): Tail 4.25″ (11 cm). Small with large ears. Eyes large. Upperparts ochre chestnut. Belly white, turning to straw color on sides.
Behavior. Alone or in nestbound families. Usually silent; will squeak if frightened or when fighting. Omnivorous, although diet mainly includes a variety of vegetable materials.
   Builds soft nests in concealed places, often near houses. Litters of 5 or 6 young. Born from early spring through summer.
Status and Habitat. Common resident in dry, scrub desert. Also around and in farm buildings. *One adult found lethargic following a cool night in a man-made hole in the ground near an isolated field station on east shore of Golfo San José, Chubut, May 1981.*
Range. Patagonia; much of central and northern Argentina, Chile to southern Peru.
Similar Species. Similar to the following species but much smaller; has finer fur and richer coloring on flanks and throat.

199. DARWIN'S LEAF-EARED MOUSE / Rata Orejuda Panza Gris
Phyllotis darwinii

Description. Body 4.75″ (12 cm); tail 5.5″ (14 cm). Ratlike with large eyes and ears. Upperparts bay with chestnut, brown, or gray tones. Belly gray. Tail very long (longer than body length), covered with short, fine hair.
Behavior. Alone or in nestbound families. Active at night. Omnivorous; diet includes a variety of vegetable materials. Usually silent; squeaks if frightened or when fighting.
Status and Habitat. Common resident in dry scrub desert.
Range. Southern continental Patagonia and western Argentina.

200. SHORT-TAILED LEAF-EARED MOUSE / **Rata Orejuda Patagónica**
Phyllotis miccropus

Description. Body 3.5″ (12 cm); tail 4.25″ (5 cm). Ratlike with large ears. Upperparts dark chestnut. Belly gray. Tail short (shorter than body length), covered with short, fine hair.

Behavior. Hides during daytime, becomes active at night. Omnivorous; diet includes variety of vegetable materials.

Status and Habitat. Dry, rocky terrain and scrub desert.

Range. Southern and western continental Patagonia.

201. COMMON LEAF-EARED MOUSE / **Rata Orejuda Común**
Graomys griseoflavus   *Plate 28*

Description. Body 5.5″ (14 cm); tail 5.75″ (15 cm). Ratlike with large ears and big eyes. Gray-brown with white underparts and yellowish flanks and throat. Tail very long (longer than body), covered with short fine hair, ending in small, dark plume at tip.

Behavior. Usually found alone or in nestbound families. Although at times individuals tolerate one another, it is, in general, strongly territorial. Omnivorous; diet is varied. Usually silent, it squeaks loudly if frightened. Fairly active even during daytime although usually hidden in secluded places. Becomes more active at dusk.

Nests are made of soft vegetable matter and built in secluded places under bushes, inside crevices, and in caves. When near farms, cloth, wool, cotton, foam rubber, plastic, paper, etc., are used for nesting material, and nests are made in almost any dark, hidden, and relatively undisturbed place. Has several litters of 5 or 6 young a year, born from September through March.

Status and Habitat. Common resident. One of the most abundant field rats around and inside farm buildings. *Several dozen on the ground under bushes and in the open, as well as climbing the walls and up into the eves of an isolated field station on the shores of Golfo San José, Chubut, after nightfall in warm weather in February 1987.* Dry scrub desert.

Range. Central and northern Patagonia; most of central and northern Argentina; Bolivia and Paraguay.

Similar Species. Can be confused with the following species which is larger and has a short tail.

202. RABBIT RAT / **Rata Conejo**
Reithrodon physodes (auritus)   *Plate 28*

Description. Body 7.75″ (20 cm); tail 4″ (10.5 cm). Large, oval-shaped ears lend a small, rabbitlike appearance. Head and back grayish chestnut, richer on sides. Underparts white.

Behavior. Hard to see because of its nocturnal and secretive behavior. Digs tunnels that lead vertically downward from an entrance that measures approximately 2″ (5 cm) in diameter (certain wasps dig similar holes). Burrows have 3 or 4 of these entrances. Active burrows can be recognized by fresh, droplet-shaped fecal pellets around entrance. Feeds on grasses.

Breeds from September to April. Gestation lasts 27 days. Female gives birth to 4 young and mates again immediately after parturition. Is sexually mature at 4 months.

Status and Habitat. Dry, mixed grass and bush-covered steppe and hillsides to 9000 ft (3000 m). Never near human dwellings.

Range. Argentina, Chile, and Uruguay.

OLD WORLD RATS AND MICE / Ratones Múridos
(Family Muridae, subfamily Murinae)

Large family, found throughout Old World land masses. Many were inadvertently introduced in other parts of the world where they have proliferated. Of over 400 species, 3 have been introduced in eastern Patagonia.

203. NORWAY, COMMON, OR BROWN RAT / Rata Noruega
Rattus norvegicus

Description. Body 8.5″ (22 cm); tail 6″ (15 cm). Very large. Small ears. Tail shorter than body. Gray-brown upperparts with paler, or yellowish, underparts.

Behavior. Gregarious. Principally active at night; also forages in daylight. Omnivorous and opportunistic. Feeds on a variety of grains and vegetable and animal products. Lives in close association with man.

Builds nests in concealed places.

Status and Habitat. Abundant in urban and rural areas; the rodent of sewers. Towns, cities, and ports.

Range. Introduced indirectly from Europe, Africa, and Asia. Found in many parts of the world.

204. ROOF RAT / Rata Europea
Rattus rattus

Description. Body 8″ (20 cm); tail 7″ (18 cm). Large. Relatively large ears. Tail only slightly shorter than body. Upperparts brownish or blackish; underparts paler.

Behavior. Gregarious. Active during day and night. Feeds on vegetable—often grain—and animal products. Lives in close association with man. Nests in concealed places.

Status and Habitat. Common in towns, cities, and ports. More widely dispersed than the previous species.

Range. Introduced indirectly from Europe. Found worldwide.

Similar Species. Similar to Norway rat but has larger ears and longer tail.

205. HOUSE MOUSE / Laucha Europea
Mus musculus

Description. Body 4″ (10 cm); tail 3″ (8 cm). Slender and with a long tail. Upperparts gray-brown; underparts white or pale gray.

Behavior. Gregarious. Mainly active at night. Feeds on varied vegetable—often grain—and animal matter. Lives in close association with man. Nests in secluded places.

Status and Habitat. Common in towns and cities. Particularly abundant in barns and granaries.

Range. Indirectly introduced from Europe. Found worldwide.

Similar Species. Can be confused with Vesper Mouse, but more slender and with a long tail.

CAVIES AND MARAS / Cuises y Maras
(Family Caviidae)

Pleasant-looking, mostly small to medium-sized rodents, although the largest is the size of a hare. They have robust bodies, large heads, big rounded eyes, and no tail. The best-known cavy is the domestic guinea pig, commonly kept as a pet worldwide. Unlike rats and mice, cavy litters are small and offspring are well developed at birth. An exclusively South American family, widely distributed throughout the continent. Contains 5 genera with a total of 14 species; 2 are found in eastern Patagonia.

206. PATAGONIAN LESSER CAVY / Cuís Chico
Microcavia australis   *Plate 27*

Description. Body 8.5″ (22 cm); weight 7 oz (200 g). Rounded body with a large head and no tail. Eyes large, surrounded by a pale ring. Small, rounded ears. Upperparts gray-brown; underparts and feet paler. Three digits on the hind feet and four on the front feet.

Behavior. Active during daytime. Colonial and gregarious. Forages on ground for leaves and grasses (*Stipa* sp.), also stands on hind legs to reach lower branches and climbs up inside bushes (*Zuaeda, Lycium, Schinus, and Atriplex*) as much as 6 ft (2 m) off the ground to reach taller fronds.

Rests and sleeps in scrapes under bushes. Digs complex networks of tunnels about 12″ (30 cm) below ground and extending on average 100 ft (26 m). Burrows lack enlarged chambers or nests. Several entrances, usually concealed under bushes, have well-worn paths or "runways" leading from them through the vegetation above ground.

Each burrow is used by up to 40 individuals. Males commonly use a home range of around 2 acres (0.75 hectare), and females about half that area. Usually silent; produces a variety of squeaks and snorts, particularly when threatened.

When female enters estrus, she is chased by as many as 6 courting males. Gestation lasts 54 days. Young are born from August to April but mostly between September and November. Average litter size is 2 (occasionally 1–5). Young weigh one ounce (35 g) at birth and are fully developed. They follow their mother until they are totally weaned at 3 or 4 weeks. Female becomes sexually mature between 40 and 85 days old. Usually lives 3–4 years, occasionally up to 7.

Status and Habitat. Common resident. Populations blossom and dwindle enormously from year to year, possibly as a result of food availability, predation, and

disease. *Resident populations in bush-covered areas close to shore around Golfo San José Península Valdés, Chubut.* Common in mixed grass and bush steppe and savanna.
Range. From Santa Cruz to all of Patagonia and western Argentina to Jujuy.

207. MARA OR PATAGONIAN HARE / Mara o Liebre Patagónica
Dolichotis patagonum   *Plate 27*

Description. Body 32″ (80 cm). Square head with large, rounded ears. Large body with round rump. Tail is merely a stump. Color fawn brown turning to gray on hindback and ending in a distinct white band around rump. Legs long. Forelegs ending in 4 toes; hindlegs ending in 3.

Behavior. Usually in pairs. Occasionally several dozen may gather to feed on grasses that carpet shallow, dried-up lake beds. Spends daytime grazing on tips of grasses, herbs, desert flowers, fruit, and seed pods. Rarely drinks water. Sleeps under bushes at night. Curious bouncing, antelope-like gait or "stoting." Capable of bursts of speed of over 30 mph (45 kph).

Strictly monogamous. Should one of the pair die, the other takes a new mate only after some time has passed. During the year, each pair occupies a range of about 500 acres (200 hectares), but uses only about 75 acres (30 hectares) at any given time. Pairs avoid one another, particularly outside the breeding season. Partners produce a continual dialogue of alternating low-volume calls. Emits high-pitched whistling contact call, audible 90 ft (30 m) away.

Mating begins in June, when pairs are dispersed. Sexual receptivity lasts only a few hours but may occur twice a year. Gestation lasts 90 days. Births occur between August and January. Two pups, less commonly one or 3, are born. Usually only one litter born per year. Young are reared in dens that are often used by several pairs. *Twenty-two pairs were observed sharing a single den on Península Valdés, 1984 (A. Taber).* Dug by pregnant females, den has wide entrance surrounded by bare soil and short tunnel 3–6 ft (1–2 m) long which leads into an irregular

16. The Mara stots like a small antelope, leaping into the air for a better view.

17. The Mara grazes either standing or sitting.

chamber about 3 ft (1 m) below the surface. Same den is used year after year. Once completed, mothers do not enter burrow again and it is used only by their pups. Each time she returns from foraging to the burrow, the female produces high-pitched whistles and low grunting sounds to call her pups. When about 6 weeks old, pups follow their parents during the day and begin grazing. Weaning occurs at 11 weeks. Maximum longevity is 15 years.

Status and Habitat. Locally common in parts of the northern coastal areas of Patagonia. *Highest densities have been recorded near the center of Península Valdés with one animal every 20 acres (8 hectares) in 1984 (A. Taber).* Mixed grass and scrub desert. Often along edges that separate scrub from grassland. *Three or 4 adults in a grassy area near the coast at Cabo Blanco, Santa Cruz, in early 1996 (M. Oliva Day).*

Range. Central Argentina to southern Patagonia (Río Santa Cruz).

VIZCACHAS AND CHINCHILLAS / Vizcachas y Chinchillas
(Family Chinchillidae)

Robust, pleasant-looking rodents with rounded features and soft dense fur, large ears, and longish tails. Some species are as large as the European hare. An exclusively South American family with 6 species that include the plains vizcacha of the pampas, the mountain vizcacha, and the chinchillas of the Andean regions of Peru and Bolivia. One species is found in eastern Patagonia.

18. The Mara pup is fully developed and able to open its eyes at birth.

19. (a) Both male and female Maras scent-mark the ground. (b) The female Mara suckles her pups—usually two—until they are about eleven weeks old.

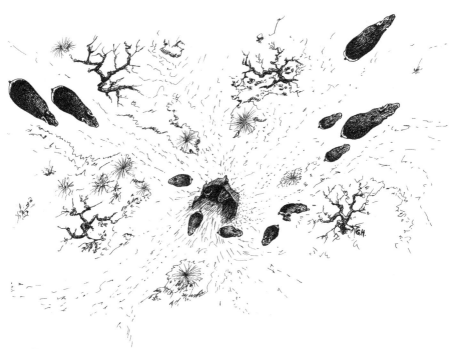

20. Maras commonly use communal burrows in which up to fifteen adult pairs deposit their young. In the above, a female is leading her pups away to suckle while her mate accompanies them close by (top right-hand corner). Another adult pair approaches and several pups remain in and around the burrow.

208. MOUNTAIN VIZCACHA / Vizcacha Serrana o Pilquín
Lagidium viscacia

Description. Body 18" (45 cm); tail 16" (40 cm). Large, with heavy head and large ears. Tail long and covered with long hairs. Eyes large. Body fur thick and soft, usually sandy gray; belly white.

Behavior. Gregarious. Fairly unafraid if not molested. Sits motionless on exposed areas among the rocks. Leaps from rock to rock with surprising agility.

Status and Habitat. Fairly common resident in areas where valley walls of the Chubut River become steep and rocky. *Recorded among the rocks on the high walls of the Chubut valley, below the Dique Ameghino dam, Chubut.*

Range. Northern Santa Cruz and Chubut along the Andes as far as Peru.

TUCO-TUCOS / Tuco-Tucos
(Family Ctenomyidae)

Small, robust rodents with large heads, small eyes and ears, and short, stumpy tails. They are armed with well-developed incisors and strong claws for digging; the hind toes are fringed with short, strong bristles, which gave rise to the family name "Ctenomys," meaning comb. Underground, they produce a surprisingly loud, characteristic, heartbeat-like sound, which is audible at the surface.

An exclusively South American family with a sole genus containing 33 species. One species is found in eastern Patagonia.

209. MAGELLAN'S TUCO-TUCO / Tuco-Tuco Magallánico
Ctenomys magellanicus   *Plate 27*

Description. Body 8.5" (22 cm); tail 3.25" (8.5 cm). Robust. Short, "sawn-off" tail. Small ears. Overall pale sandy color to middle gray-brown, with individual variations.

Behavior. Gregarious. Lives mostly underground; digs elaborate networks of shallow, underground tunnels, which it constantly remodels. Burrows by biting at soil with its incisors and forcing the loose dirt backward with its feet. Fresh entrances at surface are usually surrounded by a ridge of loose soil. There may be several entrances at the surface that are opened or plugged with dirt to allow air to circulate and "air condition" the burrow. *One adult observed clearing out material from its burrow early after sunrise, Chubut River valley near Los Altares, Chubut, February 1987.* Feeds on vegetable matter found at surface near entrances to burrows, and roots. Food is stored in tunnels.

Usually heard rather than seen: emits regular, paired, loud, thudding sounds underground: "Dug-dug, dug-dug, dug-dug." The heartbeat-like calls are audible at surface, 70 ft away or more, though can be hard to pinpoint. Often several call at once. These sounds can last for several minutes but are usually discontinued when there is danger. *One juvenile recorded near the eastern shore of Golfo San José, Chubut, October 1983.*

Status and Habitat. Uncommon resident. Restricted to areas of sandy soil in dry grass and bush steppe, and alluvial, sandy, grass-covered terrain. *Several individuals seen and heard along Chubut River valley, Los Altares, Chubut, January 1990.*

Range. Southern and central Patagonia to the province of Río Negro in Argentina, also southern Chile.

WHALES AND DOLPHINS / CETÁCEOS

(Order Cetacea)

Placental mammals that live their entire lives in water, where they eat, sleep, mate, and bear and nurse their young. Although they have undergone considerable anatomical modification, they maintain the basic mammalian plan and share many common features with their terrestrial relatives. Hands and arms have become flippers; noses have moved to the top of the head; body hair has almost—but not quite—disappeared, and all that is left of the hindlegs are tiny vestigial bones inside the body wall. The tail flukes have no bony structure except for the final portion of the backbone along the center. They are flattened horizontally—not vertically as in fish—and are moved up and down through the water as the whale swims forward. All cetaceans lack external ears. They have tiny ear holes a short distance behind each eye. The narrow ear duct is about the width of a pencil lead and is filled with a wax plug. Sounds are transmitted through bones in the head. The order is divided into Toothed and Baleen Whales, based on the existence of teeth or their replacement by baleen.

TOOTHED WHALES / Cetáceos Dentados
(Suborder Odontoceti)

Cetaceans with teeth (not baleen) in either or both jaws. They echolocate their prey and guide themselves by emitting short pulses of sounds (clicks and other sounds) whose reflections from objects underwater can be heard analyzed and located by the whale. The animal can in this way build up a sonic picture of its surroundings. Found in all oceans. There are 68 species in 9 families.

Mass Stranding. Various species of toothed whales sometimes come ashore and die. The reason groups of animals strand intentionally and fatally is not understood. Several theories have been advanced, from "suicide" to parasite infestation in the inner ear of whales, causing loss of direction. So far there is no conclusive proof for any one theory and the mystery is unresolved.

BEAKED WHALES / Zífidos
(Family Ziphiidae)

Medium-sized whales 20–40 ft (6–12 m) long with 2 grooves under the throat. The flukes have no notch in the center of the trailing edge. The adults are sexually dimorphic. Most have patterns of scars on their bodies resulting from fights. Many—males in particular—have single pairs of teeth on the bottom jaw. Little is known about beaked whales' natural history. They appear to live in deep seas beyond continental shelves and feed on deep-sea fish and squid. Many have only rarely been recorded alive, and one species is only known from dead specimens. Of the 18 species, 6 occur off the coast of Patagonia.

210. SHEPHERD'S BEAKED WHALE / Zífido de Tasmania
Tasmacetus shepherdi

Description. 20 ft (6 m). Small dorsal and pectoral fins. Top and bottom jaws lined with small conical teeth. Males have 2 large teeth at the tip of each jaw. Stranded specimens are dark, with a pale forehead or "melon" and lengthwise pale streaks on the sides of the body.
Behavior. Rarely observed live. The few records are from dead stranded specimens. Diet includes hake, crab, and squid.
Status and Habitat. Very rare visitor. *One adult female was found stranded dead on shore of Punta Buenos Aires, Península Valdés, Chubut, February 1973 (R. Payne).*
Range. Southern temperate oceans. Stranded specimens in Argentina (Península Valdés and Tierra del Fuego), Chile, Australia, and New Zealand.

211. CUVIER'S BEAKED WHALE / Zífido o Delfín Picudo de Cuvier
Ziphius cavirostris

Description. 20–28 ft (6–7.5 m). Small dorsal fin and flippers. Short, ill-defined beak. Lower jaw extends beyond upper jaw and has but two conical teeth at the tip (nonprotruding in females). Color varies from gray to brown or fawn, often covered with rounded scars of unknown origin and elongated scars produced by fighting.
Behavior. Small groups of 3–10 animals. Flukes are raised out of water at beginning of a dive. Feeds on squid and deep-water fish. Is known to breach out of water. Individual stranding is frequent.
Status and Habitat. No live records known for Patagonia. Avoids boats and is rarely seen at sea. Stranded animals have been recorded for coasts of Buenos Aires, Río Negro, Chubut, and Tierra del Fuego.
Range. Atlantic and Pacific Oceans of both Northern and Southern Hemispheres to 60°S; Mediterranean and part of Indian Ocean.

212. SOUTHERN BOTTLENOSE WHALE / Zífido Nariz de Botella
Hyperoodon planifrons

Description. 23–32 ft (7–9.8 m). Dolphinlike bottle-nosed beak. Large bulbous forehead or "melon." Sickle-shaped dorsal fin. Single pair of well-developed conical teeth at tip of lower jaw. Occasionally, small vestigial teeth present as well.
Behavior. Alone or in groups of up to 25 animals. Deep diver, stays submerged sometimes more than an hour. Feeds on squid and fish.
Status and Habitat. Does not approach the shore. Approaches vessels at sea. Deep, open ocean, beyond the continental shelf.

Range. Circumpolar in Southern Hemisphere from 5° to 70°S. Migrates to higher latitudes in summer.

213. ARNOUX'S BEAKED WHALE / Zífido Marsopa o Berardio de Arnoux
Berardius arnuxii

Description. 33–42 ft (10–12.8 m). Bulbous forehead or "melon." Dolphinlike beak. Lower jaw extends beyond upper jaw, with a single pair of laterally compressed teeth at tip, exposed outside the mouth in adults. Behind these there is a second pair of teeth. Small triangular dorsal fin. Slate gray to brown or black with many scars.

Behavior. In groups of 2–20 animals. Feeds on deep-sea fish, octopus, and squid.

Status and Habitat. No live sightings in Patagonia. Oceanic, occurs usually beyond edge of continental shelf.

Range. South Pacific and South Atlantic Oceans to Antarctica. Stranding records for Tierra del Fuego and Buenos Aires.

214. GRAY'S BEAKED WHALE / Zífido Negro
Mesoplodon grayi

Description. 18–20 ft (5.5–6 m). Spindle-shaped body tapering at both ends. Two small, triangular teeth on lower jaw, placed half way back from the tip. Small dorsal fin. Brown or gray, beak and underparts often whitish. Often covered with scars.

Behavior. Alone or in groups of up to 25.

Status and Habitat. Rare visitor. Not recorded live for Patagonia. *One lone adult stranded in Golfo Nuevo, Chubut, July 1983, and one in Golfo San José, Chubut, mid-1984.* Live sightings off Buenos Aires and Tierra del Fuego. Also in other Southern Hemisphere oceans deeper than 6000 ft (2000 m).

Range. Circumpolar in Southern Hemisphere. One record from the North Atlantic.

215. STRAP-TOOTHED WHALE / Zífido De Layard
Mesoplodon layardii

Description. 20 ft (6 m). Spindle-shaped body. Dark with pale areas on underside and behind eyes. Males have a pair of long "strap-shaped" teeth halfway back from tip of lower jaw.

Behavior. Very little known. Diet includes squid.

Status and Habitat. No live sightings in coastal Patagonia. Single strandings recorded in Comodoro Rivadavia and Tierra del Fuego. Oceanic.

Range. Circumpolar in Southern Hemisphere.

SPERM WHALES / Cachalotes
(Family Physeteridae)

Whales with robust bodies and bulbous heads. They have a single blowhole on top of the head, to the left of center. They usually have functional teeth only in the bottom jaw. There are 3 species; only one is found off Patagonia.

216. SPERM WHALE / Cachalote
Physeter macrocephalus

Description. 47 ft (15 m). Comparatively easy to identify at sea. Its head is enormous, blunt, and boxlike, with a single blowhole situated far forward on the head and to the left of center. The blow consequently emerges forward and to the left. A distinct dorsal hump is followed by a series of smaller humps. Flukes are broad and triangular, and posterior edge is straight with a deep notch in center. The body has a corrugated and shriveled look. The lower jaw is straight and narrow, and has 25 large conical teeth that fit into sockets in the upper jaw. Totally black.

Behavior. Singly or in groups of up to 50 or more. Deep diver; is known to reach depths of over 3300 ft (1000 m). Can stay submerged for over one hour. Stores oxygen in body tissues more efficiently than almost any other mammal. Feeds primarily on squid, also octopus and fish.

Status and Habitat. Sightings only likely from ships in high seas. *Single adult males stranded at Riacho San José, Punta Quiroga, and Comodoro Rivadavia, Chubut, in late 1980s. A lone adult male stranded live on beach, Puerto Madryn, Chubut, September 1989, and died 4 hours later.* Factory ship whaling was prohibited in 1979. Ocean waters beyond continental shelf. Seldom found in waters less than 500 ft (170 m) deep.

Range. Irregularly but widely distributed in all oceans. Most range toward the poles in summer and return to temperate zones in winter. Males migrate to higher latitudes than females.

KILLER WHALES AND OCEANIC DOLPHINS / Orcas y Delfines
(Family Delphinidae)

Mostly small to medium-sized cetaceans with elongated, very hydrodynamic bodies, beak-shaped mouths, and sickle-shaped dorsal fins. They have a single blowhole on top of the head. The flukes have a notch in the center of the trailing edge. There are 33 species worldwide, found in all oceans and in some of the larger rivers. There are 9 species off the coast of Patagonia.

217. KILLER WHALE / Orca
Orcinus orca   *Plate 29*

Description. 21–27 ft (7–9 m). Largest of all dolphins, weighing 3–7 tons. Robust, torpedo-shaped body with a large, triangular, 5 ft (1.5 m) tall dorsal fin and large, paddle-like flippers. Black or gray-black upperparts with a well-defined white, ventral pattern, extending from the lower jaw, between the flippers and forming a "trident" on lower belly. Oval-shaped white patch extending back from each eye. Dusky gray "saddle" patch behind dorsal fin, the shape of which differs from individual to individual. Underside of flukes white or light gray. 10–13 pairs of conical teeth in each jaw. *Female:* 18 ft (6 m). Smaller and slighter than male; dorsal fin 3 ft (1 m) and sickle-shaped as in juveniles.

Behavior. Travels alone or more commonly in groups or "pods" of 2–7 animals. Pods are highly stable social units centered around one or more matriarchs (related females) and their offspring. Members of a pod travel and hunt together and come to the rescue of trapped or injured companions.

Normal cruising speed is 2.5–7 mph (4–12 kph); can maintain 12 mph (20 kph) when traveling fast, with short bursts of up to 30 mph (50 kph).

Remains submerged 4–7 min, occasionally 14 min or more, and can cover over 3 miles (5 km) underwater. Will surface repeatedly 4 or 5 times after a lengthy dive. Dives of almost 1000 ft (290 m) lasting 21 min have been recorded. All members of the pod rise to the surface approximately together to breathe. Sometimes breaches and lobtails. Hunts prey in coordination with other members of group. Diet includes fish, birds (penguins, Steamer Ducks, cormorants), sea lions, elephant seals, dolphins, sharks, and occasionally young Right Whales. *Hunts sea lion pups at Punta Norte, Península Valdés, Chubut, between mid-March and end of April each year. Beaching itself intentionally, it snatches pups directly off the shore when these venture into or near the sea for the first time. As part of a learning process groups often "play" with prey, catapulting even full-grown sea lions from the ocean into the air, with a blow from the flukes.* Emits clicking sounds at rates of between one and 300 per sec which it uses to echolate objects in water. When not hunting marine mammals, produces whistles and pulsed calls or "screams." Screams are very intense and can even be heard on the surface. Each pod has its own set of calls or "pod dialect," which probably enables members to maintain contact while foraging 6 miles (10 km) or more apart.

Polygynous. Gestation lasts 15 months. Female gives birth to one calf every 3–5 years. Measures 5–6 ft (2.1–2.5 m) and weighs as much as 440 lb (200 kg) at birth. Calf nurses about one year.

Sexual maturity occurs at 9 or 10 years in the female and at 15 years or even older in the male. Male lives 35 years on average and female may live more than 50.

Status and Habitat. Common resident, but local population low. *The number regularly sighted off the wildlife reserve at Punta Norte on Península Valdés was estimated at 30 animals in 1978 (J. C. López & D. López).* More common on shores facing open ocean than inside bays. Regularly covers large distances and also migrates as different prey become available. *Known individuals from Península Valdés have been seen 124 miles (200 km) north, in Bahía San Blas, Buenos Aires province, and the same distance south at Rawson, Chubut, as well as 200 miles (300 km) out to sea near edge of continental shelf.*

Range. Oceans throughout the world; more common in higher latitudes.

218. FALSE KILLER WHALE / Falsa Orca
Pseudorca crassidens

Description. 18 ft (5.5 m). Head small and rounded. Body long and slender. Dorsal fin, situated halfway down the back, tall and sickle-shaped. Flippers have a hump on middle of leading edge, which is characteristic of the species. Mouth long, extending almost as far back as the eye. 8–11 large conical teeth in each jaw. Body black except for ventral blaze, and occasionally sides of head gray. *Female:* Slightly smaller, 16 ft (4.9 m). Calf measures 6 ft (1.8 m) at birth.

Behavior. Gregarious; in large groups, often together with other dolphins. Will ride bow waves and sometimes leap clear of the water. Feeds primarily on squid and large fish.

Status and Habitat. Rare visitor. No live sightings. *One stranding record for Golfo Nuevo in 1974.* Oceanic and rarely seen near land unless there is deep water offshore.

Range. Widely distributed in warm, temperate, and tropical waters around the world.

Similar Species. Can be confused with Killer Whale and Pilot Whale, but former has an unmistakably large, tall dorsal fin and striking white color pattern, whereas latter has a very bulbous head, broader and lower dorsal fin, very long flippers, and small peglike teeth.

219. LONG-FINNED PILOT WHALE / Calderón o Ballena Piloto
Globicephala melaena

Description. 20 ft (6.2 m). Bulbous head. Long flippers. Low sickle-shaped dorsal fin, situated well forward on the back. Slate gray to black, with pale markings on underside. The single blowhole is slightly to the left of center on top of head. 8–12 peglike teeth in upper and lower jaws. *Female:* Slightly smaller, 18 ft (5.4 m), and lighter build.

Behavior. Gregarious; usually in small groups; at times, in several hundreds, commonly together with other dolphins. Often lies motionless at surface; does not bow-ride and rarely breaches. Feeds on squid and fish.

Gestation lasts 16 months. Calves born in late summer, nurse for 12 months.

Status and Habitat. Occasional visitor. Sighted from shore in summer, both inside bays and along open ocean shores. Individual and whole herds of Pilot Whales strand more frequently than any other whale or dolphin. Attempts to return the animals to sea are sometimes successful but more commonly fail. *Mass strandings in Chubut include Punta Norte (mid-1970s), Punta Tombo (early 1980s), mainland near Isla Escondida (1988); over 400 animals near Bahía Bustamante in October 1991.* Oceanic and near-shore waters.

Range. Southern Hemisphere oceans. North Atlantic.

220. DUSKY DOLPHIN OR FITZ ROY'S DOLPHIN / Delfín Oscuro o de Fitz Roy
Lagenorhynchus obscurus   *Plate 29*

Description. 5–7 ft (1.7–2 m). Slender, streamlined body. Small but well-defined dark beak. Dorsal fin sickle-shaped; lighter on trailing edge. Upperparts steel gray with a conspicuous, oblique, pale gray "fork" on flanks, extending from ventral region to level with dorsal fin. Sides of head gray extending back behind flippers. Rest of underparts white.

Behavior. Gregarious, usually in small pods of 6–15 but up to several hundred animals. When resting, travels at about 2.5 mph (4 kph). When foraging is capable of speeds over 25 mph (40 kph) over short distances. Emits strings of clicks, which it uses for echolocation. Feeds on fish and squid. *Between September and March, 200–300 dolphins gather to feed together around Península Valdés on school-*

ing Argentine anchovy (Engraulis anchoita). Large flocks of terns, Kelp Gulls, Black-browed Albatrosses, Magellanic Penguins, cormorants, and shearwaters join to feed on the tightly schooling fish. Breaches spectacularly and lobtails noisily, probably fulfilling social functions. Swims actively with Southern Right Whales (*Eubalaena australis*). Sometimes will approach moving boats and ride the bow wave.

Mating takes place between October and March. Gestation lasts about 11 months. Calves born between November and March, nurse for approximately 18 months.

Status and Habitat. Common all year round in Golfo San José, Golfo Nuevo, Golfo San Matías, and open Atlantic around Península Valdés south to Golfo San Jorge. Most frequently sighted from shore between September and April, when weather is fine and calm or with wind velocity less than 12 mph (20 kph). Oceanic, primarily coastal.

Range. Oceans bordering South America, South Africa, and New Zealand.

221. PEALE'S DOLPHIN / Delfín Austral
Lagenorhynchus australis

Description. 6 ft (2 m). Falcate dorsal fin. Black or dark gray face and chin, upperparts, and dorsal fin. White patch in front of and behind flippers and belly. Sides gray, crossed with single pale stripe from lower flanks to anterior dorsal region.

Behavior. Very coastal. In groups of 2–10, often in kelp forests. Diet includes hake, Mixinides, squid, shrimp, and octopus. Sometimes leaps into the air. At times follows ships or rides bow waves.

Status and Habitat. One of the most commonly sighted dolphins when crossing Strait of Magellan. *Very common along coast of Santa Cruz and southern Chubut, particularly south of Camarones (M. Iñiguez).* In Tierra del Fuego, population much reduced because it was hunted for many years for use as crab bait in traps.

Range. Golfo San Matías to Tierra del Fuego. Also up the Chilean coast to Valparaiso.

222. COMMERSON'S DOLPHIN / Tonina Overa
Cephalorhynchus commersonii   *Plate 29*

Description. Male 4.5 ft (1.5 m). Small but conspicuous. Stocky with a low "melon," and rounded dorsal fin. Striking, unique color pattern. Black, with white "shawl" extending across front of dorsal fin, down the flanks and under belly except for genital region. Chin white. 29–30 pairs of small pointed teeth in each jaw. *Female:* Smaller dorsal fin. *Calf:* 30″ (70 cm) at birth; white "shawl" present; brownish gray instead of black markings.

Behavior. Usually in small groups of 2 or 3, very occasionally in large pods. *Aggregations of 100 or more have been sighted off Comodoro Rivadavia, Falkland Islands (Islas Malvinas) and Strait of Magellan.* Commonly breaches. Feeds on crabs, squid, and fish such as silverside and Fuegian sardine. Sometimes approaches moving boats and rides the bow wave. Uses boats, piers, and shore to enclose prey.

Calving peaks between December and January. *First calves are born in September in Ría Deseado (M. Iñiguez).*

Status and Habitat. Very common though local; year-round resident, around Cabo Dos Bahías, off pier of Comodoro Rivadavia, Chubut; Ría Deseado and Bahía San Julián, Santa Cruz. Occasional visitor on coast of northern Patagonia. *Sightings off the port of Rawson, Caleta Valdés, Chubut, October 1981.* Oceanic, coastal, to very shallow water, at times just beyond the surf zone.

Range. Drake's Passage to Punta Arenas in Chile and as far as mouth of the Río Negro in Argentina; Falkland Islands (Islas Malvinas). A separate population around Kerguelen Islands in Indian Ocean.

223. RISSO'S DOLPHIN OR GRAMPUS / Delfín Gris
Grampus griseus

Description. 12–13 ft (3.6–4 m). Relatively large dolphin. Head rounded and blunt. Large triangular dorsal fin (more curved in female). Pale brown to light gray, whitish around head; flippers and dorsal fin darker. Body extensively scarred with lines. Seven pairs of peglike teeth in bottom jaw.

Behavior. In small groups of 2–5, or large pods of up to several dozen. Feeds on squid and fish. Local summer visitors known to remain in one area of coastal water for several successive days.

Status and Habitat. Occasional visitor from October to March. Prefers deep, warm to temperate ocean, usually greater than 600 ft (200 m). Occasionally ventures into shallow inshore waters. *Five adults spent over one week in coastal waters near eastern shore of Golfo San José, Chubut, January 1986.*

Range. Tropical and warm temperate Atlantic and Pacific Oceans. Some individuals range to higher latitudes. *Several stranded animals found in Tierra del Fuego (N. Goodall).*

224. BOTTLE-NOSED DOLPHIN / Tonina Común
Tursiops truncatus gephyreus   *Plate 29*

Description. 10 ft (3 m). Distinct beak, clearly delineated from forehead. Dorsal fin moderately tall and curved. Markings and scars on dorsal fin often help in telling individuals apart. Flukes deeply notched. Dark gray, paler below, often with a pale stripe extending back from sides of head. 16–18 teeth in each jaw. *Juvenile:* pale gray.

Behavior. In small groups of 5–25. Each group has a specific "beat," ranging from a few hundred yards to several miles, which it patrols continually. These beats shift from time to time, so the group may be resident in an area for several months or even years. *In Golfo San José, Península Valdés, Chubut, 7 individual animals photographed in 1974 were seen again 12 years later in 1986.*

Travels at 3–9 mph (5–14 kph). Although sometimes rides bow waves, usually avoids or ignores boats. Diet is varied and includes squid and fish such as hake (*Merluccius hubbsi*) and bottom-rock-dwelling fish (*Pinguipes fasciatus*). Breaches, head slaps, tail slaps, nose-outs, and "kelp tossing" are common and probably have social meanings. Occasionally swims with Southern Right Whales (*Euba-*

laena australis), which respond by lunging forward and thrashing their flukes. Produces strings of clicking sounds, underwater, for echolocation.

Gestation lasts 12 months. Calves born during spring, summer, and fall. Females bear one calf every 2 or 3 years. Calves remain close to their mothers for several months.

Status and Habitat. Common though sporadic on the coast of Chubut; *one doubtful record for the coast of Santa Cruz (M. Iñiguez)*. Like other dolphins, difficult to observe when wind is greater than 12 mph (20 kph). Oceanic, although truly coastal, preferring water depths less than 33 ft (10 m). Known to travel distances over 186 miles (300 km). The most common dolphin in captivity in aquariums around the world.

Range. Is widely—but probably thinly—distributed in all oceans, except for high latitudes.

225. COMMON DOLPHIN / Delfín Común
Delphinus delphis

Description. 8 ft (2.5 m). Medium sized. Long, well-defined beak. Prominent, curved dorsal fin. Upperparts brownish black, belly whitish. Gray, white, or yellowish tan wavy markings on sides, cross below dorsal fin, producing an "hour glass" design. 40–50 teeth in each jaw.

Behavior. In large groups, sometimes of several hundred individuals. Can dive to 918 ft (280 m), and stay underwater for 8 min. Feeds on squid and fish. Commonly breaches; rides bow waves.

Status and Habitat. Common visitor in Golfo San Matías (Río Negro and Chubut). Mostly pelagic, occurring in waters beyond the 100 fathom or 600 ft (200 m) contour.

Range. Coast of northern Patagonia. All tropical and temperate oceans.

PORPOISES / Marsopas
(Family Phocoenidae)

Small and dolphinlike mammals, with mouth not beaked. Porpoises have spade-shaped teeth, whereas dolphins have conical teeth. Of the 6 species known in the world, 2 are found in eastern Patagonia.

226. BURMEISTER'S PORPOISE / Marsopa Espinosa
Phocoena spinipinnis

Description. 6 ft (1.8 m). Small with a somewhat blunt head. Low, distinctive, wing-shaped dorsal fin, placed far back. Fine, grainlike spines along ridge (only visible closeup). Body dark brown in life, dark gray when stranded. 13–20 small spadelike teeth in each jaw.

Behavior. In small groups of 5–8 animals. Unobtrusive. Does not breach or lobtail. All members of group surface 2 or 3 times within same period of time and then are gone, sometimes for several minutes, reappearing several hundred yards away. Emerges at shallow angle, barely disturbing water; breaks the surface with top of its head, and with a faint ducking motion immediately begins to dive. Situated far down the back, the dorsal fin often does not even break the surface. The flukes never show above the water. Diet includes fish and squid. Is not attracted to boats.

Calving occurs in autumn. *One female, washed up dead on shores of Golfo San José, Chubut, showed signs of recent pregnancy (enlarged empty uterus and colostrum in mammary glands), June 1986.*

Status and Habitat. Common though local year-round resident. Occasionally, on mirror-calm days, from October through March, in Golfo Nuevo and San José, Chubut, within 1500 ft (500 m) from shore.

Numbers low. Coastal waters between 16 and 33 ft (5 and 10 m) deep, usually in areas where bottom is rocky rather than sandy.

Range. Temperate waters of South America from Tierra del Fuego to Uruguay on the Atlantic and to Peru on the Pacific.

227. SPECTACLED PORPOISE / Marsopa de Anteojos
Phocoena dioptrica

Description. 7 ft (2.2 m). Small with a round head. Rounded triangular dorsal fin. Upperparts black, contrasting with white underparts along a horizontal line extending through the eye and down the flanks. 16–23 teeth in both jaws.

Behavior. Unknown.

Status and Habitat. Accidental visitor (?). No records of live sightings. One stranding record in Golfo Nuevo, Chubut. Many for Tierra del Fuego.

Range. Possibly circumpolar in sub-Antarctic latitudes near continents and islands. Coast of South America from Tierra del Fuego to Uruguay.

BALEEN WHALES / CETÁCEOS CON BARBAS

(Order Mysticeti)

Large to very large cetaceans characterized by the replacement of teeth by baleen. Baleen is a hornlike material fixed like the teeth of a comb to each of the upper maxillaries. The inner surface is shredded into fine hairs which act as a sieve to trap small prey upon which the whale feeds by filtering small food from the sea. Paired blowholes on top of the head serve for breathing and produce the characteristic whale "spout," which is often visible as a jet of water particles and condensation when the animal exhales. Although baleen whales produce different—mostly low-frequency—sounds, they are not known to echolocate. There are 3 families: rorquals, right whales, and gray whales. The two former are represented off Patagonia. The last, with a single species, is found only in the northern Pacific.

RORQUALS / Rorcuales o Ballenas de Aleta Dorsal
(Family Balaenopteridae)

Streamlined, fast-swimming whales with dorsal fins and parallel grooves on the throat. The largest whales of all belong to this group. Rorquals have distendable throats. They feed by chasing prey, usually fish. As they draw near, they take a gigantic mouthful of prey-filled seawater. The water is then expelled through the relatively short baleen and the prey is swallowed. Rorquals are found in all oceans. Of the 6 species, 5 occur in Patagonia; only one is a regular visitor.

228. BLUE WHALE / Ballena Azul
Balaenoptera musculus   *Plate 30*

Description. 82–98 ft (25–30 m). The largest living animal, and probably the largest ever. Bluish gray, mottled paler. Dorsal fin extremely small and placed very far back. Head broad and flat and U-shaped when viewed from above. The shape of the spout when the whale blows is high, slender, and vertical. Has 55–68 ventral grooves that reach the navel.

Behavior. Seen singly or in pairs. Feeds near surface of the ocean, principally on krill—small shrimplike crustaceans. Produces very low frequency sounds underwater, inaudible to the human ear, which travel hundreds of miles.

Gestation lasts 12 months. Calves nurse approximately 8 months, during which time they increase in weight as much as 320 lb (90 kg) a day.

Status and Habitat. Rare visitor. One unconfirmed sighting off Península Valdés, Chubut; and one stranding record. Open ocean and coastal waters off continents. Hunted commercially until, on edge of extinction, was given international protection in 1965. Since then numbers have not recovered. Only about 9000 remained in 1985.

Range. North Pacific, North Atlantic, and all Southern Hemisphere oceans. Southern population generally from sub-Antarctic to ice edge between September and March. From April to August, moves northward into more temperate waters.

229. FIN WHALE / Rorcual Común
Balaenoptera physalus   *Plate 30*

Description. 88 ft (27 m). Very large. Dorsal fin curved and relatively large (larger than that of the blue whale), placed very far back. Head, viewed from above, is pointed. Upperparts uniform dark gray; underparts white. Right lower lip and baleen on same side white. Left lip and baleen dark gray. Has 56–100 ventral grooves that reach the navel.

Behavior. Alone or in pods of up to 7 animals. Dives to depths of 754 ft (230 m). Can swim at 20 mph (32 km), although usually travels between 2 and 9 mph (3–15 kph). Diet includes krill, squid, and schooling fish.

Gestation lasts one year. Female bears a calf every 2 or 3 years and nurses about 8 months.

Status and Habitat. Hypothetical. No live records. Open ocean and coastal waters off continents.

Range. Worldwide. Temperate waters in winter, migrates toward the poles in summer.

230. SEI WHALE / Ballena Sei o Rorcual Mediano
Balaenoptera borealis   *Plate 30*

Description. 56–59 ft (17–18 m). Large and streamlined with a prominent, sickle-shaped dorsal fin, set not as far back as that of previous two species. Head V-shaped when viewed from above, but less pointed than that of Fin Whale; a single central ridge runs between the tip and the blowhole. Upperparts, including lower lips, dark gray. Belly white. Has 30–60 ventral grooves ending well before the navel.

Behavior. Alone or in small groups of up to 5 individuals. Fast-swimming; surfaces at a shallow angle; head still visible above the surface when dorsal fin appears. With a shallow dive, the body disappears; fin remains visible at surface a short while longer. A straight line of "fluke-prints" is often visible disturbing the surface of the sea, indicating the whale's passage below. When traveling, surfaces regularly to breathe, approximately every 30 sec. Feeds near surface on copepods, krill, and small schooling fish.

Sound produced when exhaling at surface is brief and more explosive compared with that of the Southern Right Whale. Spout is an inverted cone.

Gestation lasts about one year. One calf is born every 2 or 3 years; it is nursed for 5–9 months. *A single adult female and noticeably smaller calf swam several miles offshore in Golfo San José, Chubut, February 1984.*

Status and Habitat. Rare, and sightings extremely chancy; however, this is the only other species of baleen whale, besides the Southern Right Whale, that comes close to shore with any frequency in Patagonia. *One lone individual came within 328 ft (100 m) of shore in water less than 33 ft (10 m) deep in Golfo San José, Chubut, October 1986. One lone adult stranded in Golfo San José, Chubut, December 1973.* Open ocean to coastal waters off continents.

Range. Principally temperate oceans throughout the world.

231. MINKE WHALE / Ballena Minke o Rorcual Menor
Balaenoptera acutorostrata   *Plate 30*

Description. 33 ft (10 m). Relatively small and slender, the smallest rorqual. Head very slender and pointed with a single central ridge. Tall curved dorsal fin. Upperparts black or dark gray, paler below. Usually has a conspicuous white patch on flippers. Ventral grooves end in front of navel.

Behavior. Occurs singly or in twos and threes. Feeds on krill and small schooling fish. Occasionally breaches. Sometimes inspects boats.

Status and Habitat. Rare visitor. *One young whale stranded dead on eastern shores of Golfo San José, Chubut, January 1986.* Open ocean as well as coastal waters, in bays and inlets.

Range. Widely distributed in tropical, temperate, and polar waters of both hemispheres. Some individuals migrate enormous distances. Congregates on feeding grounds in high latitudes in summer and moves toward equator in winter.

232. HUMPBACK WHALE / Yubarta o Ballena Jorobada
Megaptera novaeangliae   *Plate 30*

Description. 49 ft (15 m). Large and robust. Dorsal fin low and of varied shape. Small, rounded projections on various parts of head. Body dark gray with white patches on belly and under tail surface. Flippers very long and mostly white, with knoblike projections on the leading edge. Has 14–35 wide ventral grooves extending to navel. *Female:* Slightly larger, 52 ft (16 m).

Behavior. Alone or in groups of 2 or 3, and 12–15 on its breeding and feeding grounds. When traveling, swims at 4–7 mph (6–12 kph). Commonly breeches and slaps its flippers or flukes on surface of water. Feeds on krill and schooling fish. Traps fish in bubble nets produced by swimming around a school while releasing air from its blowholes.

Male sings intricate songs on its breeding grounds. These songs are loud and musical and can be detected underwater as much as 19 miles (30 km) away. Also produces low sounds that can be detected more than 100 miles (180 km) away.

Status and Habitat. Hypothetical visitor. No live records. *Recorded off coasts of Buenos Aires and Tierra del Fuego.* Migration routes in open ocean may occasionally bring it close offshore. Open ocean to continental and oceanic island waters.

Range. Widely distributed in all oceans. Makes extensive migrations from winter breeding grounds in tropical seas to high-latitude feeding grounds.

RIGHT WHALES / Ballenas Francas
(Family Balaenidae)

Robust whales with arched rostrums and long baleen. They lack the expandable throats of the previous family. Slow-swimming, they feed by advancing with their mouths open, "skimming" small invertebrates from the ocean. Of the 4 species, 2 occur off Patagonia.

233. SOUTHERN RIGHT WHALE / Ballena Franca Austral
Eubalaena australis   *Plate 30*

Description. 40–46 ft (12–14 m). Large and robust. Lacks dorsal fin and ventral grooves. Head is rounded and very large, accounting for almost a third of entire body length. Completely black, sometimes mottled with gray, brown, or white, with an irregular white patch on abdomen. Weighs 30–35 tons. On head, irregular patches of thickened skin called callosities. These are covered with a thin layer of parasitic crustaceans, called cyamids, which give the callosities a white appearance. Callosities form patterns unique to each individual and remain unchanged throughout life (see below). Produces a V-shaped cloud of mist and water particles when it exhales. Has 250 baleen plates on either side of the mouth, which measure 10″ (25 cm) at birth and grow to over 6 ft (2 m) when

21. The Southern Right Whale breaches often, leaping almost clear of the water.

22. Probably to thermoregulate, the Southern Right Whale frequently holds its tail out of the water for several minutes.

fully adult. *Female:* Slightly larger than male, 40–50 ft (13.5–16 m). Hard to distinguish from male unless it turns to expose its belly showing a short genital slit with a mammary slit on each side.

Behavior. Gregarious. Alone, in small groups, or large, loose pods. Breath rate is once every 15 sec–4 min; can remain submerged up to 30 min. Feeds by filtering zooplankton from the sea. Occasionally, 2 or more whales feed together, swimming side by side. Commonly leaps out of water (breaching) and smacks the surface of the ocean with its tail (lobtailing) or flippers, producing loud sounds that are probably useful for communication. Calf begins breaching within a few months of birth. Often holds its tail vertically in the air for 10 min or more at a time, and sometimes appears to "sail." Produces low-frequency calls under water (50–500 Hz), similar to a cow's mooing, as well as a variety of audible, breathing sounds at the surface.

Mating off Península Valdés takes place from June to November. Several males gather around one or more females and follow them for as much as 6–8 hr, jostling for position in their attempts to mate. Gestation probably lasts about 12 months. Females have one calf every 3 years. Calving begins in May and ends in October. Measuring 16 ft (5.5 m) and weighing 4 tons at birth, the calf grows over 1.5″ (3.5 cm) a day during its first months. It suckles frequently for periods lasting as much as 15 min. Calf remains with its mother for one year, and separates when they return together to their calving ground. Female is sexually mature at 6 years of age. Life span is probably between 50 and 70 years.

23. A Southern Right Whale mother and her calf.

Status and Habitat. Very common between April and December, with maximum numbers occurring between September and October. Historically very abundant. Estimates indicate an original population of over 100,000 animals before the arrival of man. Hunted to verge of extinction by end of 19th century. *(American whalers alone took an estimated 200,000 right whales between the end of the 1700s and late 1800s).* Nowadays is protected by international agreements and by national and provincial laws in Argentina. In the years since research in Península Valdés, Chubut, began in 1970, over 1000 right whales were identified by their callosity patterns (R. Payne, 1995). *There may have been fewer than 5000 alive worldwide in 1995; the Península Valdés population was estimated at around 1500 individuals.* Mothers and calves form a loose herd close to shore, in depths of around 15 ft (5 m). Adults without calves and juveniles usually swim in deeper water, a little farther offshore, at this time and tend to leave Península Valdés altogether in November, one month before the mothers and calves. Where the Península Valdés population goes between January and March is unclear, although there appears to be a certain amount of dispersal in the Southwest Atlantic when it becomes pelagic. Population increased 7% per annum from 1970 to 1990 (R. Payne).

Range. All of the Southern Hemisphere from 20°S to the Antarctic, although more common between 30° and 50°S. Major populations occur off Argentina, Uruguay, and southern Brazil; South Africa, Australia, and New Zealand.

234. PYGMY RIGHT WHALE / Ballena Franca Pigmea
Caperea marginata   *Plate 30*

Description. 21 ft (6.4 m). Small and slender, compared to other members of the family. Head less robust with a strongly arched mouth and prominent sickle-shaped dorsal fin. Upperparts dark gray, below white. Two furrows on throat.

Behavior. Alone; occasionally in pairs or small groups. Unobtrusive. Diet includes copepods.

Status and Habitat. No live sightings in Patagonia. *One stranded adult found in Riacho San José, Chubut, 1985.*

Range. Temperate waters of the Southern Hemisphere.

CARNIVORES / CARNÍVOROS

(Order Carnivora)

A varied group of placental mammals that share a similar unique tooth structure evolved for cutting flesh: the first lower molars and last upper premolars have jagged cusps. Most are meat-eating and many capture live prey, but some are omnivorous and others are even vegetarian.

FOXES / Zorros
(Family Canidae)

Long-muzzled, long-legged carnivores adapted to chasing prey. Domestic dogs belong to this family. Canids originated 40 or 50 million years ago during the Eocene in North America. From there they extended throughout the world. Of the 35 species, two are found in eastern Patagonia.

235. COLPEO FOX / Zorro Colorado
Dusicyon culpaeus magellanicus   *Plate 31*

Description. Body 33″ (85 cm); tail 12–18″ (30–45 cm); weight 11–28.5 lbs (5–13 kg). Sturdier and more wolflike than the following species, with slightly smaller ears. Overall color rusty reddish. Upperparts yellowish underfur with black guard hairs. Head, legs, and tail tawny.

Behavior. Nocturnal. Hides in caves and under vegetation during daytime. Home range covers an area of 8 square miles (20 sq km) or more. *One adult seen killing a one-month old guanaco "chulengo" at Monte León, Santa Cruz, December 1996 (F. Larrivière).* Feeds primarily on rodents and hares. Sheep make up 20% of its diet. Also feeds on reptiles and insects.

Female comes into heat in August and September. Several males follow her and attempt to mate. Gestation lasts 55–60 days, and one litter of 5 or 6 young is born annually. Pupping takes place in a den.

Status and Habitat. Common though inconspicuous resident in open to tree-and-bush-covered hilly country and mountains. Less commonly, open plains. Rare on coast in northeastern Patagonia.

Range. Tierra del Fuego, continental Patagonia, and the Andes to Peru. *One adult by a roadside 30 miles (50 km) South of Cabo Blanco, Santa Cruz, December 1989 (G. Harris & W. Conway).*

236. ARGENTINE GRAY FOX / Zorro Gris
Dusicyon griseus   *Plate 31*

Description. Body 19.5″ (50 cm); tail 12″ (30 cm). Slight; with large ears and pointed muzzle. Coat gray with yellowish underfur. Legs, head, and tail pale tawny.

Behavior. Alone or in small family groups. Curious, becomes easily accustomed to people where it is protected and where food is available. Fairly diurnal as well as nocturnal. Feeds mainly on birds, small rodents, insects, reptiles, and berries. Occasionally chases insects and mice on the macadam at night. Call is a sharp yap, "Ra-a-a," made especially during breeding season.
    Gestation lasts 55–60 days, and usually one litter of 5 or 6 pups is born each year. *A female with a 2-month-old litter of 5 near Bahía Bustamante, Chubut, December 1992.*

Status and Habitat. Common resident; in dry, bush-covered steppe and low, hilly country. Does not compete with sheep farming. Is trapped for its fur, at times extensively and with little control. From 1976 to 1979 between 680,000 and 990,000 pelts were exported annually through the port of Buenos Aires.

Range. Patagonia and western Argentina.

FERRETS, SKUNKS, ETC. / Hurones, Zorrinos, etc.
(Family Mustelidae)

A large group of carnivores, typically short-legged and long-bodied, with much variation, found in almost every habitat, including in fresh water and saltwater. They occur on all continents except Australia and Antarctica. Of the 66 species, 3 occur locally.

237. PATAGONIAN WEASEL / Huroncito
Lyncodon patagonicus   *Plate 32*

Description. Body 11.75″ (30 cm); tail 2.75″ (7 cm). Small, slender, and supple-bodied, with a small head. Ears smallish. Legs and tail short. Upperparts gray, darker on nape, head, lower neck, and forelegs. Wide white band extending back from the forehead and down either side of the neck.

Behavior. Usually alone. Nocturnal. Terrestrial; digs burrows. Like all members of the family, produces a strong-smelling fluid from a pair of anal glands which is used to scent-mark. Silent.

Status and Habitat. Rare resident. *One adult recorded preying upon Elegant Crested Tinamous at Punta Norte; one skull from northern Península Valdés. One animal dug its burrow under wildlife warden's house at Cabo Dos Bahías and scavenged food, November 1979.* Dry bush-covered steppe and hilly country.

Range. Patagonia and western Argentina to Salta.

238. LITTLE GRISON / Hurón Menor
Galictis cuja — Plate 32

Description. Body 19.5″ (50 cm); tail 11.75″ (30 cm). Small-headed, slender, and supple, but larger than the previous species with a longer tail and larger ears. Upperparts gray. White line extends from forehead down the sides of neck. Underparts dark brown.

Behavior. Alone or in small groups. Terrestrial. Fairly diurnal. Ignores people. Very active, is always on the go. Nose held close to the ground, it bounds along on short legs with an undulating motion. With quick hurried movements, forages under bushes, particularly along lesser cavy runways. Besides lesser cavies, hunts other small rodents and vertebrates and occasionally feeds on carrion. Like all mustelids, produces a strong, slightly pungent-smelling scent from two anal glands. Dens in burrows. Silent.

Breeds in dens between August and February. Female ovulation is induced by copulation.

Status and Habitat. Fairly common resident. *One small den in the walls of a small dry stream bed with an entrance 6″* (15 cm) tall and 10″ (25 cm) wide, October 1986. Savanna, woodland; dry bush- and grass-covered steppe and hillsides.

Range. From northern Patagonia to central America.

239. PATAGONIAN SKUNK / Zorrino Patagónico
Conepatus humboldti — Plate 32

Description. Body 15.5″ (40 cm); tail 7.75″ (20 cm). Robust body with a bushy tail. Black or brown with 2 white lines extending back from forehead on either side of the back.

Behavior. Alone or in family groups. Terrestrial. Female remains within a territory of one-half to one square mile all year round. Home range of male is larger. Fairly diurnal although more active at night. Forages about the desert floor in search of insects, grubs, small vertebrates, vegetable matter, and carrion on which it feeds. Digs a burrow for a den and may remain inactive during severe cold weather. Burrow is similar to that of armadillo but, if fresh, shows a profusion of fine scratch marks around the walls and entrance. Fairly tame and confident. When startled, it faces the threat, raises its tail warningly, and stamps the ground with its front feet. Its well-known pungent scent is produced by a gland on each side of the anus. When attacked, it sprays clear fluid from these glands with remarkable accuracy. Spray can be momentarily blinding if it comes in contact with the eyes. Silent.

Gestation lasts 42 days. Has 2–4 young per litter. *One adult female seen alternately carrying her two almost fully grown young across a road, Península Valdés, Chubut, February 1983.*

Status and Habitat. Fairly common resident in dry grass- and bush-covered steppe and open hillsides. Becomes easily accustomed to people and scavenges food from farmhouses.

Range. All of Patagonia.

WILD CATS / Gatos Monteses
(Family Felidae)

A well-known group of mammals—the most truly flesh eating of all carnivores—divided into large and small cats. Domestic cats belong to the latter. A curious difference between large cats (*Panther*) and small cats (*Felis*) is that large
cats roar but cannot purr, whereas small cats can purr but not roar. Cats are found
on all continents except Australia and Antarctica. There are 35 species; 3 species
of small cats (which include the Puma) occur on the coast of Patagonia.

240. PAMPAS CAT / Gato del Pajonal
Felis colocolo   Plate 31

Description. Body 23.5″ (60 cm); tail 11.75″ (30 cm). Robust body with a comparatively broad face; thick legs and tail. Dense, slightly mottled, sandy-colored
coat with conspicuous black stripes at back of the front legs. Claws can be
retracted.

Behavior. Usually alone. Primarily nocturnal, is sometimes active during the day.
Shy. Feeds mainly on small to medium-sized rodents, birds, lizards, and insects.
Usually silent.

Status and Habitat. Uncommon resident. Population unknown. Occasionally
seen fleetingly on roads at night. *Three daytime sightings of lone adults in bush-covered areas between September and March on Península Valdés, Chubut. One daytime sighting for Punta Tombo, Chubut, in summer (D. Boersma).* Grassland, forest, savanna,
dry bush-covered steppe and hillsides.

Range. Patagonia, central, and much of northern Argentina to Ecuador.

241. GEOFFROY'S CAT / Gato Montés
Felis geoffroyi   Plate 31

Description. Body 23.5″ (60 cm); tail 13.5″ (35 cm). More slender build than previous species, with a smaller head. Tail thinner and longer. Upperparts pale
sandy gray, paler below, with conspicuous black spots.

Behavior. Solitary. Nocturnal, occasionally seen during daytime. Feeds on birds,
rodents, reptiles, and insects, captured on ground and in bushes. *One adult up
in the branches of a bush, hunting mockingbirds that came to drink water at a water hole
on Península Valdés, Chubut, January 1985.* If pressed, can swim well. Usually silent.
Begins breeding in August. Gestation lasts 9 weeks.

Status and Habitat. Uncommon resident. Occasionally seen fleetingly on roads
at night. Savanna, forests, grass- and bush-covered steppe; hilly country.

Range. Central and northern Patagonia

242. PUMA / Puma
Felis concolor

Description. Body 5 ft (1.5 m); tail 30″ (75 cm). Large and powerful body with a
long tail. Thick, pale, sandy gray coat. Retractable claws.

Behavior. Solitary and shy. Primarily nocturnal but also fairly active during day. Summer ranges may cover 50,000 to 75,000 acres (150–200 sq km). Hunts guanacos, maras, rheas, and sheep.

Status and Conservation. Uncommon resident on coast of Patagonia. Historically resident on Península Valdés, Chubut. *One adult visited the wildlife reserve at Isla de Los Pájaros, Chubut, in early 1970 (J. C. López).* Locally common in bushcovered steppe and open or wooded highlands of central and western Patagonia. Is hunted in most of its range.

Range. All of Patagonia; much of South, Central, and North America to Canada.

PINNIPEDS / PINIPEDOS

(Order Pinnipedia)

Derived from the Latin words "pinna" meaning feather or wing, and "pedis" for foot, "pinnipedia" aptly means "wing-footed." Hind- and forelimbs are flipper-shaped, adapted for swimming. Pinnipeds forage at sea but must return to land or ice to give birth and suckle their young. Some species produce sounds under water. The order comprises 3 families: sea lions (Otariidae), seals (Phocidae), and walruses (Odobenidae).

SEA LIONS AND FUR SEALS / Lobos Marinos
(Family Otariidae)

Marine mammals that come ashore to breed and rest. They have external ears, which are visible behind the eyes, and their testicles are situated in a scrotal sack between the rear limbs. To move on land, all members of this family advance their rear flippers and walk or "gallop" on all fours. They propel themselves through the water using their large foreflippers, while their rear flippers are used principally as rudders. There are 14 species of otariids, 2 of which inhabit the coast of Patagonia.

243. SOUTH AMERICAN SEA LION / Lobo Marino del Sur
Otaria flavescens (byronia)   *Plate 33*

Description. Male 7–8 ft (2.3–2.6 m); weight 700 lb (340 kg). Very muscular and compact. Thick neck, large, upturned, blunt muzzle. Large, conspicuous mane. Coat is composed of a single layer of guard hairs. Rich chestnut brown with lighter-colored mane. *Female:* 6 ft (1.8–1.9 m); weight 300 lb (144 kg), much smaller and more graceful. Pale rust brown. *Pup:* Entirely black at birth; molts to light chestnut one month later.

Behavior. Very gregarious. At sea in groups of 2 or 3 or more. Forms colonies on

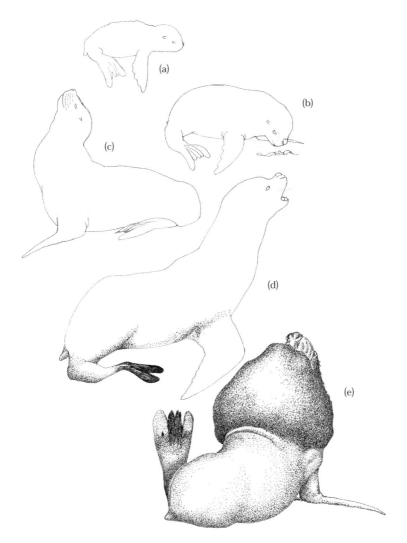

24. South American Sea Lion. (a) Newborn pup. (b) Month-old pup. (c) Adult female. (d) Young male. (e) Adult male.

the coast for resting or breeding. Can "gallop" rapidly on land, its speed matching that of a man running. Feeds principally in shallow waters near the coast. *Animals from Patagonia have been followed over 60 miles (100 km) offshore (C. Campagna).* Diet includes fish, crustaceans, and mollusks. Also feeds on fish discarded by fishermen. Timid on land, is curious and fearless at sea. Molting of old fur is gradual and occurs annually between April and August. Male has 33–42 long, bristlelike hairs or "vibrissae" on the muzzle, which it extends forward dur-

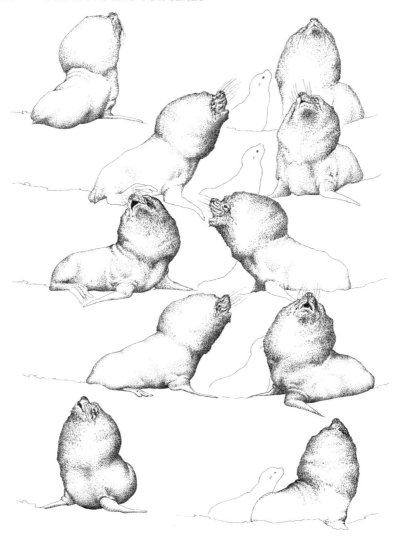

25. To keep their harems, dominant male South American Sea Lions thrust rapidly at each other. Real fights are less common than thrusting.

ing fights. Male produces rasping roars and snorts; female loud, sheeplike bleating calls; each pup produces a lamblike bleating which its mother can identify.

At the end of December the males start competing for females and territories. Females group and males claim positions within the compact colony. Each male can secure 1–10 females. The dominant male sits among the females with his massive head thrust skyward and defends his position from other males. Disputes are continuous and fights between males get serious. Around the edges of the colony are to be found displaced males. Gestation lasts a about a year. Within a week of arrival, the female gives birth to a pup. Born mainly in January, pups measure almost 2.2 ft (80 cm) and weigh about 25 lb (12 kg). Female becomes receptive about 6 days after giving birth and mates. Between one and 3 days after mating, she leaves her pup for 1–4 days while she feeds at sea. One month after birth, the pup enters the sea with its mother.

In March, breeding colony diminishes in size as females and pups move toward their wintering colonies. Pups suckle for about 10 months and are then weaned. Adult males, some of which may not have fed or rested for 2 months, return to sea to feed. The male does not share in the care of pups. Males form all-male colonies.

The female becomes sexually mature when about 4 years old, whereas the male cannot defend a harem until 7 or 8 years of age. Lives approximately 18 years.

Status and Habitat. Common resident. Before arrival of Europeans the population was much greater than at present. *Over 260,000 were slaughtered between 1917 and 1953 for their skins and oil on Península Valdés alone. The current population of coastal Patagonia is around 60,000 and shows signs of increasing (E. Crespo).* Breeding and resting colonies are on rocky points, protected beaches, and coastal islands. Some individuals make a habit of climbing on boats and piers to obtain food. Coastal waters.

Range. Inhabits Atlantic and Pacific coasts from Tierra del Fuego to the south of Brazil on the eastern coast and up to Peru on the west of South America; also Staten Island, Falkland Islands (Islas Malvinas), and the Island of Diego Ramírez. Many of the pups born on Península Valdés, Chubut, winter at Punta Bermejo, Río Negro.

244. SOUTH AMERICAN FUR SEAL / Lobo Marino de Dos Pelos
Arctocephalus australis   *Plate 33*

Description. 6 ft (1.90 m); weight 300 lb (159 kg). Heavy-set with a thick neck. Muzzle moderately long and pointed. Coat dark gray to brown; underparts paler, often yellow rust. Mustachial "vibrissae" are very long. *Female:* 5 ft (1.42 m); weight 110 lb (50 kg), much smaller and more graceful than the male.

Behavior. Gregarious. Forms large colonies, sometimes together with previous species. Males gather in all-male colonies. Very timid on land. The whole colony may take to the water if frightened. Walks on all fours and is particularly adept at climbing steep, irregular rocky shores. In hot weather, spends long hours in the water near the colony, with one or 2 flippers held in the air to keep cool. Swims rapidly, using its foreflippers, and often porpoises out of the water. Feeds at sea on the continental shelf and beyond. *Recorded over 200 miles (300 km) from the coast.* Diet includes Argentine anchovy (*Engraulis anchoita*) and other fish, cephalopods, gastropods, and crustaceans. Does not follow fishing vessels at sea.

Male produces low roars and repeated high-pitched calls. Female makes loud barking calls and pup produces a lamblike bleating. Both sexes also produce an alarm "cough."

In November, males fight to establish territories on shore within the colony and begin restraining females. Territories have ill-defined limits and harems range from one to 13 females. Female gives birth to a single offspring within the harem. At birth, pup weighs about 9 lb (4 kg). Female becomes receptive shortly after giving birth and mates with the harem bull. After she has mated, the dominant bull allows her to return to sea to feed. Breeding season extends into mid-January. Gestation is actually about 7 months but appears to last a little under a year because of delayed implantation (*see* Southern Elephant Seal). Pups gather in crèches toward end of December while their mothers are away at sea feeding. Female nurses her offspring for almost a year.

Female becomes sexually mature when 3 years old; male is able to defend a harem only when 6 or 7 years old.

Status and Habitat. Scarce in Patagonia. Resident on some islands. Occasional visitor on the continental coast. Mainly coastal waters, coming ashore on steep, inaccessible, rocky shores. Generally occupies steep shores while the sea lion prefers level spaces.

Range. Tierra del Fuego up to São Paulo (Brazil) on the Atlantic and the south of Peru on the Pacific; Falkland Islands (Islas Malvinas). *Colony on Isla Rasa, Chubut, varied seasonally in 1993–96 between 2000 and 11,000 adults (E. Crespo).* Small, nonbreeding colonies on Isla Escondida, Chubut, and Cabo Blanco, Santa Cruz.

Similar Species. Smaller than the previous species, with a very pointed snout. Fur much finer and grayer.

TRUE SEALS / Focas, Elefantes Marinos
(Family Phocidae)

Marine mammals that rest and breed on land. They lack visible, external ears. Testicles are hidden within the abdominal cavity; rear flippers are not extended forward, and members of this family cannot walk on all fours but instead advance by "hitching" along on their bellies. They swim with their rear flippers using their relatively small foreflippers for maneuvering under water. In consequence, the vertebrae of the lumbar region are large and strong.

True seals can make prolonged dives because their blood contains relatively large amounts of oxygen-carrying hemoglobin. They have a larger proportion of blood in the body per unit of weight, in comparison with terrestrial mammals, and they are able to store more oxygen in their muscles. Some true seals make very deep dives. Before diving they breathe most of the air out of their lungs. As the seal descends, residual air is forced out of the alveoli into the relatively nonabsorbing, noncollapsible forward air passages. This avoids nitrogen of the residual air becoming dissolved in the blood and then converting into bubbles of gas when pressure is relieved as the animal returns to the surface. This excruciating phenomenon, called the "bends," is well known to divers and can be fatal. There are 18 species of true seals in the world, one of which is found in coastal Patagonia.

245. SOUTHERN ELEPHANT SEAL / Elefante Marino del Sur
Mirounga leonina   *Plate 33*

Description. Male 13–20 ft (4–5 m); weight 5000–7500 lb (2400–3600 kg). Spindled-shaped body. Large proboscis, which gives rise to its name. Foreflippers small and very flexible; hindflippers webbed. All slate gray. As the year advances, the pelt wears and turns chestnut, cream, or yellowish. *Female:* 10 ft (3 m); weight 1300 lb (600 kg), much smaller than male and has no proboscis. Color similar. *Pup:* Black at birth. Before weaning, when 3 weeks old, molts to silvery gray with paler underparts.

Behavior. Gregarious on the coasts. Swims using its hind flippers. Maximum speed in water is around 12–15 mph (20–25 kph). Does not breach. Dives continuously at sea, day and night, to depths averaging 1200–2000 ft (350–650 m) and occasionally beyond 3000 ft (1000 m). Each dive lasts an average of 20 min, then seal rises to the surface where it remains breathing for about 3 min and dives again. *Longest dive recorded lasted 2 hours (Campagna et al. 1995).* It feeds on fish and cephalopods. On land, it advances by "hitching" on its belly. Male emits loud, harsh roars as a threat display, and makes echoing hammer-on-wood-like territorial calls. Proboscis acts as a resonance box. Female produces loud, prolonged, rasping sounds, and also emits high-pitched, barklike calls during breeding season to attract her offspring. Pup produces short yelps.

Polygynous. At end of August, males start arriving at the traditional breeding beaches and immediately commence competing to establish a social rank or hierarchy. Shortly after, females start arriving. Controlled by a single dominant male or "beach master," each harem contains an average of 10–20 females, occasionally over 100. These harems are dotted along the pebble beach every 650–3000 ft (200–1000 m). Around edges of each harem, other males gather and challenge the beach master.

Although birth takes place about 11 months after copulation, gestation is little more than 7 months, as in the fur seal and sea lion. After a few early divisions, the blastocyst rests in the upper reaches of the womb for several months, no larger than a grain of sand. Then, about January, it resumes its splitting and growth, "implanting" in the uterus. Gestation takes place at sea. Female gives birth to a single pup on land 5 days after arrival. Pup measures 4 ft (1.3 m) at birth and weighs about 80 lbs (40 kg). Most births take place in September and October. Eighteen days after giving birth, female becomes receptive and mates with the harem bull. Milk is rich in fat (50%) and protein. Pup is nursed for a total of 23 days and increases rapidly in weight to almost 300 lb (130 kg). It is then weaned and abandoned by the mother. From the time she arrives on shore until she weans her pup, she does not enter the water to feed or drink and can lose more than a third of her weight. The pup remains ashore a further 5–8 weeks and then goes to sea in search of food. After she has weaned her pup, the female returns to sea to feed for two and a half months; then she returns to molt.

The dominant bull leaves as soon as he has mated with all the females in his harem, or has been forced away by another male, and returns to sea to feed. The last breeding bull does not leave the rookery until mid-November. The male returns to molt at the beginning of February. Molting occurs every year and takes between 16 and 21 days. The first animals molt in November and the last in March.

Female becomes mature at 3–5 years of age. Male cannot normally defend a harem until he is 10 years old. Both exceptionally live up to 20 years.

Status and Habitat. Common along the external shores of Península Valdés and adjacent shores. Uncommon along the rest of Patagonia. Occurs on shore much of the year but is more abundant during the breeding season. Low rocky platforms and pebble or sandy beaches along the coast in isolated areas. In 1990 the world population of Southern Elephant Seals was estimated to be around 664,000. Main concentrations occurred at South Georgia (over 350,000), Macquarie Island (78,000), and Kerguelen (189,000). The Península Valdés population of about 33,000 animals is showing signs of growth (Laws 1994). Elsewhere, most populations are diminishing.

Range. Colonies on many islands throughout the sub-Antarctic oceans between 16°S and 78°S. Although animals occasionally visit the continental shores of Antarctica, Africa, New Zealand, Tasmania, and parts of South America, the only continental breeding colony occurs on Península Valdés in Patagonia. *From here both sexes usually swim directly to edge of continental shelf, where they remain feeding along the break. Some animals travel 1200 miles (2000 km) farther afield into the Atlantic (C. Campagna).*

EVEN-TOED UNGULATES / UNGULADOS PARIDIGITADOS

(Order Artiodactyla)

A large and varied group of mammals. Domestic sheep and cows (family Bovidae) belong to this order.

GUANACOS / Guanacos
(Family Camelidae)

Camel-like animals differ from other, even-toed ungulates, such as cows, sheep, and deer, because their bodies do not rest on hooves, but on thickened pads covered with skin on the soles of each toe. The hoofs are small and situated in front of each toe, resembling nails. All camelids (camel-like animals) have harelips, long curved necks, and their legs lack tensor muscles, making the legs' insertion in the body look very high. Of the 6 species of camelids that exist in the world today, 4 are found in South America. Two of these, the alpaca and the llama, exist only in domesticated form, whereas the vicuña (pronounced "vicoonia") and the guanaco are wild. The ranges of the llama, alpaca, and vicuña are mostly restricted to the Altiplano zone of Argentina, Chile, Bo-

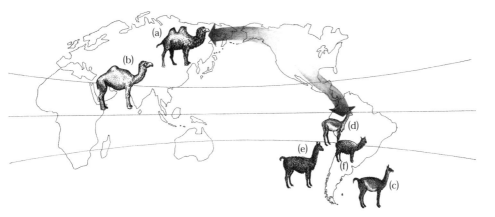

26. Camel-like animals originated in North America. They moved west into Asia across the Bering land bridge and south through the Isthmus of Panama into South America during the Pliocene, 10 million years ago. They then became extinct in North America. (a) The Bactrian camel still exists in the wild in parts of Central Asia. (b) The Dromedary only exists in domesticated form. (c) The Guanaco is the most widely distributed of the wild camels of South America. (d) The Vicuña is found only in the Altiplano. (e) The Llama exists only in domesticated form and is used as a pack animal in the Andes. (f) The Alpaca exists only in domesticated form and is reared for wool in the Andes.

livia, and Peru. The guanaco is the most widely distributed of the 4 South American camelids and the only one found in Patagonia.

246. GUANACO / Guanaco
Lama guanicoe   *Plate 31*

Description. 6 ft (1.8 m). The largest indigenous herbivore of the Patagonian steppe. Covered with very fine hair. Upperparts rust; underparts white. Muzzle and top of head blackish. Long ears, normally held erect but pressed back to signal threat. Tail short and bushy. Female very hard to distinguish other than by behavior.

Behavior. Gregarious. In groups all year round; lone individuals are rare.

Social structure is centered round the family herd: a dominant male establishes himself in a specific area covering between 250 and 1250 acres (1–5 sq km), and defends between 6 and 16 females. Dominant male marks his territory with dung piles. Nonbreeding males form groups that may number over 100 animals.

Forages during daytime, moving slowly through the scrub; returns in the evening to preferred sleeping sites. Does not need to drink for long periods. In summer, occasionally drinks brackish water from lagoons and saltwater from the sea.

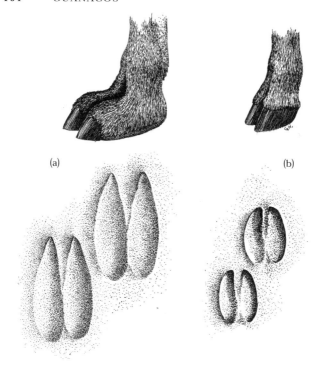

(a)   (b)

27. The foot shape and print of the Guanaco (a) compared
with that of the sheep (b). Note the position of the hoof and
the depth of the print.

Can run at 37 mph (60 kph). The young guanaco or *chulengo* is able to run
swiftly within a day of birth.

When attacking, holds its head high, and with ears back, spits fine mists of spit-
tle which, if entering the eye, could temporarily blind its aggressor. Is a strong
swimmer and sometimes crosses over to islands in search of food. Frequently
dust-bathes using pawed-out depressions in soil, the surface of which is churned
into powdery dust. Alarm call is a high neigh emitted by both males and females;
this signal serves to warn the group of potential predators.

In October, adult males challenge one another over territorial boundaries.
They thump their chests together while shaking their heads and trying to bite
each other. Usually the encounter ends in a chase in which the winner runs with
his head thrust forward, almost touching the ground. Gestation lasts 345–360
days; female gives birth to one young a year. Young are born during November
weighing 16–24 lb (8–11 kg). Two weeks after giving birth, the female mates with
the herd's dominant male. The young *chulengo* suckles for 6–12 months. Female
reaches sexual maturity at 2 years, while male is able to establish a territory and
form a family group only at 4–6 years.

28. Guanacos frequently threaten other members of the herd or outsiders, laying their ears flat and spitting.

29. In the foreground, a typical family herd with seven adult female Guanacos in December or January on the Valdés Peninsula, Patagonia. Three newborn *chulengos* have paler coats. The yearling, standing second from the left, will probably soon be expelled from the group by the herd's male, standing on the rise at right. A dung heap in the immediate foreground is made by herd members and helps mark territory. An adult female dusts herself at right. A group of bachelors browses in the background. The rounded bushes are Quillimbai (*Chuquiraga avellanedae*); the grasses are mainly Flechilla (*Stipa* sp.), in full seed. Giant fossil oysters (*Ostrea tehuelche*) form part of the Tertiary deposits in the rise at right.

30. Two male Guanacos fight over a harem, butting with their chests and biting, until one of them retreats. With his head held close to the ground, the victor chases the loser.

Status and Habitat. Common resident. Hunted for meat and skins in many parts, and its range is shrinking. *In 1995 the population on Península Valdés had shrunk to under 2500 animals, less than a third of its original size, through illegal hunting (R. Baldi).* Open, arid terrain from high-altitude plateaus to open scrub desert.

Range. Center and south of Argentina. South of Chile to Ecuador. Introduced in the Falkland Islands (Islas Malvinas).

Appendix A
Accidental Records and
Sightings

A number of species of birds and mammals have been recorded on the coast of continental Patagonia that do not breed here and their ocurrence is probably accidental rather than regular.

BIRDS

247. GREATER WAGTAIL-TYRANT / Calandrita
Stigmatura budytoides

Description. 5.5″ (14 cm). Upperparts brown. Eyebrow and underparts yellowish. Long tail, dark brown tipped with white.

Behavior. Conspicuous and active. Often holds tail erect as it forages among branches of bushes. Very vocal. Occasional loud, repeated duets.

Status and Habitat. Rare or accidental in arid bush-covered steppe. *One adult among bushes at Punta Tombo, Chubut, November (1993).*

Range. Northern edge of Patagonia, central Argentina, east of the Andes to Bolivia.

248. KELP GOOSE / Caranca
Chloephaga hybrida

Description. 20″ (52 cm). Entirely white except for primaries and wing bar, visible in flight. Legs yellow. *Female:* Head and back blackish brown, belly heavily barred black and white.

Behavior. In pairs. Forages among kelp.

Status and Habitat. Rare or accidental (?). Rocky seashores. *One pair recorded on Isla Pingüino, Santa Cruz, winter 1987 (Marcos Oliva Day).*

Range. Coast of Tierra del Fuego.

249. YELLOW-BILLED TIT-TYRANT / Torito Pico amarillo
Anairetes flavirostris

Description. 4″ (10 cm). Very similar to Tufted Tit-Tyrant but dark streaking on chest heavier and darker. Iris dark. Lower mandible pale horn.

Status and Habitat. Rare or accidental. Dry thick scrub areas. *One adult recorded at Punta Tombo, Chubut, November 1991.*

Range. Northern edge of Patagonia, central Argentina, Andes of Bolivia and Peru.

MAMMALS

250. LEOPARD SEAL / Leopardo marino
Hydrurga leptonyx

Description. 9–11 ft (3–3.6 m). Head large; wide mouth and powerful jaws; eyes placed high, giving it a reptilian appearance. Upperparts dark gray-brown mottled darker. Underparts light brown, spotted dark.

Behavior. Feeds on fish, krill, cephalopods, marine birds, and mammals. Penguins are a favorite prey.

Status and Habitat. *One thin and wounded adult appeared on the beaches of Puerto Madryn in winter 1996.*

Range. Circumpolar around Antarctica. Wanders into temperate waters of the Southern Hemisphere.

251. CRABEATER SEAL / Foca Cangrejera
Lobodon carcinophagus

Description. 5–8 ft (1.5–2.5 m). Snout fairly long and slightly upturned. Body often crossed with long, straight, parallel scars. Upperparts dark silver gray; underside pale cream or off-white. Unique to these seals, the postcanine teeth show several cusps.

Behavior. Solitary. Feeds on krill.

Status and Habitat. Accidental visitor. *One very thin adult appeared on beaches of Puerto Madryn, Chubut, August 1994.* One of the most abundant seals in the world.

Range. Circumpolar around Antarctica. Ranges up the coasts of South America, New Zealand, Australia, and South Africa.

Appendix B
Recommended Reading

General

Campbell, B., and E. Lack. 1985. *A Dictionary of Birds.* The British Ornithologists' Union. Vermilion, S.D.: Buteo Books; Calton, Waterhouses, Staffordshire, U.K.: T. and D. Poyse Ltd.

Erize, F., M. Canevari, P. Canevari, G. Costa, and M. Rumboll. 1981. *Los Parques Nacionales de la Argentina y Otras de Sus Areas Naturales.* Madrid: INCAFO.

Simpson, G. G. 1980. *Splendid Isolation: The Curious History of South American Mammals.* New Haven, Conn.: Yale University Press.

Birds

Canevari, M., P. Canevari, G. R. Carizzo, G. Harris, J. Rodriguez Mata, and R. J. Straneck. 1991. *Nueva Guía de las Aves Argentinas.* Buenos Aires: Fundación Acindar.

De Schauensee, R. M. 1970. *A Guide to the Birds of South America.* Philadelphia: Academy of Natural Sciences/Livingston Publishing.

Dunning, J. S. 1982. *South American Land Birds.* Newton Square, Pa.: Harrowood Books.

Harrison, P. 1983. *Seabirds: An Identification Guide.* Boston: Houghton Mifflin.

———. 1987. *Seabirds of the World: A Photographic Guide.* Princeton: Princeton University Press.

Hayman, P., J. Marchant, and T. Prater. 1986. *Shorebirds: An Identification Guide to the Waders of the World.* London: Christopher Helm.

Murphy, R. C. 1936. *Oceanic Birds of South America.* Vols. 1–2. New York: Macmillan.

Narosky, T., and D. Yzurieta. 1987. *Guía para la identificación de las Aves de Argentina y Uruguay.* Buenos Aires: AOP Vazquez Mazzini Editores.

Ridgely, R. S., and G. Tudor. 1989. *The Birds of South America.* Vol. 1: *The Oscine Passerines.* Austin: University of Texas Press.

———. 1994. *The Birds of South America.* Vol. 2: *The Suboscine Passerines.* Austin: University of Texas Press.

Scott, P. 1957. *A Coloured Key to the Wildfowl of the World.* Slimbridge, UK: The Wildfowl Trust.

Tuck, G., and H. Heinzel. 1978. *A Field Guide to the Seabirds of Britain and the World.* London: Collins.

Mammals

Campagna, C., and A. Lichter. 1996. *Las Ballenas de la Patagonia.* Buenos Aires: Emecé Editores.

Harris, G., and C. Garcia. 1986. *The Right Whales of Peninsula Valdes.* Puerto Madryn, Arg.: Editorial Golfo Nuevo.

Hoyt, E. 1981. *Orca: The Whale Called Killer.* Toronto: E. P. Dutton/Firefly Books.

Leatherwood, S., and R. Reeves. 1983. *The Sierra Club Handbook of Whales and Dolphins.* San Francisco: Sierra Club Books.

Lichter, A. 1993. *Huellas en la Arena Sombras en el Mar.* Buenos Aires: Editorial Terranova.

Macdonald, D. 1984. *The Encyclopedia of Mammals.* New York: Facts on File.

Payne, R. 1993. *Among Whales.* New York: Scribner.

Reeves, R. R., B. S. Stewart, and S. Leatherwood. 1992. *The Sierra Club Handbook of Seals and Sirenians.* San Francisco: Sierra Club Books.

Glossary

Adult — A fully developed physically and sexually mature individual.

Breaching — Leaping clear or almost clear of the water.

Caruncle — Unfeathered fleshy, often brightly colored structures on the heads of some species of birds (e.g., at the base top part of the beak in some cormorants).

Coverts — The feathers that cover the upper and lower surfaces of the wing from the leading edge to the base of the primaries and secondaries.

Cretaceous — Period of geological time extending from 136 to 65 million years before the present.

Cryptic — Body coloration that blends with the surroundings.

Culmen — The dorsal ridge of the upper mandible of birds.

Dabbling ducks — Ducks of the tribe anatini that feed on the surface of the water or by "upending."

Diurnal — Active during daytime.

Dorsal — Pertaining to the upper or top side.

Echolocation — The process of locating, by way of reflected sound, the position and qualities of an object.

Eocene — Geological epoch extending from 55 to 37 million years before the present.

Filoplumes — Differentiated, hairlike feathers on the head of some species of birds.

Forage — To search for food.

Gape — The mouth opening; the angle formed at the lateral corners of the open mouth.

Halux — The first toe of birds, which is usually opposed and points backward.

Melon — The rounded area on top of the head of dolphins and beaked whales.

Miocene — Geological epoch extending from 22 to 5 million years before the present.

Molt — The annual replacement of feathers or fur.

Mottled — Stained or smudged.

Nocturnal — Active at night.

Oceanic — Pertaining to the ocean.

Oceanic island — Island far from the mainland, as opposed to a coastal island.

Pelagic — Pertaining to the ocean areas beyond the continental shelf. Birds that forage on the high sea.

Pod — A group of whales or dolphins.

Polyandrous — Females that mate with more than one male during one season.

Polygynous — Males that mate with more than one female during one season.

Primaries — The flight-enabling feathers that are fixed to the hand (metacarpal) joint of the bird and form the outer portion of the wing.

Rachis — The shaft of the feather.

Ramus (pl. rami) — Lower edge of a bird's bill.

Rookery — Area chosen by colonial species of marine mammals or birds to rest or breed on shore.

Roost — Area chosen by birds for resting.

Secondaries — The flight-enabling feathers that are fixed to the forearm (ulna) of the bird and form the trailing edge of the wing.

Speculum — Brightly colored—often iridescent—area at the base of the secondaries in ducks and geese.

Steppe — Low-lying, flat, arid country of the temperate zone.

Sternum — The breastbone.

Stot — Advance by bouncing on all four legs.

Surf zone — The area of coastal water between the place where the waves break and the shore.

Tarsal joint — Sometimes called the "knee" when referring to birds; it is in fact the ankle joint. The tarsal joint is halfway down the leg in birds and many mammals, and the leg bends forward at this point.

Tarsus (pl. tarsi) — Refers to the lower leg in birds, and corresponds to the fused tarso-metatarsus.

Terrestrial — Refers to animals that live on the ground as opposed to in bushes or trees.

Tertiary — Geological period of time extending from 65 to 2 million years before the present and containing the Paleocene, Eocene, Oligocene, Miocene, and Pliocene epochs.

Ulna — Together with the radius forms the forearm. In birds it has a series of knobs to which the quills of the secondaries are attached.

Underparts — Refers to the throat, anterior portion of the neck, chest, and belly of a bird or mammal.

Upperparts — Refers to the top of the head, neck, and back of a bird and mammal.

Vane — Also known as "vexillum," the flattened portions of the feathers on both sides of the rachis, made up of evenly spaced barbs.

Ventral — The underside of the body.

Vibrissae — Long hairs on muzzle in mammals and surrounding the beak in some birds.

Washup — Refers to the carcasses, found on beaches, of birds or mammals that died at sea.

Wrists — The carpal joint. In birds this joint is at the bend in the leading edge of the wing.

Bibliography

American Ornithologists' Union. 1983. *Checklist of North American Birds.* 6th ed.

Boersma, P. D. 1987. Penguins oiled in Argentina. *Science* 236: 135.

————. 1996. Marine conservation: Protecting the exploited commons. *Society for Conservation Biology Newsletter* 3, no. 4.

Boersma, P. D., D. L. Stokes, and P. M. Yorio. 1990. Reproductive variability and historical change of Magellanic Penguins (*Spheniscus magellanicus*) at Punto Tombo, Argentina. In L. S. Davis and J. T. Darby, eds., *Penguin Biology,* 15–43. Chicago: Academic Press.

Boswall, J., and D. MacIver. 1975. The Magellanic Penguin (*Spheniscus magellanicus*). In B. Stonehouse, ed., *The Biology of Penguins,* 271–305. London: Macmillan.

Boyd, I. L., T. R. Walker, and J. Poncet. 1996. Status of southern elephant seals at South Georgia. *Antarctic Science* 8 (3): 237–244.

Brownell, R. L., Jr., P. B. Best, and J. H. Prescott, eds. 1986. *Right Whales: Past and Present Status.* Reports of the International Whaling Commission. Special Issue 10. Cambridge, U.K.

Cabrera, A., and J. Yepes. 1960. *Mamíferos Sudamericanos,* vols. 1–2. Buenos Aires: Ediar S. A. Editores.

Campagna, C., and B. J. Le Boeuf. 1988. Reproductive behaviour of southern sea lions. *Behaviour* 104 3/4.

Campagna, C., B. J. Le Boeuf, S. B. Blackwell, D. E. Crocker, and F. Quintana. 1995. Diving behaviour and foraging location of female southern elephant seals from Patagonia. *Journal of Zoology* (London) 236: 55–71.

Campagna, C., and M. Lewis. 1992. Growth and distribution of a southern elephant seal colony. *Marine Mammal Science* 88(4): 387–396.

Campagna, C., M. Lewis, and R. Baldi. 1993. Breeding biology of southern elephant seals in Patagonia. *Marine Mammal Science* 9(1): 34–47.

Corbet, G. B., and J. E. Hill. 1980. *A World List of Mammalian Species.* London and Ithaca, N.Y.: British Museum and Cornell University Press.

De Schauensee, R. M. 1970. *A Guide to the Birds of South America.* Philadelphia: Academy of Natural Sciences/Livingston Publishing.

Doello Jurado, M. 1917. *Sobre aves de Puerto Deseado. Revista El Hornero.* Vol. 1. Buenos Aires.

Dubost, G., and H. Genest. 1974. Le comportement social d'une colonie de maras (*Dolichotis patagonum*) dans le Parc de Branfere. *Z. Tierpsychol.* 35: 225–302.

Frere, E., P. Gandini, and V. Lichtschein. 1996. Variación latitudinal en la dieta del pingüino de Magallanes (*Spheniscus magellanicus*) en la costa Patagónica, Argentina. *Ornitología Neotropical* 7: 35–41.

Gandini, P. A., P. D. Boersma, E. Frere, M. L. Gandini, T. Holik, and V. Lichtschein. 1994. Magellanic Penguins (*Spheniscus magellanicus*) affected by chronic petroleum pollution along coast of Chubut, Argentina. *Auk* 111: 20–27.

Gandini, P., E. Frere, and P. D. Boersma. 1996. Status and conservation of Magellanic Penguins (*Spheniscus magellanicus*) in Patagonia, Argentina. *Bird Conservation International* 6: 307–316.

Genest, H., and G. Dubost. 1974. Pair living in the Mara (*Dolichotis patagonum Z.*). *Mammalia* 38, no. 2: 155–162.

Harris, G., and C. Garcia. 1990. Ballenas francas Australes El Lento Camino de la Recuperación. *Ciencia Hoy* 2, no. 7: 36–43.

Jehl, J. R. 1975. *Pluvianellus socialis:* Biology, ecology, and relationships of an enigmatic patagonian shorebird. *Trans. of San Diego Soc. Nat. Hist.* 18: 29–73.

Navas, J. R., T. Narosky, N. A. Bó, J. C. Chébez. *Lista Patrón de los Nombres Comunes de las Aves Argentinas.* Buenos Aires: Asociación Ornitológica del Plata.

Nores, M. 1991. *Checklist of the Birds of Argentina.* Centro de Zoología Aplicada. Publicación 10, Universidad Nacional Córdoba.

Olrog, C. C., and M. M. Lucero. 1981. *Guía de los Mamíferos Argentinos.* Tucumán, Arg.: Fundación Miguel Lillo.

Payne, R., O. Brazier, E. Dorsey, J. Perkins, V. Rowntree, and A. Titus. 1983. External features of Southern Right Whales (Eubalaena australis) and their use in identifying individuals. In *Communication and Behavior of Whales*, ed. R. Payne, pp. 371–445. AAAS Selected Symposia Series. Boulder, Colorado: Westview Press.

Payne, R., V. J. Rowntree, J. S. Perkins, J. G. Cooke, and K. Lankester. 1990. Population size, trends and reproductive parameters of right whales (*Eubalaena australis*) off Península Valdés. *Rep. Int. Whal. Comm.* (Special Issue) 12: 271–278.

Ridgely, R. S., and G. Tudor. 1989. *The Birds of South America.* Vol. 1: *The Oscine Passerines.* Austin: University of Texas Press.

———. 1994. *The Birds of South America.* Vol. 2: *The Suboscine Passerines.* Austin: University of Texas Press.

Rumboll, M. 1974. Una nueva especie de macá (Podicipitidae). *Comunicaciones del Museo Argentino de Ciencias Naturales (Zoología)* (Buenos Aires) 4: 33–35.

Yorio, P. M., and G. Harris. 1992. Actualización de la distribución reproductiva, estado poblacional y de conservación de la gaviota de Olrog (*Larus atlanticus*). *El Hornero* 13: 200–202.

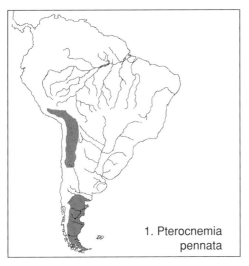

1. Pterocnemia
pennata

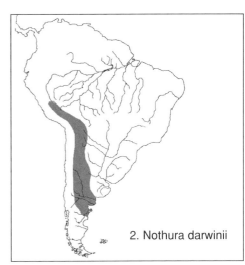

2. Nothura darwinii

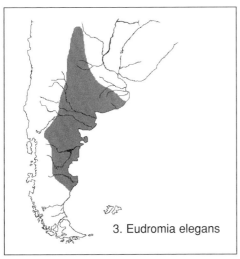

3. Eudromia elegans

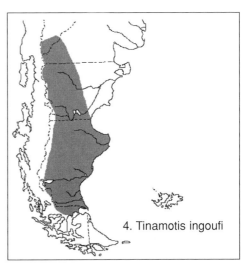

4. Tinamotis ingoufi

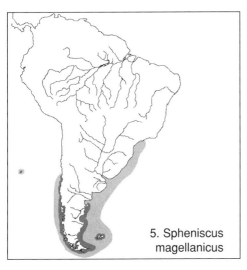

5. Spheniscus
magellanicus

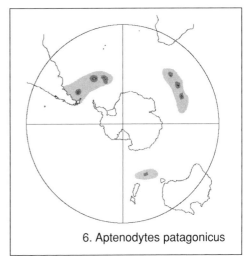

6. Aptenodytes patagonicus

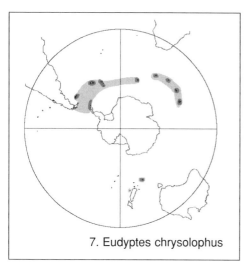

7. Eudyptes chrysolophus

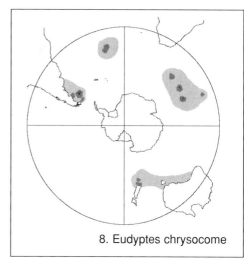

8. Eudyptes chrysocome

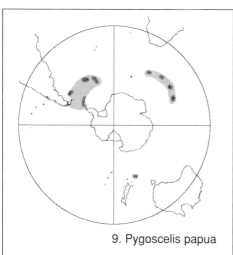

9. Pygoscelis papua

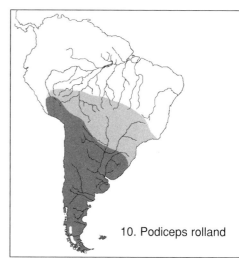

10. Podiceps rolland

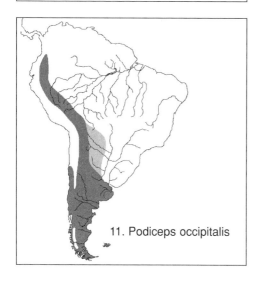

11. Podiceps occipitalis

12. Podiceps gallardoi

13. Podiceps major

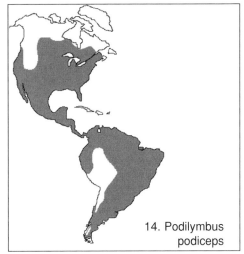

14. Podilymbus podiceps

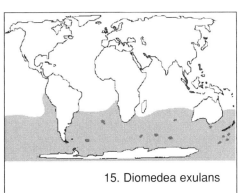

15. Diomedea exulans

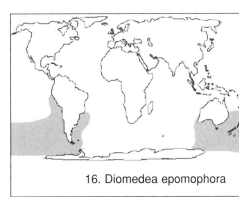

16. Diomedea epomophora

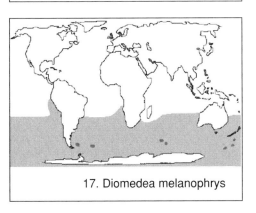

17. Diomedea melanophrys

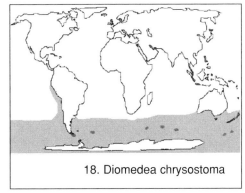

18. Diomedea chrysostoma

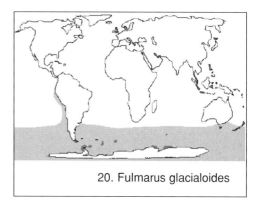

19. Macronectes giganteus

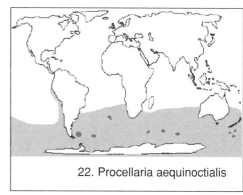

20. Fulmarus glacialoides

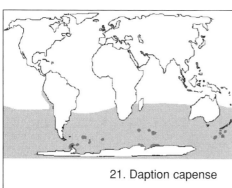

21. Daption capense

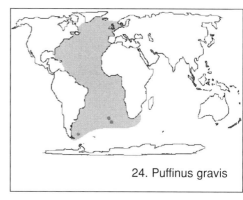

22. Procellaria aequinoctialis

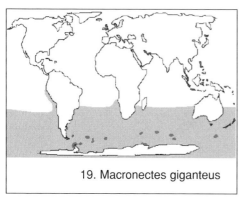

23. Procellaria (Adamastor) cinerea

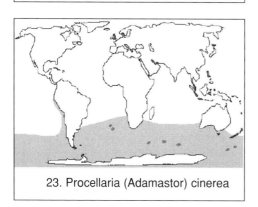

24. Puffinus gravis

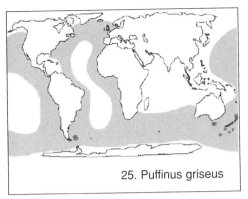

25. Puffinus griseus

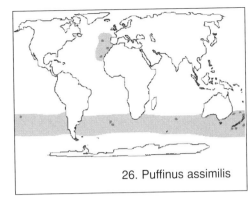

26. Puffinus assimilis

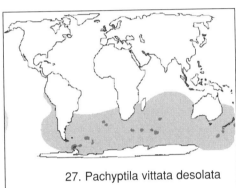

27. Pachyptila vittata desolata

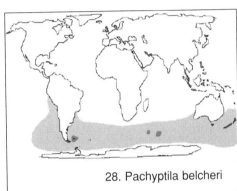

28. Pachyptila belcheri

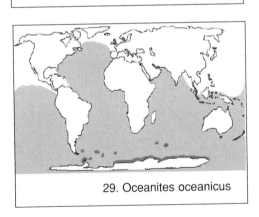

29. Oceanites oceanicus

30. Phalacrocorax olivaceus

31. Phalacrocorax
magellanicus

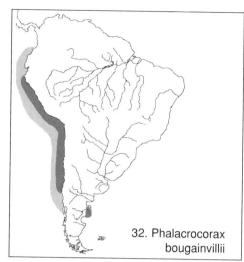

32. Phalacrocorax
bougainvillii

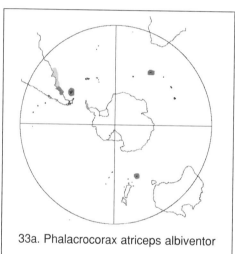

33a. Phalacrocorax atriceps albiventor

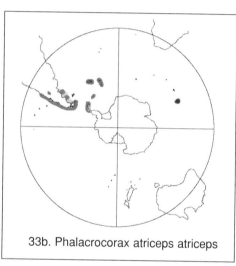

33b. Phalacrocorax atriceps atriceps

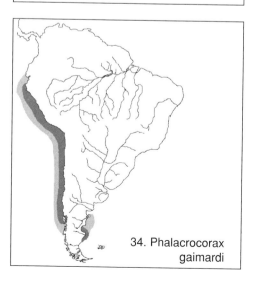

34. Phalacrocorax
gaimardi

35.
Ardea cocoi

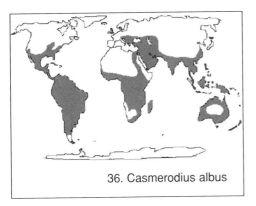

36. Casmerodius albus

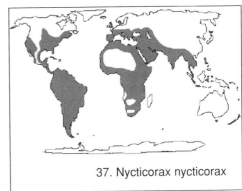

37. Nycticorax nycticorax

38. Egretta thula

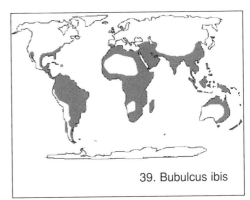

39. Bubulcus ibis

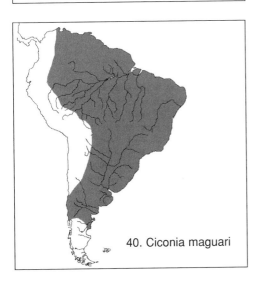

40. Ciconia maguari

41. Theristicus caudatus

42. Plegadis chihi

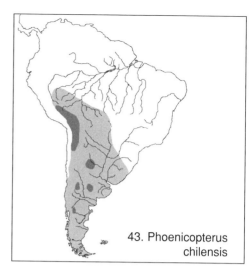

43. Phoenicopterus chilensis

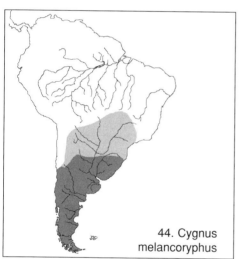

44. Cygnus melancoryphus

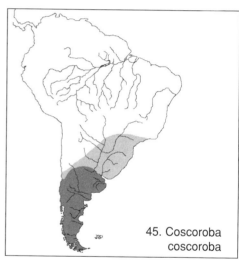

45. Coscoroba coscoroba

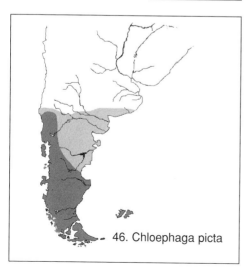

46. Chloephaga picta

47. Chloephaga poliocephala

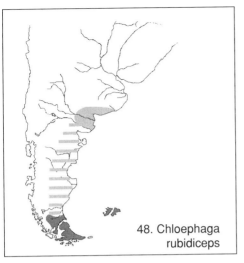

48. Chloephaga
rubidiceps

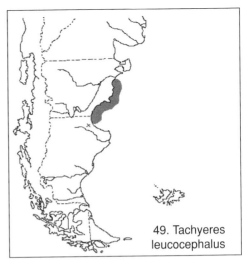

49. Tachyeres
leucocephalus

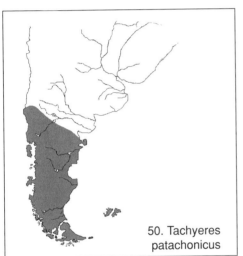

50. Tachyeres
patachonicus

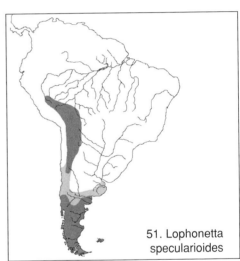

51. Lophonetta
specularioides

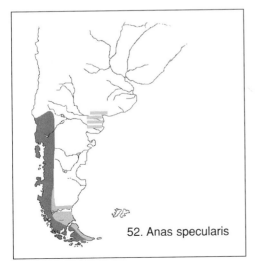

52. Anas specularis

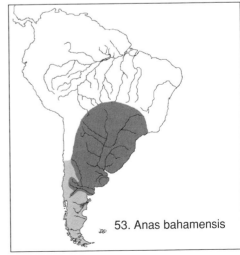

53. Anas bahamensis

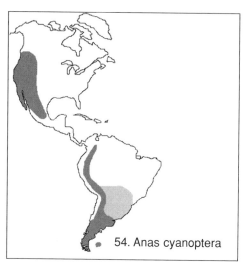

54. Anas cyanoptera

55. Anas platalea

56. Anas sibilatrix

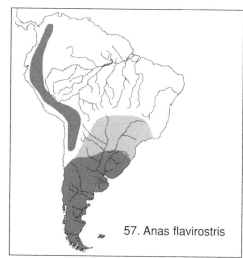

57. Anas flavirostris

58. Anas versicolor

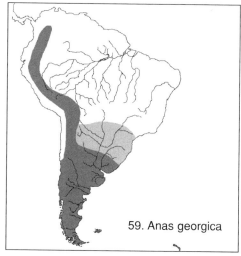

59. Anas georgica

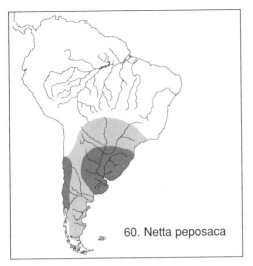

60. Netta peposaca

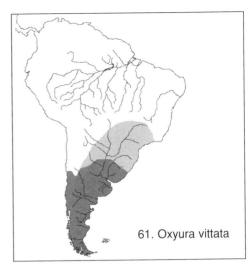

61. Oxyura vittata

62. Cathartes aura

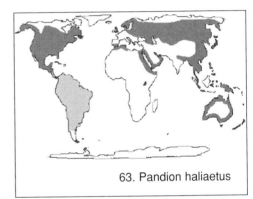

63. Pandion haliaetus

64. Geranoaetus melanoleucus

65. Buteo polyosoma

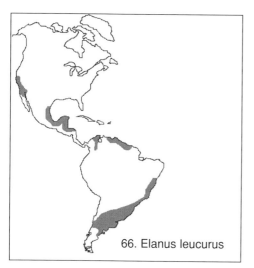

66. Elanus leucurus

67. Circus cinereus

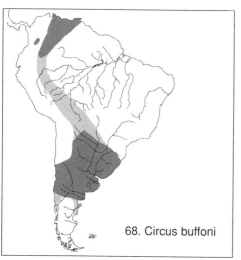

68. Circus buffoni

69. Milvago chimango

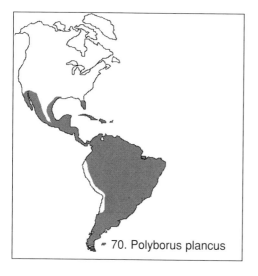

70. Polyborus plancus

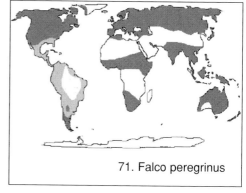

71. Falco peregrinus

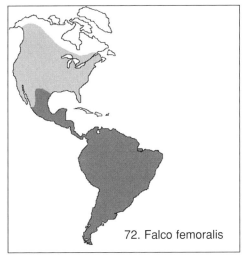

72. Falco femoralis

73. Falco sparverius

74. Pardirallus sanguinolentus

75. Fulica leucoptera

76. Fulica armillata

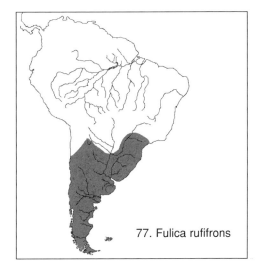

77. Fulica rufifrons

78. Gallinula
melanops

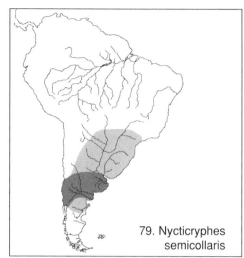

79. Nycticryphes
semicollaris

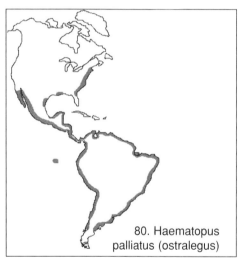

80. Haematopus
palliatus (ostralegus)

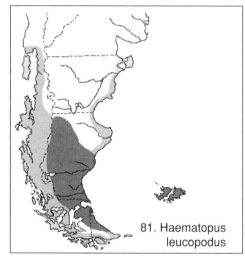

81. Haematopus
leucopodus

82. Haematopus ater

83. Vanellus chilensis

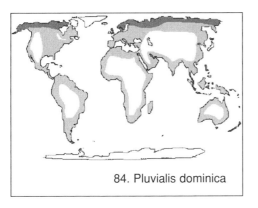

84. Pluvialis dominica

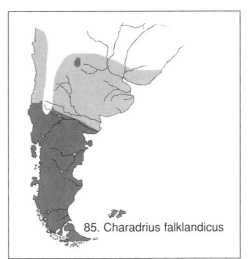

85. Charadrius falklandicus

86. Charadrius
semipalmatus

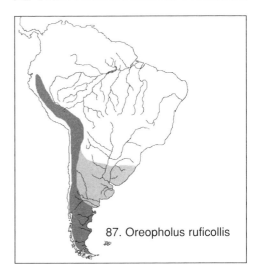

87. Oreopholus ruficollis

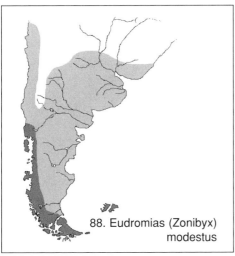

88. Eudromias (Zonibyx)
modestus

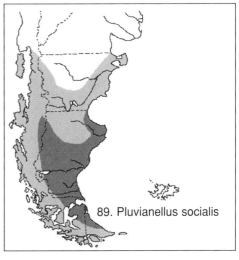

89. Pluvianellus socialis

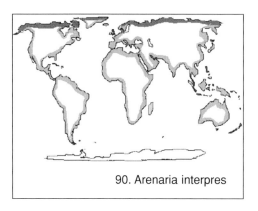

90. Arenaria interpres

91. Limosa haemastica

92. Tringa flavipes

93. Tringa melanoleuca

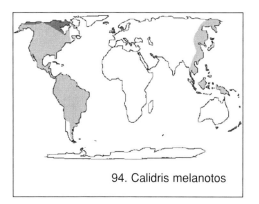

94. Calidris melanotos

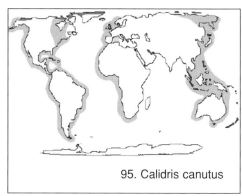

95. Calidris canutus

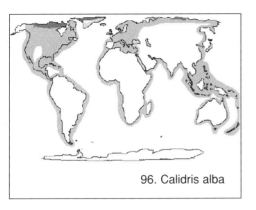

96. Calidris alba

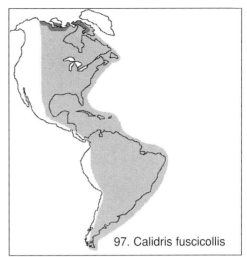

97. Calidris fuscicollis

98. Calidris pusilla

99. Calidris bairdii

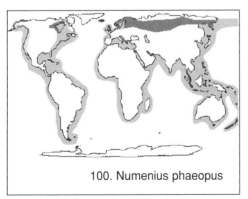

100. Numenius phaeopus

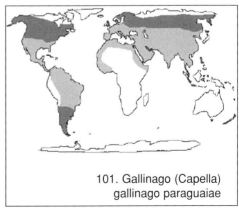

101. Gallinago (Capella)
gallinago paraguaiae

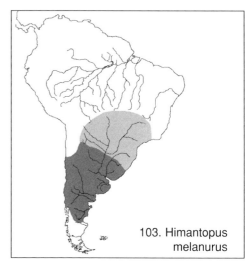

102. Phalaropus tricolor

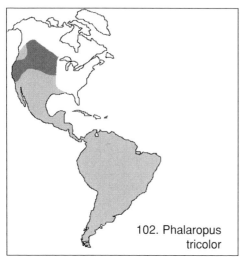

103. Himantopus melanurus

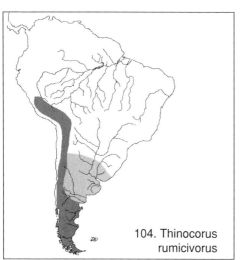

104. Thinocorus rumicivorus

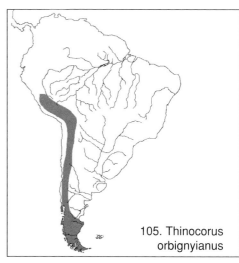

105. Thinocorus orbignyianus

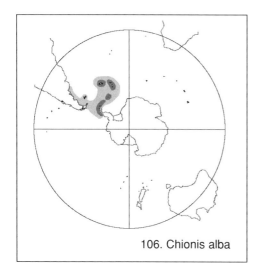

106. Chionis alba

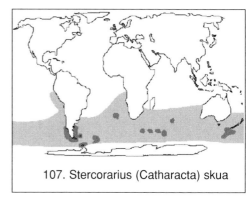

107. Stercorarius (Catharacta) skua

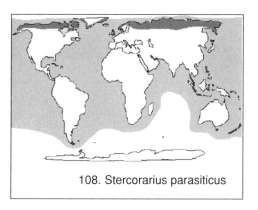

108. Stercorarius parasiticus

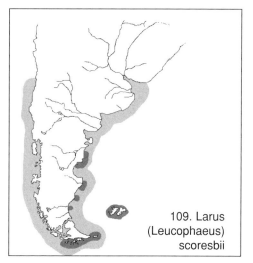

109. Larus (Leucophaeus) scoresbii

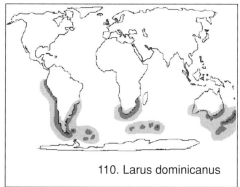

110. Larus dominicanus

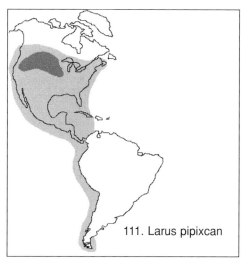

111. Larus pipixcan

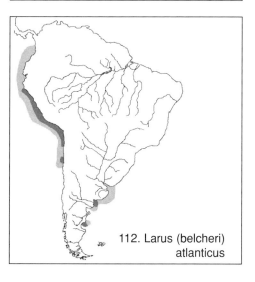

112. Larus (belcheri) atlanticus

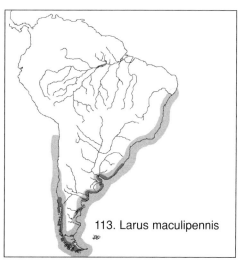

113. Larus maculipennis

114. Sterna
hirundinacea

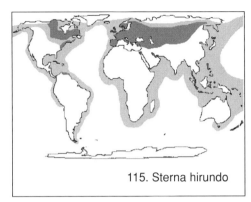

115. Sterna hirundo

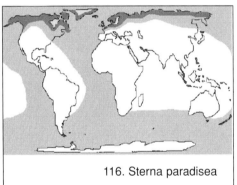

116. Sterna paradisea

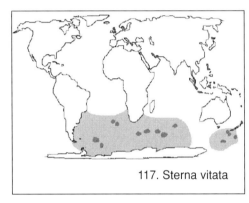

117. Sterna vitata

118. Sterna
eurygnatha

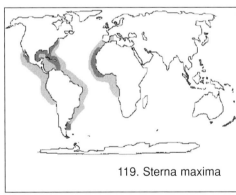

119. Sterna maxima

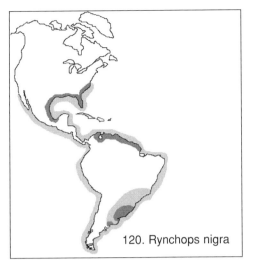

120. Rynchops nigra

121. Zenaida auriculata

122. Columbina picui

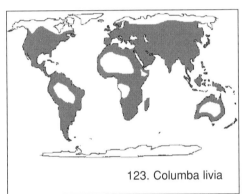

123. Columba livia

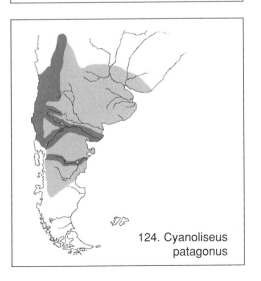

124. Cyanoliseus patagonus

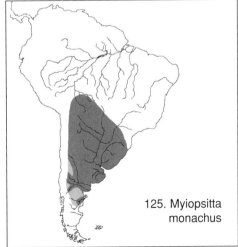

125. Myiopsitta monachus

126. Guira guira

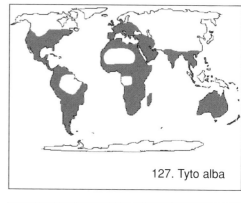

127. Tyto alba

128. Bubo virginianus

129. Athene (Speotyto) cunicularia

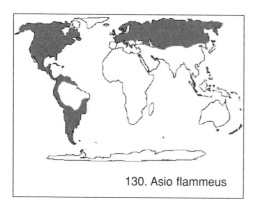

130. Asio flammeus

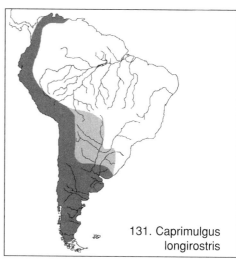

131. Caprimulgus longirostris

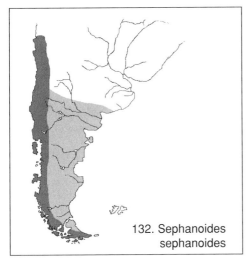

132. Sephanoides
sephanoides

133. Ceryle torquata

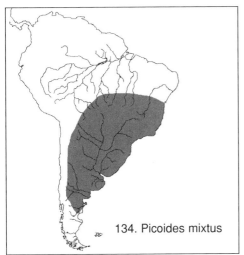

134. Picoides mixtus

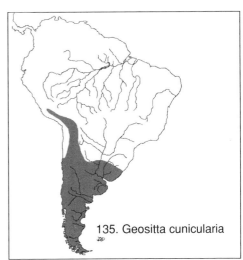

135. Geositta cunicularia

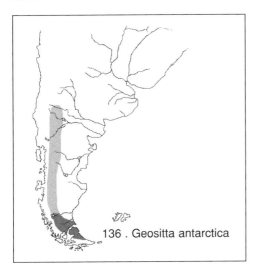

136 . Geositta antarctica

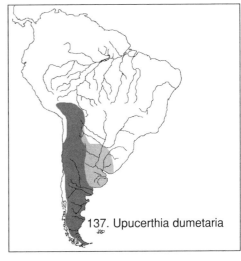

137. Upucerthia dumetaria

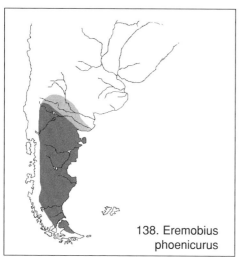

138. Eremobius
phoenicurus

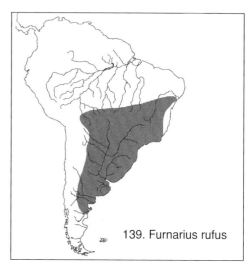

139. Furnarius rufus

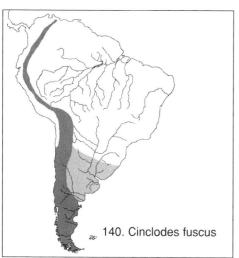

140. Cinclodes fuscus

141. Phleocryptes
melanops

142. Leptasthenura
aegithaloides

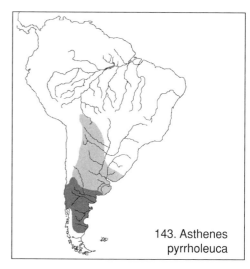

143. Asthenes
pyrrholeuca

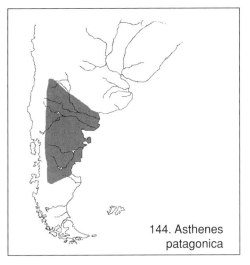

144. Asthenes patagonica

145. Thripophaga (Asthenes) modesta

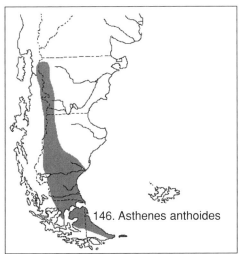

146. Asthenes anthoides

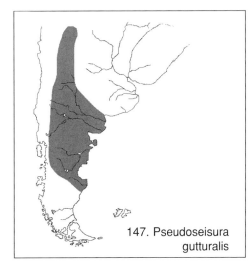

147. Pseudoseisura gutturalis

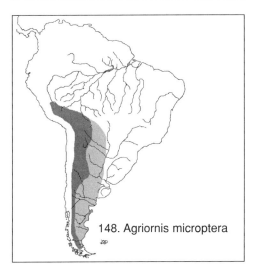

148. Agriornis microptera

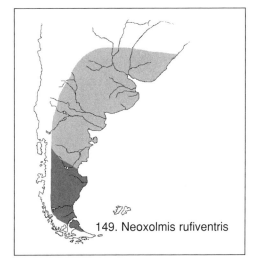

149. Neoxolmis rufiventris

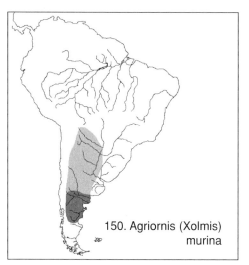

150. Agriornis (Xolmis)
murina

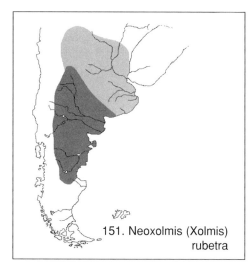

151. Neoxolmis (Xolmis)
rubetra

152. Muscisaxicola
macloviana

153. Lessonia rufa

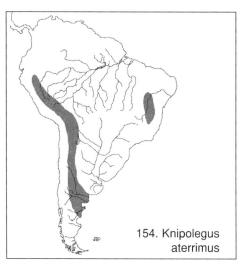

154. Knipolegus
aterrimus

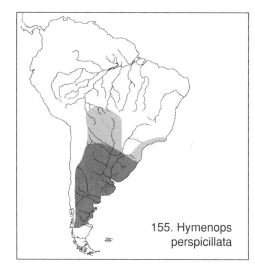

155. Hymenops
perspicillata

156. Pitangus
sulphuratus

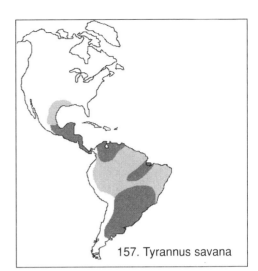

157. Tyrannus savana

158. Serpophaga
subcristata

159. Pseudocolopteryx
flaviventris

160.Tachuris
rubrigastra

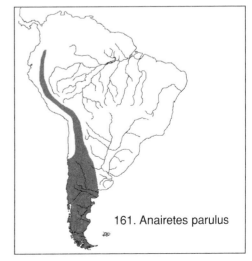

161. Anairetes parulus

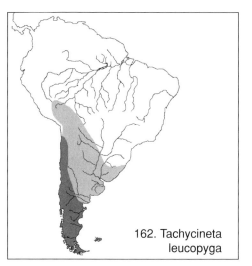

162. Tachycineta
leucopyga

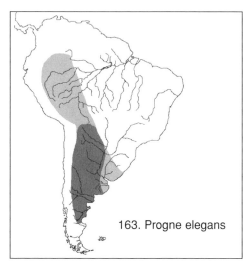

163. Progne elegans

164. Notiochelidon
cyanoleuca

165. Hirundo rustica

166. Cistothorus
platensis

167. Troglodytes
aedon

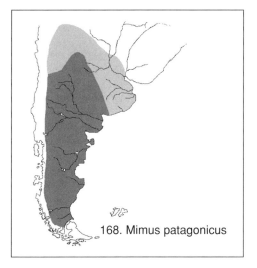

168. Mimus patagonicus

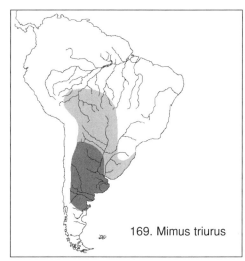

169. Mimus triurus

170. Turdus falklandii

171. Anthus correndera

172. Molothrus
bonariensis

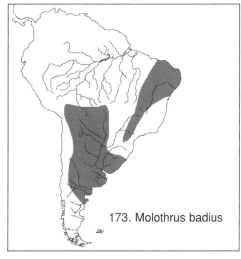

173. Molothrus badius

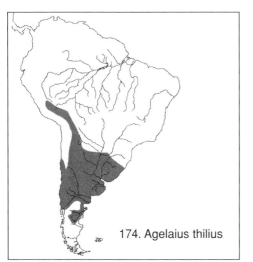

174. Agelaius thilius

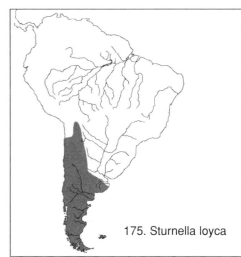

175. Sturnella loyca

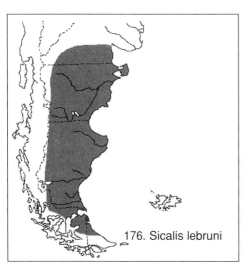

176. Sicalis lebruni

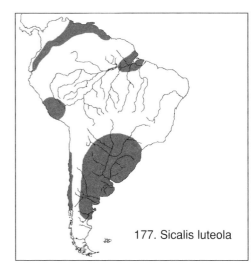

177. Sicalis luteola

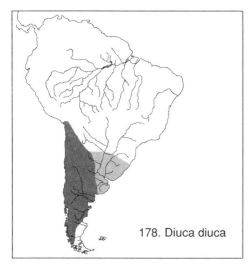

178. Diuca diuca

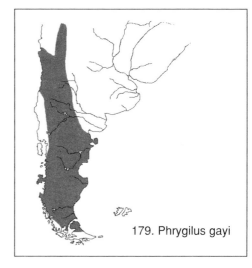

179. Phrygilus gayi

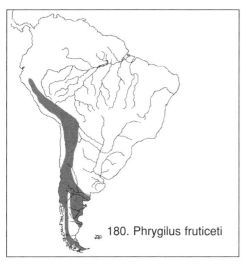

180. Phrygilus fruticeti

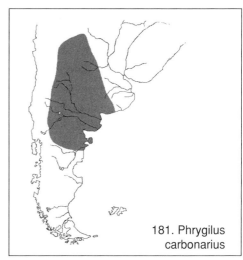

181. Phrygilus carbonarius

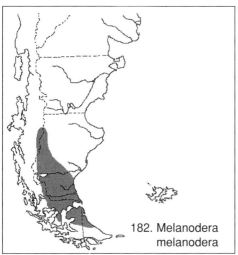

182. Melanodera melanodera

183. Zonotrichia (Junco) capensis

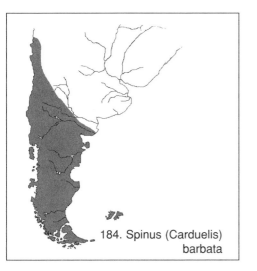

184. Spinus (Carduelis) barbata

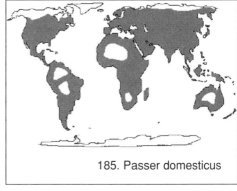

185. Passer domesticus

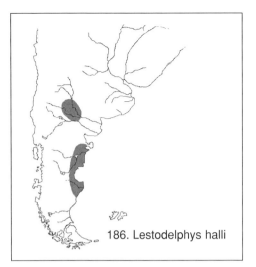

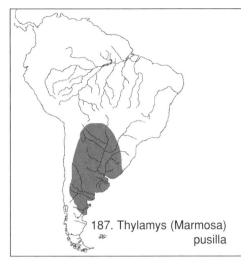

186. Lestodelphys halli

187. Thylamys (Marmosa) pusilla

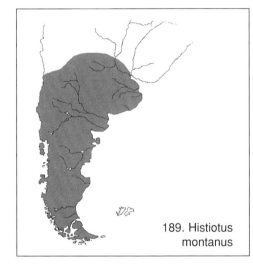

188. Tadarida brasiliensis

189. Histiotus montanus

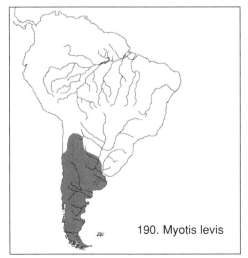

190. Myotis levis

191. Chaetophractus villosus

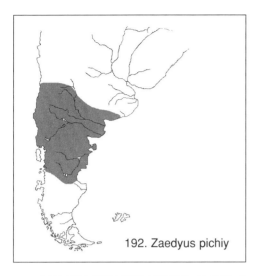

192. Zaedyus pichiy

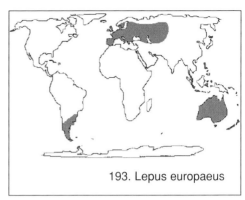

193. Lepus europaeus

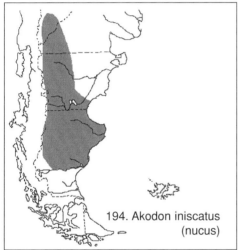

194. Akodon iniscatus
(nucus)

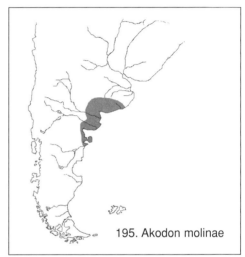

195. Akodon molinae

196. Akodon xanthorinus

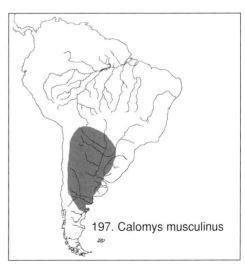

197. Calomys musculinus

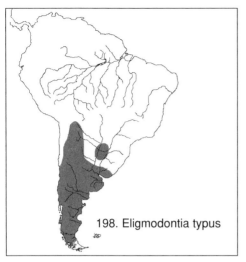

198. Eligmodontia typus

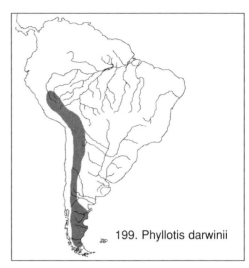

199. Phyllotis darwinii

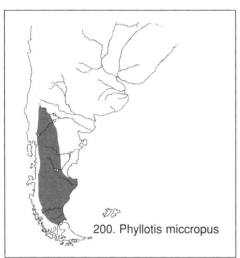

200. Phyllotis miccropus

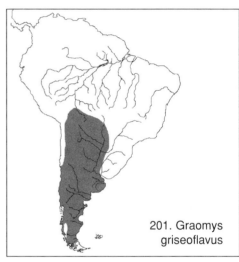

201. Graomys
griseoflavus

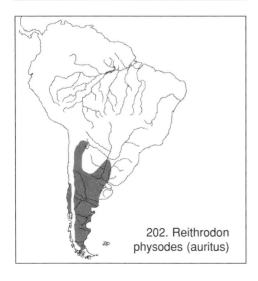

202. Reithrodon
physodes (auritus)

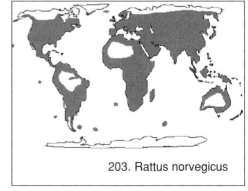

203. Rattus norvegicus

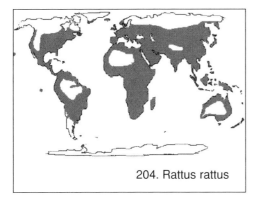

204. Rattus rattus

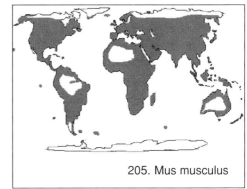

205. Mus musculus

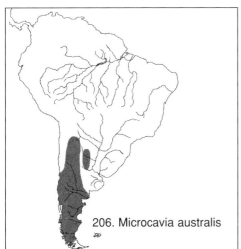

206. Microcavia australis

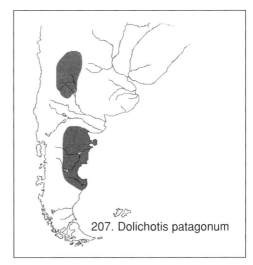

207. Dolichotis patagonum

208. Lagidium viscacia

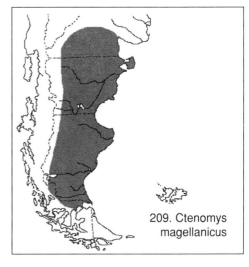

209. Ctenomys magellanicus

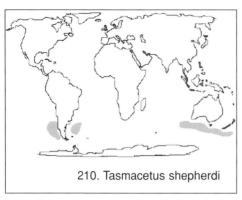

210. Tasmacetus shepherdi

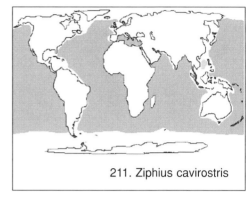

211. Ziphius cavirostris

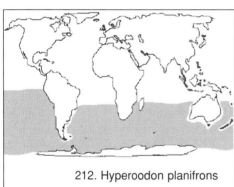

212. Hyperoodon planifrons

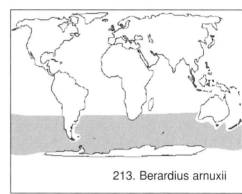

213. Berardius arnuxii

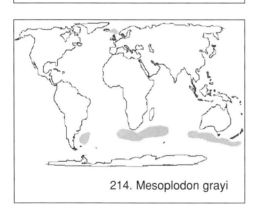

214. Mesoplodon grayi

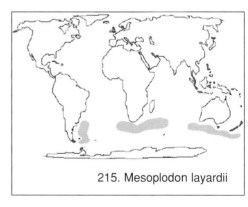

215. Mesoplodon layardii

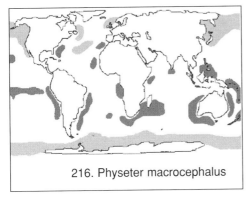

216. Physeter macrocephalus

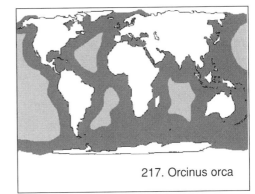

217. Orcinus orca

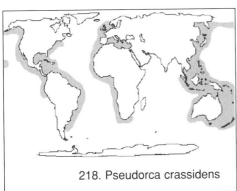

218. Pseudorca crassidens

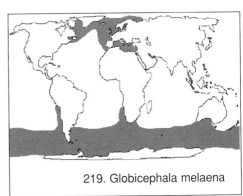

219. Globicephala melaena

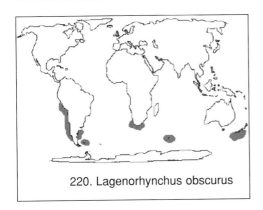

220. Lagenorhynchus obscurus

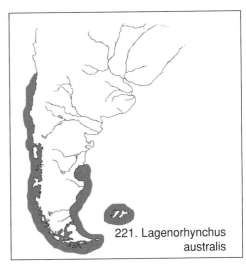

221. Lagenorhynchus australis

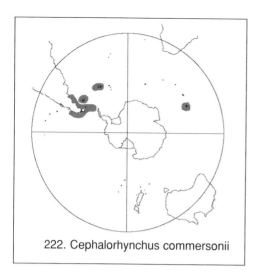

222. Cephalorhynchus commersonii

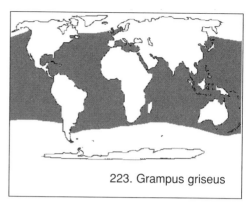

223. Grampus griseus

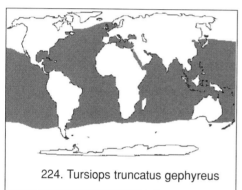

224. Tursiops truncatus gephyreus

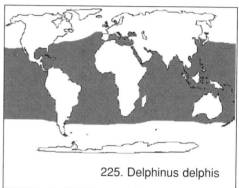

225. Delphinus delphis

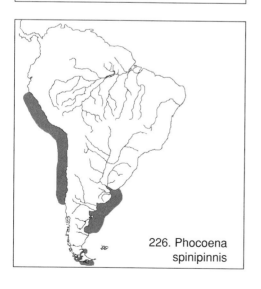

226. Phocoena spinipinnis

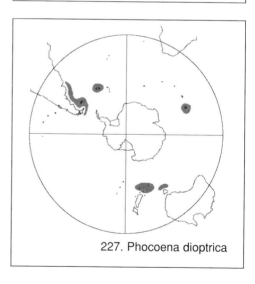

227. Phocoena dioptrica

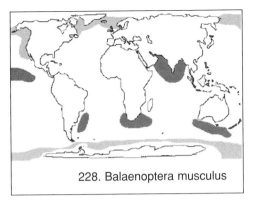

228. Balaenoptera musculus

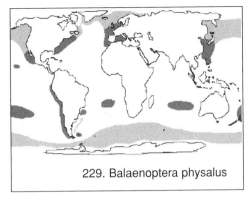

229. Balaenoptera physalus

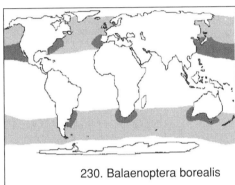

230. Balaenoptera borealis

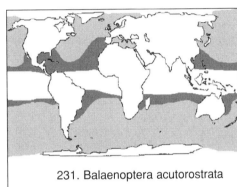

231. Balaenoptera acutorostrata

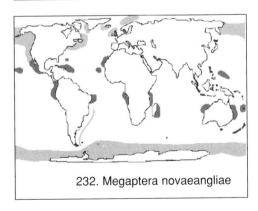

232. Megaptera novaeangliae

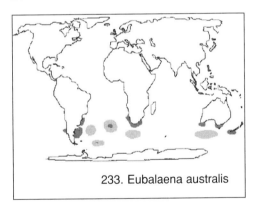

233. Eubalaena australis

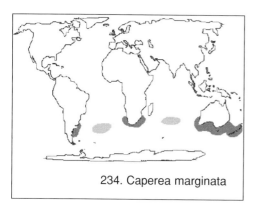
234. Caperea marginata

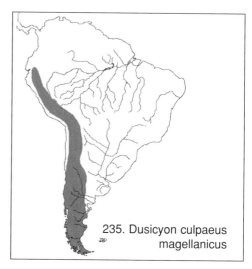
235. Dusicyon culpaeus magellanicus

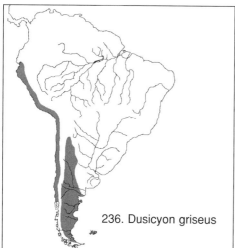
236. Dusicyon griseus

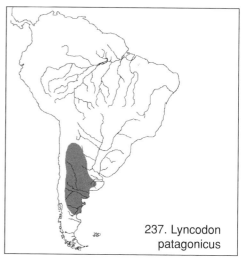
237. Lyncodon patagonicus

238. Galictis cuja

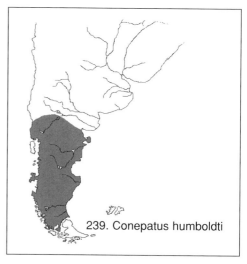
239. Conepatus humboldti

240. Felis colocolo

241. Felis geoffroyi

242. Felis concolor

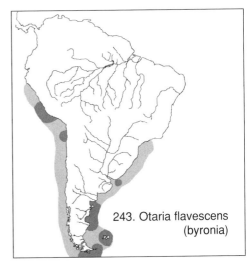

243. Otaria flavescens (byronia)

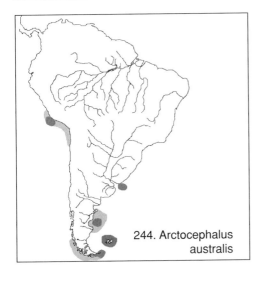

244. Arctocephalus australis

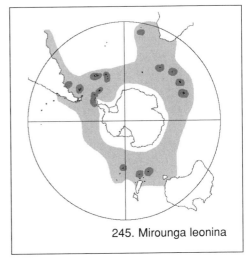

245. Mirounga leonina

246. Lama guanicoe

247. Stigmatura
budytoides

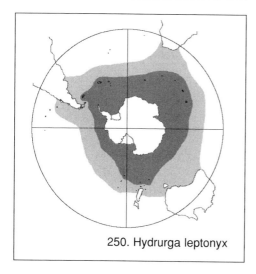

248. Chloephaga
hybrida

249. Anairtetes
flavirostris

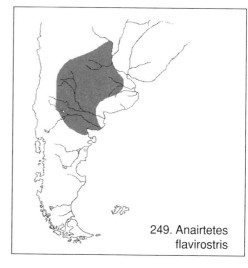

250. Hydrurga leptonyx

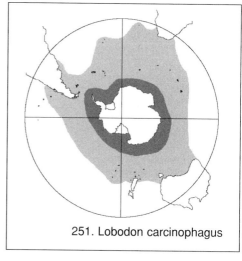

251. Lobodon carcinophagus

Index

GRAHAM HARRIS was born in Argentine Patagonia, received an advanced degree in veterinary science from the Universidad Nacional de Buenos Aires, and returned to Patagonia to work for wildlife conservation. He is co-founder and president of Fundacion Patagonia Natural. He has contributed articles and illustrations to books, journals, and magazines and is co-author of *The Right Whales of Península Valdés* and co-author as well as co-illustrator of the authoritative two-volume *Nueva Guia de Aves Argentinas* (published by Fundacion Acindar).